PENGUIN BOOKS
UNSETTLING AMERICA

Maria Mazziotti Gillan, born of Southern Italian immigrant parents, is director of the Poetry Center at Passaic County Community College in Paterson, New Jersey, and editor of *Footwork: The Paterson Literary Review,* as well as the author of several poetry collections including, *Winter Light, The Weather of Old Seasons,* and *Taking Back My Name.* Her latest collection, *Where I Come From: New and Selected Poems,* will be published by Guernica Editions in 1994.

Jennifer Gillan, half Italian American and half Irish American, is an instructor of English and composition at State University of New York at Stony Brook. She is currently working on *Recasting America: Indianness and the Construction of American Identities,* a critical study of the "Wild West" as a national origin story and its relationship to the construction of American identities. This interdisciplinary study examines some literary, historical, and cinematic texts from 1890 to the present that represent conceptions of Americanness and Indianness.

Unsettling America

AN ANTHOLOGY OF CONTEMPORARY

MULTICULTURAL POETRY

■ ■ ■

EDITED BY

Maria Mazziotti Gillan

and Jennifer Gillan

PENGUIN BOOKS

PENGUIN BOOKS
Published by the Penguin Group
Penguin Books USA Inc., 375 Hudson Street,
New York, New York 10014, U.S.A.
Penguin Books Ltd, 27 Wrights Lane,
London W8 5TZ, England
Penguin Books Australia Ltd, Ringwood,
Victoria, Australia
Penguin Books Canada Ltd, 10 Alcorn Avenue,
Toronto, Ontario, Canada M4V 3B2
Penguin Books (N.Z.) Ltd, 182–190 Wairau Road,
Auckland 10, New Zealand

Penguin Books Ltd, Registered Offices:
Harmondsworth, Middlesex, England

First published in simultaneous hardcover and paperback editions
by Viking Penguin and Penguin Books, divisions of
Penguin Books USA Inc. 1994

1   3   5   7   9   10   8   6   4   2

LIBRARY OF CONGRESS CATALOGING IN PUBLICATION DATA
Unsettling America: an anthology of contemporary multicultural
poetry/edited by Maria Mazziotti Gillan and Jennifer Gillan.
p.   cm.
ISBN 0-670-85170-1 (hardcover)
ISBN 0 14 02.3778 X (paperback)
1. American poetry—Minority authors.   2. United States—Race
relations—Poetry.   3. Ethnic groups—United States—Poetry.
4. Minorities—United States—Poetry.   5. American poetry—20th
century.   I. Gillan, Maria M.   II. Gillan, Jennifer.
PS591.M54U58   1994
811'.54080355—dc20   94–722

Printed in the United States of America
Set in Granjon
Designed by Ann Gold

Acknowledgments

An anthology like *Unsettling America* would not be possible without advice, assistance, and support from a variety of people. In particular, we want to express our great appreciation for her encouragement of this project to Daniela Gioseffi, a wonderful poet, fiction writer, editor, and friend. We also offer our gratitude to Robert Creeley, Maxine Kumin, Mary Jo Bona, Joseph Papaleo, and Arthur Clements for their letters of support, as well as Dawn Seferian, Michael Hardart, and Shelley Roth for their confidence in this project and their diligence in bringing about the publication of this volume.

We particularly want to acknowledge the considerable support of this project provided by Elliott Collins, president of Passaic County Community College, and the Passaic County College Board of Trustees, as well as by the Paterson Museum and its director, Giacamo De Stefano. We also wish to thank Hector Ortiz, T. J. Naik, Aline Papazian, Dorothy Starr, Pam Macklin, Deborah Iozia, Bruce Balistrieri, Sam Balistrieri, Ellen Denuto, Rose Romano, Fred Gardaphe, Anthony Tamburri, Paolo Giordano, Alexander Taylor, and Luis J. Rodriguez for their contributions to this anthology.

Finally, we are grateful to Dennis Gillan for his sensitivity and tolerance during the long process of compiling *Unsettling America*.

Contents

NEGOTIATING 213

Introduction

Despite the efforts of revisionist historians, specific mythic scenes have become frozen into tableaus of American identity—democratic forefathers signing the Declaration of Independence, pilgrims giving thanks for survival in the New World, soldiers fighting bravely to protect a nation conceived in liberty and justice. Yet, by settling on these characters in the nation's historical drama, many other ways of conceiving of American identity have been denied.

The actual physical settlement of America and its expanding boundaries was accompanied by violent confrontations as well as the violence of erasure. As Sherman Alexie reminds us in "Vision (2)," these histories are not part of the official American story; in the Great American Movie starring Christopher Columbus, Cotton Mather, and Andrew Jackson, "you can see an Indian leaning against the back wall. You won't find his name / among the end credits; you can't hear his voice or his song. / Extras, we're all extras."

The nostalgic vision of a simple, harmonious past, emphasizing the strenuous but rewarding settlement of this country by heroic pioneers, obscures the long history of oppression within the United States: the decimation of native peoples, the enslavement of African Americans, the exclusion of Chinese Americans, the lynching of Italian Americans, the internment of Japanese Americans during World War II, the increase in anti-Semitism and neo-Nazi violence, and the economic exploitation of migrant workers. The official version of the settlement of America and its national character leaves out these severe and often violent aspects of what stabilizing the national identity entailed.

When compiling *Unsettling America*, we did not try to be all-inclusive, to create a pluralistic play of voices, or to make a simplistic call for diversity, but rather we chose poems that directly address the instability of American identity and confront the prevalence of cultural conflict and exchange within the United States. Through the organization of the book, we hope to highlight the constant erecting, blurring, breaking, clarifying, and crossing of boundaries that are a consequence of the complex intersections among peoples, cultures, and languages within national borders, which themselves are revised constantly.

While it was necessary to organize the book into sections, we hope that this complexity will be reflected in the thematic organization of the book: the cultural dislocation of both immigration and relocation in *Uprooting;* the representation and performance of American identity in *Performing;* the articulation of one's experience, as well as the labeling of those experiences by others, in *Naming;* the uncomfortable position of in-betweenness as both American and Other in *Negotiating;* and the rethinking and re-imagining of American identity in *Re-envisioning.*

As these poets attempt to re-envision American identity, they must confront deeply entrenched conceptions of Americanness. Within the United States, skin color, language, ethnicity, and religion are often used to measure Americanness; when these four yardsticks are employed, people from African, Arabic, Asian, Italian, Jewish, Latino(a), and indigenous American backgrounds are represented as "Other" in the prevailing American tableaus. Many writers describe how they internalize these monolithic representations of Americanness at the same time that they recognize their implied Otherness.

In "Dear John Wayne," Louise Erdrich deals with the complexity of this process of identification as she describes a group of Native American teen-agers at a John Wayne drive-in movie. She recounts the power of Wayne's blue eyes and ultra-American toughness as he voices his hatred of Indians:

> How can we help but keep hearing his voice,
> the flip side of the sound-track, still playing:
> *Come on, boys, we've got them*
> *where we want them, drunk, running.*
> *They will give us what we want, what we need:*
> *The heart is a strange wood inside of everything*
> *we see, burning, doubling, splitting out of its skin.*

Erdrich expresses her double consciousness as both American and Other. Her specific history as a Chippewa will not allow her to have the same relationship to the John Wayne myth as other moviegoers; while the western heroic narrative encourages her to identify with the hero, she also recognizes herself as the villain. Unfortunately, she cannot choose to ignore the myth, since it operates in the way others view her and the way she views herself.

As Erdrich discovers, cinema is a powerful tool for disseminating the codes of Americanness and establishing the un-American. Pat Mora finds comfort in the darkened movie theater, but only by ignoring how American culture has excluded her family:

> So I buy the dark with my last fifteen cents.
> I try not to think of the bare ice box, my mother's
> always sad eyes, of my father who never understood
> this country, of the price of eggs and names and skin.
> —from "Depression Days"

Mora's poem suggests that despite the absence of their reality from the screen, many still grow up desiring the versions of Americanness served up at the cinema. Chitra Banerjee Divakaruni recognizes the emptiness of the Hollywood image, yet still wants to believe in the promise of the world that cinema offers:

> . . . Here while the film-songs still echo
> in the corridors and restrooms, we can trust
> in movie truths: sacrifice, success, love and luck,
> the America that was supposed to be.
> —from "Indian Movie, New Jersey"

While surrounded by these movie images, she can still believe in the promise of the land of opportunity. Similarly, Joseph Papaleo's poem "American Dream: First Report" describes how television offered assimilation to his family:

> First nobody liked us; they said we smelled
> and looked too short and dark.
> Then the TV proposed marriage, and we said yes.
> Momma and sisters kept the commercials going,
> to prove we were married in the palaces of soap.

This marriage is an unstable one as the "well-dressed citizens / devoted to the disinfection of [their] carpets" realize all that has been lost in the contract.

Part of what deteriorates in the aspiration for the American look or attitude—whether that means dyed-blond hair, a small, straight nose, or an Americanized name—is often a sense of cultural connection or pride. For Miguel Algarín, access to his culture has been reduced and watered down to easily accessible transmissions from the electronic media:

> I learn off the radio waves
> of 98.7 Kiss F.M. salsa/disco jams,
> that come from a Sony,
> bought even though I need a coat,
> even though I'm behind on my payments
> for the Trinitron Remote Control Color T.V.
> that I picked up at Crazy Eddie's last month.
> —from "At the Electronic Frontier"

For Algarín, as for many others, it is difficult to separate what is American from what is not. Many poets describe their realization of the impossibility of this split. Gregory Djanikian's "In the Elementary School Choir" portrays how a boy adapts American identities to his bicultural position:

> "Land where my fathers died," I bellowed,
> And it was not too hard to imagine
> A host of my great uncles and -grandfathers
> Stunned from their graves in the Turkish interior
> And finding themselves suddenly
> On a rock among maize and poultry
> And Squanto shaking their hands.

When he plugs his ancestors into the Thanksgiving scene, he revises the American origin story to fit his needs; unfortunately, in order to do so he has to erase his ancestors' stories.

At the same time that writers must struggle against these external cultural pressures, they must also manage the complicated demands of their own communities. For Gregg Shapiro, the home becomes a site of struggle, a location fraught with the pain of dislocation. In "Tattoo," he describes the legacy of the Holocaust passed from father to son:

> My father won't talk about the numbers
> 3-7-8-2-5 between the wrist and elbow
> blue as blood on his left forearm
> Instead, he spreads himself over me
> spilling his protection, like acid, until it burns

Writers in this position of in-betweenness must struggle to articulate the complexities of their experiences while they confront legal, educational, and cinematic systems that attempt to define their experience for them. In "failure of an invention," Safiya Henderson-Holmes tries to combat the power of the names and labels imposed on her:

> i am not any of the faces
> you have put on me america
>
> every mask has slipped
> i am not any of the names
>
> or sounds you have called me
> the tones have nearly
>
> made me deaf
> this dark skin, both of us
>
> have tried to bleach

When people are caught between these shifting boundaries, they often suffer the insecurities of that straddling. In order to define ourselves as Americans, we must jettison our cultural baggage; we are allowed our cultures only as they fit into familiar stereotypes. Chrystos recognizes that Hollywood Indians, bedecked in feathers and dancing at a powwow, are presented as real Indians. In "The Real Indian Leans Against," she declares her frustrated refusal of cardboard cultural reproductions:

> I want to bury these Indians dressed like cartoons of our
>   long dead
> I want
> to live
> somewhere
> where nobody is sold

For Chrystos, unsettling means a refusal to be defined in another's terms.

Unfortunately, cultures are misunderstood, lives misread and redefined by others. In "Nikki-Rosa," Nikki Giovanni laments that an outsider writing about her life would only focus on all that she did not have, and would miss the cultural connections that nourished her:

> childhood remembrances are always a drag
> if you're Black
> you always remember things like living in Woodlawn
> with no inside toilet
> and if you become famous or something
> they never talk about how happy you were to have
> your mother
> all to yourself and
> how good the water felt when you got your bath
> from one of those
> big tubs that folk in chicago barbecue in

Giovanni implies that her culture, when absorbed by another, is reflected back as somehow distorted or diminished.

Many poets recount the way they internalize negative images of their cultures and become embarrassed by their own backgrounds. Some depict the way they initially reject their family or heritage to prove their allegiance to America; in "After the Funeral of Assam Hamady," Hamod (Sam) describes his embarrassment at his father and grandfather, who stop their car on a South Dakota highway to chant their prayers. While Hamod initially rejects his past, later he replays the scene and attempts to re-envision his connection with his heritage:

> I hear them still singing
> as I travel half-way across
> America
> to another job
> burying my dead
> I always liked trips, traveling at high speed
> but they have surely passed me
> as I am standing here now
> trying so hard to join them
> on that old prayer blanket—
> as if the pain behind my eyes
> could be absolution

Hamod's poem demonstrates the resilience of cultural ties. While the poem initially seems to be about cultural alienation, it suggests that despite the pressures of dislocation, communities still manage to persist and pass on the tools of cultural survival.

The poems in *Unsettling America* tell American stories; they proclaim the complexity of the American identity and articulate alternative histories of American cultural relations. By refusing to be defined or named in another's terms, poets like Hamod, Chrystos, and Nikki Giovanni challenge stereotypes about their cultures, artistic productions, and bodies; through the power of their writing, they refuse to accept the designated boundaries that say that the issue of who or what is American is settled once and for all.

Jennifer Gillan
Stony Brook, New York

Uprooting

■ ■ ■

The experience of disconnection, whether it is from a home country or a cultural heritage, indicates a painful process of separation. While *uprooting* refers to immigrant experiences, it also focuses on the cultural dislocation of those who are born in the United States but trace their cultural heritage to non–Anglo Saxon roots. In "Dust World," Adrian C. Louis relates an alternative vision of the history of American settlement:

> Whirlwinds of hot autumn dust
> paint every foolish hope dirty.
> I stand in the impudent ranks of the poor
> and scream for the wind to abate.
> Prayers to Jesus might be quicker
> than these words from blistered hands
> and liquor, but the death wind
> breaks the lines to God.
> I have no sylvan glades of dreams,
> just dust words
> for my people dying.

Where Is My Country?

Where is my country?
Where does it lie?

The 4th of July approaches
and I am asked for firecrackers.
Is it because of my skin color?
Surely not because
of my husband's name.

In these skyways
I dart in and out.
One store sells rich ice cream
and I pick bittersweet nuggets.

In the office someone asks me
to interpret Korean,
my own Cantonese netted
in steel, my own saliva.

Where is my country?
Where does it lie?

Tucked between boundaries
striated between dark dance floors
and whispering lanterns
smoking of indistinguishable features?

Salted in Mexico
where a policeman speaks to me in Spanish?
In the voice of a Chinese grocer
who asks if I am Filipino?

Channeled in the white businessman
who discovers that I do not sound Chinese?
Garbled in a white woman
who tells me I speak perfect English?
Webbed in another
who tells me I speak with an accent?

Where is my country?
Where does it lie?

Now the dress designers flood us
with the Chinese look,
quilting our bodies in satin
stitching our eyes with silk.

Where is my country?
Where does it lie?

                              Nellie Wong

Dreams in
Harrison Railroad Park

We sit on a green bench in Harrison Railroad Park.
As we rest, I notice my mother's thighs
thin as my wrists.
I want to hug her
but I am afraid.

A bearded man comes by, asks for a cigarette.
We shake our heads, hold out our empty hands.
He shuffles away and picks up
a half-smoked stub.
His eyes light up.
Enclosed by the sun he dreams
temporarily.

Across the street an old woman hobbles by.
My mother tells me: She is unhappy here.
She thinks she would be happier
back home.
But she has forgotten.

My mother's neighbor dreams
of warm nights in Shanghai,

of goldfish swimming in a courtyard pond,
of having a young maid
anoint her tiny bound feet.

And my mother dreams
of wearing dresses that hang in her closet,
of swallowing soup without pain,
of coloring eggs
for an unborn grandson.

I turn and touch my mother's eyes.
They are wet
and I dream
and I dream
of embroidering
new skin.

                                                        Nellie Wong

Heavy Blue Veins

Heavy blue veins streaked across my mother's legs, some of them
bunched up into dark lumps at her ankles. Mama engorged veins
with a razor and drains them into a porcelain-like metal pail called
a tina. I'm small and all I remember are dreams of blood, me
drowning in a red sea, blood on the sheets, on the walls, splashing
against the white pail in streams out of my mother's ankle. But
they aren't dreams. It is mama, my blood, by the side of the bed,
me on the covers, and her slicing into a black vein and filling the
pail into some dark, forbidden red nightmare which never stops
coming, never stops pouring, this memory of Mama and blood
and Watts.

                                                  Luis J. Rodriguez

We Never Stopped Crossing Borders

We never stopped crossing borders. The Río Grande (or Río Bravo, which is what Mexicans call it, giving the name a power "Río Grande" just doesn't have) was only the first of countless barriers set in our path.

We kept jumping hurdles, kept breaking from the constraints, kept evading the border guards of every new trek. It was a metaphor to fill our lives—that river, that first crossing, the mother of all crossings. The L.A. River, for example, became a new barrier, keeping the Mexicans in their neighborhoods over on the vast east side of the city Don't speak Spanish, don't be Mexican—you don't belong. Railroad tracks divided us from communities where white people lived, such as South Gate and Lynwood across from Watts. We were invisible people in a city which thrived on glitter, big screens and big names, but this glamor contained none of our names, none of our faces.

The refrain "this is not your country" echoed for a lifetime.

                                                          Luis J. Rodriguez

Wired In

My entire life
has been spent
in refugee camps
in spite of television
electric lights
running water
cadillac footprints down asphalt roads
all moments lived
have been in the camps
on the outskirts of American cities
So many hours
blinded by juke box lights

of Saturday night mornings
only those of us inside understand
the nature of
captivity
or madness

Lamont B. Steptoe

Such a Boat of Land

Against a backdrop of Pennsylvania hills
woodsy, farmed and framed
in Amtrak window, Amish men
black-suited like Lincolns just off
the assembly line
silver beards tangled with mists and crows
buggey toward the horizon
such a boat of land moved by sails of sky
cornfields talk at night
tally the body counts of Pittsburgh and Philadelphia
city dwellers know this land
but only come robed in the stuff of dreams
this other country
barned, hexed
so much space in this different place
how to explain the closets of cities
the subterranean rivers of blood
coursing beneath the land
how to explain the cardboard Hoovervilles
rogue weeds of human despair
how to explain niggervilles, gookvilles, spicvilles . . .
how to explain the awful silence
after the shouting, the shooting, the burning,
the marching feet of soldiers and protestors
ebbing and flowing on the beaches of time
in this American land

Lamont B. Steptoe

Immigrants in Our Own Land

We are born with dreams in our hearts,
looking for better days ahead.
At the gates we are given new papers,
our old clothes are taken
and we are given overalls like mechanics wear.
We are given shots and doctors ask questions.
Then we gather in another room
where counselors orient us to the new land
we will now live in. We take tests.
Some of us were craftsmen in the old world,
good with our hands and proud of our work.
Others were good with their heads.
They used common sense like scholars
use glasses and books to reach the world.
But most of us didn't finish high school.

The old men who have lived here stare at us,
from deep disturbed eyes, sulking, retreated.
We pass them as they stand around idle,
leaning on shovels and rakes or against walls.
Our expectations are high: in the old world,
they talked about rehabilitation,
about being able to finish school,
and learning an extra good trade.
But right away we are sent to work as dishwashers,
to work in fields for three cents an hour.
The administration says this is temporary
so we go about our business, blacks with blacks,
poor whites with poor whites,
chicanos and indians by themselves.
The administration says this is right,
no mixing of cultures, let them stay apart,
like in the old neighborhoods we came from.

We came here to get away from false promises,
from dictators in our neighborhoods,
who wore blue suits and broke our doors down
when they wanted, arrested us when they felt like,

swinging clubs and shooting guns as they pleased.
But it's no different here. It's all concentrated.
The doctors don't care, our bodies decay,
our minds deteriorate, we learn nothing of value.
Our lives don't get better, we go down quick.

My cell is crisscrossed with laundry lines,
my T-shirts, boxer shorts, socks and pants are drying.
Just like it used to be in my neighborhood:
from all the tenements laundry hung window to window.
Across the way Joey is sticking his hands
through the bars to hand Felipe a cigarette,
men are hollering back and forth cell to cell,
saying their sinks don't work,
or somebody downstairs hollers angrily
about a toilet overflowing,
or that the heaters don't work.

I ask Coyote next door to shoot me over
a little more soap to finish my laundry.
I look down and see new immigrants coming in,
mattresses rolled up and on their shoulders,
new haircuts and brogan boots,
looking around, each with a dream in his heart,
thinking he'll get a chance to change his life.

But in the end, some will just sit around
talking about how good the old world was.
Some of the younger ones will become gangsters.
Some will die and others will go on living
without a soul, a future, or a reason to live.
Some will make it out of here with hate in their eyes,
but so very few make it out of here as human
as they came in, they leave wondering what good they are now
as they look at their hands so long away from their tools,
as they look at themselves, so long gone from their families,
so long gone from life itself, so many things have changed.

Jimmy Santiago Baca

We Are Americans Now,
We Live in the Tundra

Today in hazy San Francisco, I face seaward
Toward China, a giant begonia—

Pink, fragrant, bitten
By verdigris and insects. I sing her

A blues song; even a Chinese girl gets the blues,
Her reticence is black and blue.

Let's sing about the extinct
Bengal tigers, about giant Pandas—

"Ling Ling loves Xing Xing . . . yet,
We will not mate. We are

Not impotent, we are important.
We blame the environment, we blame the zoo!"

What shall we plant for the future?
Bamboo, sassafras, coconut palms? No!

Legumes, wheat, maize, old swine
To milk the new.

We are Americans now, we live in the tundra
Of the logical, a sea of cities, a wood of cars.

Farewell my ancestors:
Hirsute Taoists, failed scholars, farewell

My wetnurse who feared and loathed the Catholics,
Who called out:

         Now that the half-men have occupied Canton
         Hide your daughters, lock your doors!

                                        Marilyn Chin

Elena

My Spanish isn't enough.
I remember how I'd smile
listening to my little ones,
understanding every word they'd say,
their jokes, their songs, their plots.
          Vamos a pedirle dulces a mamá. Vamos.
But that was in Mexico.
Now my children go to American high schools.
They speak English. At night they sit around
the kitchen table, laugh with one another.
I stand by the stove and feel dumb, alone.
I bought a book to learn English.
My husband frowned, drank more beer.
My oldest said, "*Mamá*, he doesn't want you
to be smarter than he is." I'm forty,
embarrassed at mispronouncing words,
embarrassed at the laughter of my children,
the grocer, the mailman. Sometimes I take
my English book and lock myself in the bathroom,
say the thick words softly,
for if I stop trying, I will be deaf
when my children need my help.

Pat Mora

What Were You Patching?

needling
threading nighttime sewing machine
from Odessa to Massachusetts
Ma/Ma were you patching the world?

dead in your bed now
accurate as medical photography
your arm is curved in grace
serene in rigor mortis and hair

like moons of silver. How do I pack up
the house of your life?

this inventory so enormous
opens paper cartons like mouths at my throat
offering no anaesthesia
while my eyes sink
in the worst procedure
following the coffin with its Jewish
star. Driven to a lawn of cedar trees
I think of you draped inside
the brightest red shawl and dress
saved for special events
barefoot with others
yet your posture clings
to boxes of buttons, pins, stockings
and shoes outlining your walk
near medicine chests of aspirin, milk
of magnesia in blue bottles where
half your teeth still soak
saying nothing
in a yellow coffee cup.

Ma/Ma
how do I arrange my new maturity
how do I arrange these details, the endless
notebooks from English classes
how do I arrange the three branches of government
you memorized for my country's correct answer
studying citizenship, studying respect
and what do I do with aluminum
pots, scrubbed in communion of polished
mahogany, postcards, letters
and plants watered
in Russian history with your stubborn desire
to learn the syntax of America?

trapped by your attachment to love
trapped by hugs and kisses on needlepoint
trapped in chromosomes
trapped in passports from Odessa
my head freezes

in your refrigerator
packed with food.

Ma/Ma what were you patching?

How do I answer forms in triplicate?
Government departments want to know you.
You've become everybody's statistic now
while I carry your death certificate in my purse
these days.

The windows you cleaned last week for Passover
shine along Van Cortlandt park
blinding me like knives. The plants
you watered and watered
are dry. I keep wishing they'd die, wishing
like a child you'd suddenly arrive
ringing my doorbell
demanding I be home on the spot
demanding in your red tam-o'-shanter
demanding in your bifocal glasses
demanding what life is really about
in the cruelest week of April
dying in secrets of Tolstoy
secrets of stanzas I search
shaped in visions of your face
on pillows of words that hurt
like the Kaddish
I stumble on
scratching, scratching goosefeathers
across my eyelids
open now even in sleep.

Ma/Ma what were you patching?

Ruth Lisa Schechter

In Texas Grass

all along the railroad
tracks of texas
old train cars lay
rusted & overturned
like new african governments
long forgotten by the people
who built & rode them
till they couldn't run no more
& they remind me of old race horses
who've been put out to pasture
amongst the weeds
rain, sleet & snow
till they die & rot away
like photos fading
in grandma's picture book
of old black men & women, in mississippi
texas, who sit on dilapidated porches
that fall away
like dead man's skin
like white people's eyes
& inside the peeling photos
old men sit, sad eyed
& waiting, waiting for worm dust
thinking of the master & his long forgotten
promise of forty acres & a mule
& even now, if you pass across
this bleeding flesh
ever changing landscape
you will see the fruited
countryside, stretching, stretching
& old black men & young black
men, sitting on porches, waiting
waiting for rusted trains
silent in texas grass

Quincy Troupe

The Old Italians Dying

For years the old Italians have been dying
all over America
For years the old Italians in faded felt hats
have been sunning themselves and dying
You have seen them on the benches
in the park in Washington Square
the old Italians in their black high button shoes
the old men in their old felt fedoras
                          with stained hatbands
have been dying and dying
                          day by day
You have seen them
every day in Washington Square San Francisco
the slow bell
tolls in the morning
in the Church of Peter & Paul
in the marzipan church on the plaza
toward ten in the morning the slow bell tolls
in the towers of Peter & Paul
and the old men who are still alive
sit sunning themselves in a row
on the wood benches in the park
and watch the processions in and out
funerals in the morning
weddings in the afternoon
slow bell in the morning Fast bell at noon
In one door out the other
the old men sit there in their hats
and watch the coming & going
You have seen them
the ones who feed the pigeons
               cutting the stale bread
                     with their thumbs & penknives
the ones with old pocketwatches
the old ones with gnarled hands
                          and wild eyebrows
the ones with the baggy pants
                     with both belt & suspenders

the grappa drinkers with teeth like corn
the Piemontesi the Genovesi the Siciliani
                smelling of garlic & pepperonis
the ones who loved Mussolini
the old fascists
the ones who loved Garibaldi
the old anarchists reading *L'Umanità Nova*
the ones who loved Sacco & Vanzetti
They are almost all gone now
They are sitting and waiting their turn
and sunning themselves in front of the church
over the doors of which is inscribed
a phrase which would seem to be unfinished
from Dante's *Paradiso*
about the glory of the One
                who moves everything . . .
The old men are waiting
for it to be finished
for their glorious sentence on earth
                to be finished
the slow bell tolls & tolls
the pigeons strut about
not even thinking of flying
the air too heavy with heavy tolling
The black hired hearses draw up
the black limousines with black windowshades
shielding the widows
the widows with the long black veils
who will outlive them all
You have seen them
madre di terra, madre di mare
The widows climb out of the limousines
The family mourners step out in stiff suits
The widows walk so slowly
up the steps of the cathedral
fishnet veils drawn down
leaning hard on darkcloth arms
Their faces do not fall apart
They are merely drawn apart
They are still the matriarchs
outliving everyone

the old dagos dying out
in Little Italys all over America
the old dead dagos
hauled out in the morning sun
that does not mourn for anyone
One by one Year by year
they are carried out
The bell
never stops tolling

                    Lawrence Ferlinghetti

Dust World

FOR SHERMAN ALEXIE

I
Whirlwinds of hot autumn dust
paint every foolish hope dirty.
I stand in the impudent ranks of the poor
and scream for the wind to abate.
Prayers to Jesus might be quicker
than these words from blistered hands
and liquor, but the death wind
breaks the lines to God.
I have no sylvan glades of dreams,
just dust words
for my people dying.

II
With pupil-dilated *putti* in arms
three teenaged mothers
on the hood of a '70 Chevy
wave at me like they know me.
Inside the video rental
a small fan ripples sweat
and scatters ashes upon two young attendants
practicing karate kicks and ignoring me
because they're aware I could dust

their wise asses individually or collectively.
They're products of Pine Ridge High
which means they would have had two strikes
against them even if they did graduate
and these two clowns never did.
I guess they're almost courting me,
in a weird macho way almost flirting,
because I'm fatherly, half buzzed-up,
and have biceps as thick as their thighs.
Heyyyy . . . ever so softly,
this is the whiskey talking now.

III
With pupils dilated and beer in hand
three teenaged mothers court frication
more serious than their sweet Sioux butts
buffing the hood of their hideous car.
When I glide my new T-bird
out of the video store parking lot
they wave like they really know me.
One of the girls, beautiful enough
to die for except for rotten teeth
smiles and I suck in my gut
and lay some rubber.
I cruise through a small whirlwind
of lascivious regrets
and float happily through the dark streets
of this sad, welfare world.

This is the land that time forgot.
Here is the Hell the white God gave us.
The wind from the Badlands brings
a chorus of chaos and makes everything dirty.
I meander past my house and stop briefly
before driving back to where
the young girls are.
I park my car and re-enter the store.
The two young boys are still dancing
like two cats in mid-air, snarling, clawless
and spitting. No harm done.
I stare them down and place two cassettes,

both rated X, on the counter.
It's Friday night and I'm forty years old
and the wild-night redskin
parade is beginning.

Adrian C. Louis

Father from Asia

Father, you turn your hands toward me.
Large hollow bowls, they are empty
stigmata of poverty. Light pours
through them, and I back away,
for you are dangerous, father
of poverty, father of ten children,
father of nothing, from whose life
I have learned nothing for myself.
You are the father of childhood,
father from Asia, father of sacrifice.
I renounce you, keep you in my sleep,
keep you two oceans away, ghost
who eats his own children,
Asia who loved his children,
who didn't know abandonment,
father who lived at the center of the world,
whose life I dare not remember,
for memory is a wheel that crushes,
and Asia is dust, is dust.

Shirley Geok-lin Lim

from Moving

so we move now
my new wife and I, my children
move further away   like lost
shipmates crying to me for help
asking for some sound, some signal to understand

about this Arabic I sometimes speak   what Islam means to
   horizons
trying to grasp at these new patterns in the early morning darkness
floating out into the distance
and me their father—too far
away to be of much help
to be of any use
when they wake up afraid at night
wondering what that noise is
they wonder and wander without choice in this matter
it is when we are at sea this way
that I sometimes think about a life
I've never known except for a little while
in some old country of time that I remember my father and
   grandfather
talking about, when I kept wanting to go out to play baseball,
a certain amount of a reality
where at least the whole tribe moved *together*
it was that way in my "old country" of
stories of truth my father and grandfather and their grandfather
   before them
everyone   everything stuck together   things stayed
and when they moved
grandfathers   grandmothers   fathers

Hamod (Sam)

Katori Maru, October 1920

Two weeks across a strange sea,
big waves, the ship
spilling its toilets.
People sick of the ocean
run from bulkhead to bulkhead,
trying to keep their balance
on the slick iron deck.

My mother asks herself in Japanese
why her oldest sister had to die,
why now she must marry the stranger

who speaks Japanese & English
and swears with the crew.
She thinks back to Nagano-ken,
pictures her mother
cracking a brown egg
over a bowl of rice
while her father washes raw soil
from his thick hands.
Today she could trade her future
for the bottom of the ocean.

Waves, floating waves,
rise above the railing,
drift out of sight. Vancouver Island
is a memory of home, hills
soft & green as crushed velvet.

In Tacoma, Minoru buys
Western clothes: a pink taffeta dress
full of pleats, wide-brimmed hat,
white gloves, a leather handbag
and awkward high heels.
No more flowered silk,
obi sash and getas.
He brings out a used coat from the closet,
thick maroon wool, brown fur collar.
It is too full in the shoulders,
the size & color
fit her sister.
But for now she accepts it.
The rain feels heavy
on the gray sidewalks of America.

James Masao Mitsui

Restroom

I push out of Customs, stumble, almost fall, legs numb from twelve hours in the plane, bladder like it's caught between the *bajra*-crushing stones they use back in the village. I hadn't known

how to tell the man next to me, so large and red-faced, to move
so I could go to the toilet. Even if my mouth could shape the
strange guttural sounds, I couldn't have said it for the shame of
it, the voices in my head, mother, grandmother, widow-aunt, tell-
ing me women did not speak of body-things.

I press my thighs together, look for him. Eight years. Will I
recognize him? Will he walk briskly like the pale men streaming
past me, swinging a case, a grey coat thrown over his arm? Will
he know me? I shift the heavy bag from hand to hand, flex sore
muscles. The thin plastic straps have cut into my fingers, a couple
of nails broken from gripping the armrest, take-off time, that
sharp angled rush into the sky, the houses and streets of Bombay
flattened and falling away. Teeth biting down to keep in the cry-
ing, the hot bile so much worse than morning sickness. Hollow
pit inside me, like after my daughter's birth. Had to leave her
with my mother-in-law because he said we couldn't afford a child
with us now. I'll have to work in the store all day, and who would
watch her. I know how important the store is. How he saved for
it, one meal a day, rice and water, washed his pants and shirt by
hand each night. Now it's half his. A bad part of town, he wrote,
but good money, especially in liquor. I know I'll be a good worker.
I'm used to it, digging in the *bajra* fields all morning, then home
to cook *chapatis* for twelve over the open wood fire, pulling water
from the well through the burning afternoon. Soon we'll have
enough to bring our daughter, and maybe, if God wills, we'll have
another, this time a strong son to carry the family name.

But why isn't he here? And this man, so huge in his blue suit,
thrusting at me a card with his picture and letters that scurry like
black ants so I can't read? He's saying something. I try so hard
to hear, my head hurts. I finally catch a name. His name. The
word Hospital. Legs shaking so much I have to sit down on the
suitcase. A gun, shiny-black, on the man's hip. He speaks slowly,
very loudly, opening his mouth wide each time. Robbery. Shoot-
ing. He points to his left shoulder. Shakes his head. Not dead.
Hospital. He waits. I keep my eyes open so the redness won't
cover me. Band of steel around my chest, tongue too heavy to
move. He is carrying my suitcase, so I follow. Then I see the sign,
WOMEN. I know what that means. Niru-ben explained it to me. I
make hand-gestures to the man, pointing. He nods, OK, OK.

I've never seen anything like this before. Long lights every-
where, lines of mirrors. Taps, four, six, eight of them, faucets
gleaming, the white sinks shining like in a fairytale. And the

women with their bright red lips, hair short and curling around
their faces in golds and browns, bare, daring honey-colored legs,
their short skirts, black, maroon, the thin, thin points of their high
heels. I go into a stall, just like the others are doing. Can't figure
out the lock, so I have to hold on to the door. The porcelain is
cold against the backs of my thighs, but it feels so good, all that
pent-up fluid leaving me in a clean rush. Soft women voices hold
me, a sudden laugh, silk-rustlings. The redness is far now. The
air fills with a perfume I don't know. I step out, breathe deeply,
fill my lungs with it. If I can count to twenty without letting go,
everything will be all right. I turn on the faucet. Water flows and
flows over my hands, warm and full of light, like a blessing.

Chitra Banerjee Divakaruni

The Brides Come to Yuba City

The sky is hot and yellow, filled
with blue screaming birds. The train
heaved us from its belly
and vanished in shrill smoke.
Now only the tracks
gleam dull in the heavy air,
a ladder to eternity, each receding rung
cleaved from our husbands' ribs.
Mica-flecked, the platform
dazzles, burns up through thin
chappal soles, lurches
like the ship's dark hold,
blurred month of nights, smell of vomit,
a porthole like the bleached iris
of a giant unseeing eye.

Red-veiled, we lean into each other,
press damp palms, try
broken smiles. The man
who met us at the ship whistles
a restless *Angrezi* tune
and scans the fields. Behind us,
the black wedding trunks, sharp-edged,

shiny, stenciled with strange men-names
our bodies do not fit into:
Mrs. Baldev Johl, Mrs. Kanwal Bains.
Inside, folded like wings,
bright *salwar kameezes* scented
with sandalwood. For the men,
kurtas and thin white gauze
to wrap their uncut hair.
Laddus from Jullundhar, sugar-crusted,
six kinds of lentils, a small bag
of *bajra* flour. Labeled in our mothers'
hesitant hands, pickled mango and lime,
packets of seeds—*methi, karela, saag*—
to burst from this new soil
like green stars.

He gives a shout, waves
at the men, their slow
uneven approach. We crease our eyes
through the veils' red film,
cannot breathe. Thirty years
since we saw them. Or never,
like Harvinder, married last year
at Hoshiarpur to her husband's photo,
which she clutches tight to her
to stop the shaking. He is fifty-two,
she sixteen. Tonight—like us all—
she will open her legs to him.

The platform is endless-wide.
The men walk and walk
without advancing. Their lined,
wavering mouths, their
eyes like drowning lights.
We cannot recognize a single face.

Note: Yuba City in Northern California was settled largely by Indian railroad
workers around the 1900s. Due to immigration restrictions, many of them were
unable to bring their families over—or, in the case of single men, go back to
get married—until the 1940s.

Chitra Banerjee Divakaruni

Grandmother, a Caribbean Indian, Described by My Father

Nearly a hundred when she died,
mi viejita
was an open boat,
and I had no map
to show her the safe places.
There was much to grieve.
Her shoulders were stooped.
Her hands were never young.
They broke jars
at the watering holes,
like bones, like hearts.

When she was a girl,
she was given the island
but no wings.
She wanted wings,
though she bruised
like a persimmon.
She was not ruined
before her marriage.
But after the first baby died,
she disappeared in the middle
of days to worship
her black saint;
after the second,
to sleep with a hand towel
across her eyes.

I had to take care
not to exhume
from the mound of memory
these myths, these lost ones.
Born sleek as swans
on her river, my brother,
the man you have met

who has one arm,
and I glided into the sun.
Other children poured forth,
and by the time I was sixteen
I lost my place
in her thatched house.

She let me go,
and she did not come to the pier
the day the banana boat
pushed away from her shore
towards Nueva York
where I had heard
there would be room for me.

Yvonne V. Sapia

Indian Boarding School: The Runaways

Home's the place we head for in our sleep.
Boxcars stumbling north in dreams
don't wait for us. We catch them on the run.
The rails, old lacerations that we love,
shoot parallel across the face and break
just under Turtle Mountains. Riding scars
you can't get lost. Home is the place they cross.

The lame guard strikes a match and makes the dark
less tolerant. We watch through cracks in boards
as the land starts rolling, rolling till it hurts
to be here, cold in regulation clothes.
We know the sheriff's waiting at midrun
to take us back. His car is dumb and warm.
The highway doesn't rock, it only hums
like a wing of long insults. The worn-down welts
of ancient punishments lead back and forth.

All runaways wear dresses, long green ones,
the color you would think shame was. We scrub
the sidewalks down because it's shameful work.
Our brushes cut the stone in watered arcs
and in the soak frail outlines shiver clear
a moment, things us kids pressed on the dark
face before it hardened, pale, remembering
delicate old injuries, the spines of names and leaves.

                                        Louise Erdrich

Braly Street

Every summer
The asphalt softens
Giving under the edge
Of boot heels and the trucks
That caught radiators
Of butterflies.
Bottle caps and glass
Of the '40s and '50s
Hold their breath
Under the black earth
Of asphalt and are silent
Like the dead whose mouths
Have eaten dirt and bermuda.
Every summer I come
To this street
Where I discovered ants bit,
Matches flared,
And pinto beans unraveled
Into plants; discovered
Aspirin will not cure a dog
Whose fur twitches.

It's 16 years
Since our house
Was bulldozed and my father
Stunned into a coma . . .
Where it was,

An oasis of chickweed
And foxtails.
Where the almond tree stood
There are wine bottles
Whose history
Is a liver. The long caravan
Of my uncle's footprints
Has been paved
With dirt. Where my father
Cemented a pond
There is a cavern of red ants
Living on the seeds
The wind brings
And cats that come here
To die among
The browning sage.

It's 16 years
Since bottle collectors
Shoveled around
The foundation
And the almond tree
Opened its last fruit
To the summer.
The houses are gone,
The Molinas, Morenos,
The Japanese families
Are gone, the Okies gone
Who moved out at night
Under a canopy of
Moving stars.

In '57 I sat
On the porch, salting
Slugs that came out
After the rain,
While inside my uncle
Weakened with cancer
And the blurred vision
Of his hands
Darkening to earth.

In '58 I knelt
Before my father
Whose spine was pulled loose.
Before his face still
Growing a chin of hair,
Before the procession
Of stitches behind
His neck, I knelt
And did not understand.

Braly Street is now
Tin ventilators
On the warehouses, turning
Our sweat
Towards the yellowing sky;
Acetylene welders
Beading manifolds,
Stinging the half-globes
Of retinas. When I come
To where our house was,
I come to weeds
And a sewer line tied off
Like an umbilical cord;
To the chinaberry
Not pulled down
And to its rings
My father and uncle
Would equal, if alive.

Gary Soto

The Woman Hanging from
the Thirteenth Floor Window

She is the woman hanging from the 13th floor
window. Her hands are pressed white against the
concrete molding of the tenement building. She

hangs from the 13th floor window in east Chicago,
with a swirl of birds over her head. They could
be a halo, or a storm of glass waiting to crush her.

She thinks she will be set free.

The woman hanging from the 13th floor window
on the east side of Chicago is not alone.
She is a woman of children, of the baby, Carlos,
and of Margaret, and of Jimmy who is the oldest.
She is her mother's daughter and her father's son.
She is several pieces between the two husbands
she has had. She is all the women of the apartment
building who stand watching her, watching themselves.

When she was young she ate wild rice on scraped down
plates in warm wood rooms. It was in the farther
north and she was the baby then. They rocked her.

She sees Lake Michigan lapping at the shores of
herself. It is a dizzy hole of water and the rich
live in tall glass houses at the edge of it. In some
places Lake Michigan speaks softly, here, it just sputters
and butts itself against the asphalt. She sees
other buildings just like hers. She sees other
women hanging from many-floored windows
counting their lives in the palms of their hands
and in the palms of their children's hands.

She is the woman hanging from the 13th floor window
on the Indian side of town. Her belly is soft from
her children's births, her worn levis swing down below
her waist, and then her feet, and then her heart.
She is dangling.

The woman hanging from the 13th floor hears voices.
They come to her in the night when the lights have gone
dim. Sometimes they are little cats mewing and scratching
at the door, sometimes they are her grandmother's voice,
and sometimes they are gigantic men of light whispering
to her to get up, to get up, to get up. That's when she wants

to have another child to hold on to in the night, to be able
to fall back into dreams.

And the woman hanging from the 13th floor window
hears other voices. Some of them scream out from below
for her to jump, they would push her over. Others cry softly
from the sidewalks, pull their children up like flowers and
   gather
them into their arms. They would help her, like themselves.

But she is the woman hanging from the 13th floor window,
and she knows she is hanging by her own fingers, her
own skin, her own thread of indecision.

She thinks of Carlos, of Margaret, of Jimmy.
She thinks of her father, and of her mother.
She thinks of all the women she has been, of all
the men. She thinks of the color of her skin, and
of Chicago streets, and of waterfalls and pines.
She thinks of moonlight nights, and of cool spring storms.
Her mind chatters like neon and northside bars.
She thinks of the 4 a.m. lonelinesses that have folded
her up like death, discordant, without logical and
beautiful conclusion. Her teeth break off at the edges.
She would speak.

The woman hangs from the 13th floor window crying for
the lost beauty of her own life. She sees the
sun falling west over the gray plain of Chicago.
She thinks she remembers listening to her own life
break loose, as she falls from the 13th floor
window on the east side of Chicago, or as she
climbs back up to claim herself again.

Joy Harjo

Kinged

Crumpled like an embroidered pillowcase
on the floor, the old woman cries
in the smoldering of incense and steamed glass.
She is packing to return to Ohio;
her daughter has told her, "Your two years here
are up. You should go back while the weather
is warm." She has found money
as a thumb in sponge cake
leaves little impression. A kinged checker,
she is finally moving backwards
in a history of frontiers; Canton
to Hong Kong to Ohio to Seattle.

She is surprised at how the board
has cleared so quickly, how she can move
and not see another for several turns.
Soil, beyond red and black, flavors the meats,
the sun in her laundry. Only her dreams
recycle, black on gray, gray
going grayer. Her eyes swell
like beans in water, shift up
towards her skull at night.

She wonders how maternal love fails
so utterly that hate can spread like clover,
spread so that her daughter can carve
her out of her grandchildren's lives,
so utterly weeded out. Astonished
at each thump of her heart, she thinks
a piece of her must erode and drift
into her blood for it to be creeping
so slowly now. So red. Black.

Shalin Hai-Jew

Dream Poem

I miss my grandmother
As I walk along Italian streets,
Old men sit hunched on steps,
Their words tumble like skipping stones,
In a dialect I cannot understand.

I walk past them; the cold air
Tastes foreign in my mouth.
Across the street, the house
Sways in and out of sunset light—
Dizzying my flight—a brown girl on
Skateboard whizzes through patches of black and
White, her braids burn my cheek in the metallic air.

I knock on wood. Two black dogs, handsome as men,
Snarl and wag at the door.
I scold them in the old men's language and they
Whimper in retreat.
My old comare knows why I have come: her doe eyes
Are like glass before my eyes, reflecting the street
Outside. She kisses both my cheeks, grasps my hair in
Peasant hands, turns me to the door:

> And there I see her,
> Grandma with flying braids
> Looks up at me elfish and gay
> In the urban sun.
> Her eyes are older than time.

Mary Jo Bona

The Last Wolf

the last wolf hurried toward me
through the ruined city
and I heard his baying echoes

down the steep smashed warrens
of Montgomery Street and past
the few ruby-crowned highrises
left standing
their lighted elevators useless

passing the flicking red and green
of traffic signals
baying his way eastward
in the mystery of his wild loping gait
closer the sounds in the deadly night
through clutter and rubble of quiet blocks

I heard his voice ascending the hill
and at last his low whine as he came
floor by empty floor to the room
where I sat
in my narrow bed looking west, waiting
I heard him snuffle at the door and
I watched
he trotted across the floor

he laid his long gray muzzle
on the spare white spread
and his eyes burned yellow
his small dotted eyebrows quivered

Yes, I said.
I know what they have done.

Mary TallMountain

Tattoo

My father won't talk about the numbers
3-7-8-2-5 between the wrist and elbow
blue as blood on his left forearm
Instead, he spreads himself over me
spilling his protection, like acid, until it burns
I wear him like a cloak, sweat under the weight

There were stories in the lines on his face
the nervous blue flash in his eyes
his bone-crushing hugs
I am drowning in his silence
trying to stay afloat on curiosity
Questions choke me and I swallow hard

We don't breathe the same air
speak the same language
live in the same universe
We are continents, worlds apart
I am sorry my life has remained unscathed
His scars still bleed, his bruises don't fade

If I could trade places with him
I would pad the rest of his days
wrap him in gauze and velvet
absorb the shocks and treat his wounds
I would scrub the numbers from his flesh
extinguish the fire and give him back his life

                                        Gregg Shapiro

Father of My Father

FOR MITSUJI INADA

I
The way the incense gripped,
coughing, everyone coughing,
their throats resounding in the hall . . .

Above the stage, a dragon
licked his lip.

They were moaning, bowing and moaning—
three old-kimonoed men,
their tassels flapping.

The altar bristled
lacquer and gold latches.

Then clapping wood, the gift
of incense to the bowl . . .

II
Incense. Sucking the wind from him—
face a deflated callus . . .

Then the shoes paraded, on and on,
issuing from the walls.

Finally, to be strolling
over the garden—

gaunt rocks, bonsai
knuckled at the bottom.

About, all structures
surrounding the pagoda of San Jose.

III
Have you ever seen
blue eyes in a Japanese face?

That is the main thing I remember.

She took the wrong road
nightly at their intersection,
leaving him shouting, screaming,
pacing the house with a flashlight

as if something was missing.

Have you ever lost your woman?
Have you ever lost your crops
and had to move?—
packing up without your woman,
some evacuation going on . . .

Have you ever been wakened
by blue eyes shining into your face?

You wondered who you were.

You couldn't move.

Or there were evenings
steeped in scrolls and incense . . .

Sometimes, to be alone
in that museum, cleaved
by shadows, the tongue's disfigurings . . .

In Arkansas he staked a ragged garden.
Then that Colorado wind
eroded.

I flourished in that sand.

But what comes second-hand
is not the same.

Something is missing.

I sometimes wake to streetlight
pacing in my room.

I would not hold him then.

Nothing could stop me now.

Lawson Fusao Inada

Letter to a Cretan Flute-Maker

we have not forgotten you but here they have you pretend to work
till you gulp like you're sea-sick but can't vomit. then they prescribe
wonder-drugs and tell you this is paradise

here there's not much earth left, just plenty of war-bonds

but I can taste your figs and wine and recall how we almost missed
our bus up on that mountain near Festos

there are no peasants here, but my son is learning how to swim and
play the flute

Justin Vitiello

What Do I Know of Journey

What do I know of journey,
they who came before me kept what they left
but now they are gone. Invisible shells
cast off, arise in flaming hair
orphans of collapsed Shekinah
caught between earth & heaven's end
and what do I know of journey,
a child when children were murdered
waiting on lines with their mothers and fathers,
gone in gas or the flash of atomic *ain-sof*
squinted at in movie-theaters.
Ancients sit on stoops too tired to mourn,
turn inward to blood rivers, lost *shtetls*.
They cannot take me with them
and I cannot bring them back
and what do I know of journey, I
who never spoke their language.
The old ones are dead or dying

and what is left desires less and less
and what is less is what is left
while children ran off screaming
Elohim   Elohim!
into freeways smashed with the starlight of cars.

David Meltzer

When My Grandmother Said "Pussy"

It was when we were living
in the Rochdale Avenue projects,
right after we moved in. She was bringing us
a *mandel* bread wrapped in tinfoil.
She had walked up the three flights. That stairwell
wasn't the cleanest: a smell of burned food,
bubbled green walls seared with loopy graffiti.
She hobbled in shaking her head. *"Poosy!"* she spat.
"For vat do they hev to write this? What for, *Poosy?*
All over," she waved to *all over*
with the pointy bread, "it says Poosy!
It's disgustinck!" she yelled. "It could
make you *zeeck!"* My mother laughed
a little, looked down,
took her coat.
My sister and I would snicker about it for days,
but then we smiled stupidly, painfully,
utterly paralyzed
to hear her speaking—*shouting*—such a word.

How unlike her it was, who never complained,
who shushed my grandfather's hoarse diatribes
against capitalism, never read the paper,
pretended my cousin Roberta wasn't a lesbian.
At the funeral the rabbi called her a "Yiddishe Mama"—
yes, the well-scrubbed house, Passover feasts
where no one could get her to sit;

she was fed by watching us eat,
she'd hurry back to the kitchen, offer more.

It must have been indignation, that day,
about what we kids had to see. Still, it's a strange
keepsake of her. The past runs through our fingers
like flour, leaving a hard little packet
of surprising jewelry someone's buried . . .
Roberta had me look at an old photo, once,
of my grandmother dressed up for Purim, as a boy.
Chubby in plaid knickers, cap, hair twisted up,
she's smiling, thrilled, at the photographer.
I could feel Roberta feeling she saw something
hidden to everyone else:
a quality she longed to find
in my grandmother, beneath the disguise.
And I look back, too, to pluck and pluck
embarrassment's twangy piano string,
to when she named it—my grandmother
for an instant becoming dangerous
as the writing on the wall.
To say she was pushing back
against all that was trying, and would try,
to claim my attention and consume me.

                                        Carole Bernstein

14th Street Was Gutted in 1968

14th Street was gutted in 1968.
Fire was started on one side of the street.
Flames licked a trail of gasoline to the other side.
For several blocks a gauntlet of flames.
For several days debris smoldered with the stench
of buildings we had known all our lives. Had known
all our lives. I recalled the death of Otis Redding.
My sense of place was cauterized.
Since that time the city has become a buffalo
nearly a dinosaur and,
as with everything else white men have wanted

for themselves,
endangered
or extinct.

Cheryl Clarke

Walking by the
Cliffside Dyeworks

Even the dark end of Belmont Avenue
is floodlit today as though for postcards,
as though a tire, a rusted-out camshaft,
rings that trashcans left in the snow
from now on belonged to history.

Shadows fall from the brick facets
to the windows of rundown houses,
but now they land on different faces,
not those *paesano*s
who manned the second and third shifts
through the fat Forties and lean Fifties
and, as you did, into the Sixties—
mostly spent now the bankrolls they saved
against a death out of sight of their olive groves.

One was Frank Strangis
who came, like you, from Sambiase.
Nine years for stabbing a cardshark
made Frank a kind of celebrity.
Some of the women wouldn't visit,
some tried to keep their husbands away.
But you never singled him out,
even when you covered your glass
to keep him from pouring another.

I climbed the stairs of his three-family,
standing clear of the missing railings.
I could see the infield in Hinchcliffe Stadium

or halfway down the cleft of the falls,
could overhear through the screen
the women agree it was too much wine.

I could have stood there all day,
I could be standing there now
and still never have learned
if it was months or if it hit Frank
right then knife in hand
that the cardshark understood nothing
of Calabrese chivalry.

Once when I was out of work
one of the mechanics informed me
that I could show your union card
and get a job in a place like this.
Lie down, father.
Those bootprints in the old snow
leading to the Employee Entrance
are becoming shapeless as men.
And in one of the rusted-out rooms
a warping jig's burnished axle
rises from a welter of sumac
to tell them it's ten after two.

                                        Robert Carnevale

The Old Buildings

(1422 amsterdam avenue)
everybody knew
everybody else
everybody respected
& loved everybody else
unity was happening
whenever somebody
cooked pasteles
everybody in the building
was invited to eat
this is how together

everybody was in
those days (city hall
saw this harmony happening
and got intimidated
because there is nothing
that frightens
this government more
than seeing people
living and loving
and breathing together
so they decided to
demolish the buildings
that could have been
saved by renovation
& eliminate the unity)
everybody was moved
away from each other
to so-called better places
where you do not know
anybody when you move in
& you do not know anybody
when you move out
dead or alive or in
a straitjacket
the system tailored
especially for you and
all your close relatives
who came here looking
for better days and
finding the worst nights
of their existence as
they went from funeral
parlor to funeral parlor
looking for coffins
that were not too expensive

Pedro Pietri

In Response to Executive Order 9066:

All Americans of Japanese Descent Must Report to Relocation Centers

Dear Sirs:
Of course I'll come. I've packed my galoshes
and three packets of tomato seeds. Denise calls them
love apples. My father says where we're going
they won't grow.

I am a fourteen-year-old girl with bad spelling
and a messy room. If it helps any, I will tell you
I have always felt funny using chopsticks
and my favorite food is hot dogs.
My best friend is a white girl named Denise—
we look at boys together. She sat in front of me
all through grade school because of our names:
O'Connor, Ozawa. I know the back of Denise's head very well.

I tell her she's going bald. She tells me I copy on tests.
We're best friends.

I saw Denise today in Geography class.
She was sitting on the other side of the room.
"You're trying to start a war," she said, "giving secrets
away to the Enemy, Why can't you keep your big
mouth shut?"

I didn't know what to say.
I gave her a packet of tomato seeds
and asked her to plant them for me, told her
when the first tomato ripened
she'd miss me.

Dwight Okita

The Nice Thing
About Counting Stars

FOR YOSHIO AND TAKEYO OKITA

"In the hot summers of the 30s, we would
sit on the steps and sing for hours. We
even counted the stars in the sky and it
was always beautiful."

So my mother begins
writing her life down, Jackie Onassis
thinking in the car behind dark glasses.
She recalls the luxury
of growing up—she and her sisters
buying jelly bismarcks on Sundays
and eating them in the back seat
of their father's Packard
parked on the drive.
Pretending they were going
somewhere, and they were.
Not knowing years later they would
be headed for just such an exotic place.
Somewhere far from Fresno, their white stone house
on F Street, the blackboard in the kitchen
where they learned math,
long division, remainders,
what is left
after you divide something.

"When Executive Order 9066 came telling
all Japanese-Americans to leave their
houses, we cleared out of Fresno real
fast. They gave us three days. I remember
carrying a washboard to the camp. I don't
know how it got in my hands. Someone must
have told me—Here, take this."

They were given three days to move
what had taken them years to acquire—

sewing machines, refrigerators, pianos, expensive fishing
rods from Italy. A war was on—Japs
had bombed Pearl Harbor.

Burmashave signs littered the highways:

SLAP
                                    THE JAP

"Take only what you can carry."
My mother's family left the Packard
and with it left Sundays in the back seat.
Others walked away from acres of land,
drugstores, photo albums.

I think of turtles.
How they carry their whole lives
on their backs. My neighbor Jimmi
told me one night how they
make turtle soup down south.
A huge sea turtle—take a sledge hammer
to the massive shell, wedge it open
with one simple, solid blow
till the turtle can feel
no home above him, till everything
is taken away
and there is nothing
he will carry away from this moment.

My parents had three days
to relocate.
"Take only what you can carry."
One simple, solid blow—
They felt no home above them.

       "We were sent to Jerome, Arkansas.
       Arriving there, I wondered how long
       we would be fenced in."

The nice thing about counting stars is
you can do it just about anywhere.
Even in a relocation camp
miles from home, even in Jerome, Arkansas,

where a barbed wire fence crisscrosses itself
making stars of its own—but nothing
worth counting, nothing worth singing to.

My father remembers only two things:

> washing dishes in the mess hall each morning
> beside George Kaminishi and

> listening to Bing Crosby sing "White Christmas"
> on the radio in the barracks late at night.

One morning, George looked up from a greasy skillet
at my dad and said Yosh, you're a happy-go-lucky guy.
What do you want to do with your life?
It was the first time he realized he had a life
to do things with. He was fifteen. He didn't know.
It was only later that Dad found out George
had colon cancer and had no life to do things with.
And when Bing sang "White Christmas" late at night
Dad could only think, he's not singing to me he's
singing to white people.

My mother meanwhile was in a different camp
and hadn't met my father. At night, she'd lie
in bed and think about the old family car
back in the driveway—were the windows smashed
and broken into, the thing driven away by thieves?

Or was the grass a foot tall now, erasing the
Goodyear tires that were so shiny and new?
There was a hole in the week where Sunday
used to be, and she wanted jelly bismarcks
more than ever.

> "Somehow we adjusted. There were weekly
> dances for the young. Dad sent away
> for a huge rice paper umbrella of vivid colors,
> and Peg and I hugged it during stormy
> days."

Dwight Okita

Next Year, in Jerusalem

One by one, the ancient
shapes are dying.
But an old aunt leans there
from *seder* to *seder*
with her cancerous skin
flaking off the sides
of her nose.

Jerusalem waits
where it always was.
They are growing
deaf, though in different degrees.
Thin, yellow fingers twist
at their breasts
for the hearing-aid dials.
Should I repeat it
again for you? Slowly.

Turn up the sound. I am learning
their smiles. I am pleading.
Elijah's cup is untouched.
I hear myself hearing
my breathing. Loud.

Shirley Kaufman

The Survivor

IN MEMORY OF MY COUSIN,
DAVID BER PRISHKULNICK

Nîmes, August, 1966, and I
am going home. Home is here,
you say; your hand reaches
out and touches nothing.
Russia, New York, back,

that was your father; you
took up the road, moving
at dawn or after dusk
in the corrugated Citroën
loaded with shirts and ties.
Light broke in the fields
of poplars and up ahead
was one more village fair
and the peddling.

Once upon a day in 1940
a little man had to leave
his dinner and save his life
and go with his house
on his back, sleeping nowhere,
eating nothing, a shadow
running, a dark stop. That's
how grandpa told the story.
Waking, I found you waiting,
your feet crossed and swinging,
like a child on the bench
outside the window, holding
a sack of warm rolls
for breakfast.

Gray suit, woolen vest,
collar, tie. Now you are
dispersed into the atoms
of gasoline and air
that explode an instant
and are always, dispersed
to the earth that never
warmed you and the rain
drumming down on the hoods
of trucks stalled on the bridge
to Arles. You stop a moment
in my hand that cannot
stop and rise and stumble
onward toward the heart
where there is no rest.

Philip Levine

Sam

if he could have kept
the sky in his dark hand
he would have pulled it down
and held it.
it would have called him lord
as did the skinny women
in virginia. if he
could have gone to school
he would have learned to write
his story and not live it.
if he could have done better
he would have. oh stars
and stripes forever,
what did you do to my father?

Lucille Clifton

Performing

■　■　■

When Hollywood represents Americans, rarely are they the people of African, Latino(a), or Asian heritage who live in Watts. Luis J. Rodriguez describes the absence of his community from these representations: "We were invisible people in a city which thrived on glitter, big screens and big names, but this glamor contained none of our names, none of our faces. The refrain 'this is not your country' echoed for a lifetime." Yet those who because of their skin color, ethnicity, or religion are labeled unAmerican often most vigorously attempt to embody an illusory Americanness. In "When I Was Growing Up," Nellie Wong implies that the lesson of self-hatred is learned along with the mantras of Americanness:

> when I was growing up, I hungered
> for American food, American styles
> coded: *white*　and even to me, a child
> born of Chinese parents, being Chinese
> was feeling foreign, was limiting,
> was unAmerican.

Indian Movie, New Jersey

Not like the white filmstars, all rib
and gaunt cheekbone, the Indian sex-goddess
smiles plumply from behind a flowery
branch. Below her brief red skirt, her thighs
are satisfying-solid, redeeming
as tree trunks. She swings her hips
and the men-viewers whistle. The lover-hero
dances in to a song, his lip-sync
a little off, but no matter, we
know the words already and sing along.
It is safe here, the day
golden and cool so no one sweats,
roses on every bush and the Dal Lake
clean again.
        The sex-goddess switches
to thickened English to emphasize
a joke. We laugh and clap. Here
we need not be embarrassed by words
dropping like lead pellets into foreign ears.
The flickering movie-light
wipes from our faces years of America, sons
who want mohawks and refuse to run
the family store, daughters who date
on the sly.
        When at the end the hero
dies for his friend who also
loves the sex-goddess and now can marry her,
we weep, understanding. Even the men
clear their throats to say, "What *qurbani*!
What *dosti*!" After, we mill around
unwilling to leave, exchange greetings
and good news: a new gold chain, a trip
to India. We do not speak
of motel raids, canceled permits, stones
thrown through glass windows, daughters and sons
raped by Dotbusters.
        In this dim foyer
we can pull around us the faint, comforting smell

of incense and *pakoras*, can arrange
our children's marriages with hometown boys and girls,
open a franchise, win a million
in the mail. We can retire
in India, a yellow two-storied house
with wrought-iron gates, our own
Ambassador car. Or at least
move to a rich white suburb, Summerfield
or Fort Lee, with neighbors that will
talk to us. Here while the film-songs still echo
in the corridors and restrooms, we can trust
in movie truths: sacrifice, success, love and luck,
the America that was supposed to be.

qurbani: sacrifice
dosti: friendship
Dotbusters: growing anti-Indian gangs in New Jersey
pakoras: fried appetizers

Chitra Banerjee Divakaruni

Dear John Wayne

August and the drive-in picture is packed.
We lounge on the hood of the Pontiac
surrounded by the slow-burning spirals they sell
at the window, to vanquish the hordes of mosquitoes.
Nothing works. They break through the smoke-screen for blood.

Always the look-out spots the Indians first,
spread north to south, barring progress.
The Sioux, or Cheyenne, or some bunch
in spectacular columns, arranged like SAC missiles,
their feathers bristling in the meaningful sunset.

The drum breaks. There will be no parlance.
Only the arrows whining, a death-cloud of nerves
swarming down on the settlers
who die beautifully, tumbling like dust weeds

into the history that brought us all here
together: this wide screen beneath the sign of the bear.

The sky fills, acres of blue squint and eye
that the crowd cheers. His face moves over us,
a thick cloud of vengeance, pitted
like the land that was once flesh. Each rut,
each scar makes a promise: *It is*
not over, this fight, not as long as you resist.

Everything we see belongs to us.
A few laughing Indians fall over the hood
slipping in the hot spilled butter.
The eye sees a lot, John, but the heart is so blind.
How will you know what you own?
He smiles, a horizon of teeth
the credits reel over, and then the white fields
again blowing in the true-to-life dark.
The dark films over everything.
We get into the car
scratching our mosquito bites, speechless and small
as people are when the movie is done.
We are back in ourselves.

How can we help but keep hearing his voice,
the flip side of the sound-track, still playing:
Come on, boys, we've got them
where we want them, drunk, running.
They will give us what we want, what we need:
The heart is a strange wood inside of everything
we see, burning, doubling, splitting out of its skin.

Louise Erdrich

When I Was Growing Up

I know now that once I longed to be white.
How? you ask.
Let me tell you the ways.

when I was growing up, people told me
I was dark and I believed my own darkness
in the mirror, in my soul, my own narrow vision.

> when I was growing up, my sisters
> with fair skin got praised
> for their beauty and I fell
> further, crushed between high walls.

when I was growing up, I read magazines
and saw movies, blonde movie stars, white skin,
sensuous lips, and to be elevated, to become
a woman, a desirable woman, I began to wear
imaginary pale skin.

> when I was growing up, I was proud
> of my English, my grammar, my spelling,
> fitting into the group of smart children,
> smart Chinese children, fitting in,
> belonging, getting in line.

when I was growing up and went to high school,
I discovered the rich white girls, a few yellow girls,
their imported cotton dresses, their cashmere sweaters,
their curly hair and I thought that I too should have
what these lucky girls had.

> when I was growing up, I hungered
> for American food, American styles
> coded: *white*   and even to me, a child
> born of Chinese parents, being Chinese
> was feeling foreign, was limiting,
> was unAmerican.

when I was growing up and a white man wanted
to take me out, I thought I was special,
an exotic gardenia, anxious to fit
the stereotype of an oriental chick.

> when I was growing up, I felt ashamed
> of some yellow men, their small bones,
> their frail bodies, their spitting

on the streets, their coughing,
their lying in sunless rooms
shooting themselves in the arms.

when I was growing up, people would ask
if I were Filipino, Polynesian, Portuguese.
They named all colors except white, the shell
of my soul but not my rough dark skin.

when I was growing up, I felt
dirty. I thought that god
made white people clean
and no matter how much I bathed,
I could not change, I could not shed
my skin in the gray water.

when I was growing up, I swore
I would run away to purple mountains,
houses by the sea with nothing over
my head, with space to breathe,
uncongested with yellow people in an area
called Chinatown, in an area I later
learned was a ghetto, one of many hearts
of Asian America.

I know now that once I longed to be white.
How many more ways? you ask.
Haven't I told you enough?

                                        Nellie Wong

Doreen

Doreen had a round face.
She tried to change it.
Everybody made fun
of her in school.

Her eyes so narrow
they asked if she could see,

called her Moonface and
Slits.

Doreen frost tipped her hair,
ratted it five inches high,
painted her eyes round,
glittering blue shadow up to her brow.

Made her look sad
even when she smiled.

She cut gym all the time
because the white powder on her neck
and face would streak
when she sweat.

But Doreen had boobs
more than most of us Japanese girls
so she wore tight sweaters
and low cut dresses
even in winter.

She didn't hang
with us,
since she put so much time
into changing her face.

White boys
would snicker when she passed by
and word got around
that Doreen
went all the way,
smoked and drank beer.

She told us
she met a veteran
fresh back from Korea.

Fresh back
his leg
still puckered pink
from landmines.

She told us
it was a kick
to listen to his stories
about how they'd torture
the gooks
hang them from trees
by their feet
grenades
in their crotch
and watch
them sweat.

I asked her
why she didn't dig brothers.

And her eyes
would disappear
laughing
so loud
she couldn't hear herself.

One day,
Doreen riding fast
with her friend
went through the windshield
and tore off
her skin
from scalp to chin.

And we were sad.

Because
no one could remember
Doreen's face.

Janice Mirikitani

Failure of an Invention

i am not any of the faces
you have put on me america

every mask has slipped
i am not any of the names

or sounds you have called me
the tones have nearly

made me deaf
this dark skin, both of us

have tried to bleach
i can smell the cancer.

this thick hair, these thick lips
both of us have tried to narrow

begging entrance through
the needle of your eye

some of me broken
in the squeeze

and even as I carry
a bone of yours in my back

your soul america
no matter what we've tried

i've never been able to bear

Safiya Henderson-Holmes

Today Was a Bad Day Like TB

FOR AMANDA WHITE

Saw whites clap during a sacred dance
Saw young blond hippie boy with a red stone pipe
    My eyes burned him up
He smiled   *This is a Sioux pipe* he said from his sportscar
    Yes I hiss *I'm wondering how you got it*
    & the name is Lakota not Sioux
I'll tell you he said all friendly & liberal as only
       those with no pain can be
       I turned away Can't charm me can't bear to know
thinking of the medicine bundle I saw opened up in a glass case
       with a small white card beside it
       naming the rich whites who say they
       "own" it
Maybe they have an old Indian grandma back in time
    to excuse themselves
Today was a day I wanted to beat up the smirking man wearing
a pack with a Haida design from Moe's bookstore
Listen Moe's How many Indians do you have working there?
How much money are you sending the Haida people
to use their sacred Raven design?
     You probably have an Indian grandma too
     whose name you don't know
     Today was a day like TB
     you cough & cough trying to get it out
            all that comes
                is blood & spit

Chrystos

Filipino Boogie

Under a ceiling high Christmas tree
I pose
    in my Japanese kimono

My mother hands me
                  a Dale Evans cowgirl skirt
and
    baby cowgirl boots

Mommy and daddy split
No one else is home

I take some rusty scissors
                  and cut the skirt up
     in
        little pieces
(don't give me no bullshit fringe,
Mama)

Mommy and daddy split
No one else is home

    I take my baby cowgirl boots
                   and flush them
                            down
                      the
                            toilet
(don't hand me no bullshit fringe,
Papa)

I seen the Indian Fighter
Too many times
               dug on Sitting Bull
                        before Donald Duck
In my infant dream

These warriors weaved a magic spell

      more blessed than Tinker Bell

(Kirk Douglas rubs his chin
 and slays Minehaha by the campfire)

Mommy and daddy split
There ain't no one else home

I climb a mango tree
and wait for Mohawk drums
(Mama—World War II
is over . . . why you cryin'?)

Is this San Francisco?
Is this San Francisco?
Is this Amerika?

buy me Nestlé's Crunch
buy me Pepsi in a can

Ladies' Home Journal
and Bonanza

I seen Little Joe in Tokyo
I seen Little Joe in Manila
I seen Laramie in Hong Kong
I seen Yul Brynner in San Diego
and the bloated ghost
of Desi Arnaz
dancing
in Tijuana
Rip-off synthetic ivory
to send
the natives
back home
and
North Beach boredom
escapes
the barber shops
on Kearney street
where
they spit out
red tobacco

patiently
waiting
in 1930s suits
and in another dream
I climb a mango tree

and Saturday
>   afternoon
>   Jack Palance
>   bazookas

>   the krauts
>   and
>   the YELLOW PERIL
>   bombs
>   Pearl Harbor

Jessica Hagedorn

Indian Blood

On the stage I stumbled,
my fur boot caught
on a slivered board.
Rustle of stealthy giggles.

Beendaaga' made of velvet
crusted with crystal beads
hung from brilliant tassels of wool,
wet with my sweat.

Children's faces stared.
I felt their flowing force.
Did I crouch like *goh*
in the curious quiet?

They butted to the stage,
darting questions; pointing.
>   Do you live in an igloo?
>   Hah! You eat blubber!

Hemmed in by ringlets of brass,
grass-pale eyes,
the fur of *daghooda-aak*
trembled.

Late in the night
I bit my hand until it was
pierced
with moons of dark
Indian blood.

> *beendaaga':* mittens
> *goh:* rabbit
> *daghooda-aak:* caribou parka

Mary TallMountain

At the Electronic Frontier

I search the chemistry of specific emotions,
a combination of earth and air
that evokes the vital detail,
the phrase that heats the frying pan,
the look that smiles,
offering signals that localize,
where I am, and clarify what I see.
I'm child of the Electronic Frontier.
I learn off the radio waves
of 98.7 Kiss F.M. salsa/disco jams,
that come from a Sony,
bought even though I need a coat,
even though I'm behind on my payments
for the Trinitron Remote Control Color T.V.
that I picked up at Crazy Eddie's last month.
I'm child of the Columbia Space Shuttle,
and I need to know all the electronic gimmicks
invented yesterday
that are already primitive cousins
to those developed today
from eight to five P.M. in Japan.

Miguel Algarín

Vision (2)

No money for lunch so I rode an elevator to the top of the ONB Building, highest elevation in Spokane, where I stood at a window and witnessed 500 years of America: *Over 1 Billion Illusions Served.*

There is so much of this country I love, its supermarkets and bad television, the insane demands of a dollar bill in my pocket, fireworks celebrating the smallest occasions.

I am happy I can find a cup of hot coffee 24 hours a day.

But, America, in *my* country, there are no supermarkets and television is a way of never opening the front door. The fields here are green and there are no monuments celebrating the invasion of Christopher Columbus.

Here, I imagine 1492 and 1992 are two snakes entwined, climbing up the pole some call good medicine, while others name it progress or Manifest Destiny. Maybe it's economics or an extra-inning baseball game. Maybe it's Cotton Mather and Andrew Jackson looking for rescue. Maybe it's a smallpox blanket wrapped around our shoulders in the coldest winter.

Then again, who am I to talk? In the local newspaper I read this morning that my tribe escaped many of the hardships other Native Americans suffered. By the time the twentieth century reached this far west, the war was over. Crazy Horse was gone and The Ghost Dancers were only ghosts. Christopher Columbus was 500 years and 3,000 miles away, fresh from a starring role in The Great American Movie.

I've seen that film at the reservation drive-in. If you look closely, you can see an Indian leaning against the back wall. You won't find his name among the end credits; you can't hear his voice or his song.

Extras, we're all extras.

Sherman Alexie

Translated from the American

after all the drive-in theaters have closed
for winter   I'll make camp alone
at THE NORTH CEDAR   replay westerns

The Seventh Cavalry riding double formation
endlessly   Main Avenue stretches
past The Union Gospel Mission   where I keep
a post office box   miles away

at my permanent address   I'll wrap myself
in old blankets   wait   for white boys
climbing fences   to watch this Indian speak

in subtitles   they'll surround me
and when they ask   "how"
I'll give them exact directions

Sherman Alexie

Imitation of Life

When the movies were 35¢
and people drove fishtail cars,
I went with Cousin Brenda,
my mother and Aunt Elvira
to see *Imitation of Life*.
It played at the Met
on North and Pennsylvania Avenues.
Pennsylvania Avenue was our
Broadway, where the greats performed—
Redd Foxx, Moms Mabley, Chick Webb,
Billie Holiday, and Cab Calloway.
That was when we were colored.

The Met had grandeur,
like the Opéra in Paris.

Curtains were draped on the side.
The wall lights were like fountains.
In the lobby the hot dogs smelled
better than they ever did at home.
Going to the movies in Baltimore
in 1960 was like being taken
out of the day's ordinary breath
and slipped into the crystal air
of wealth and elegance.
I forgot everything in life
so that I might see its other side,
where privilege was routine.
Life was light cast on a screen.

When the daughter in the film
came back to the mother she denied,
my mother and Aunt Elvira heaved
in giant sobs. They mourned
black women who have had to submit
to white men in a white world and
bear children who sleep in confusion,
like the children who people my ancestry,
pulsating fires in a fragile tapestry.

Michael S. Weaver

The Black and White Galaxie

TO GENE F. THOMAS

With water warm enough to make me
feel the gust of spring color,
I added dish detergent and a rag.
The rag was soft enough to caress her
but raise the dirt from her skin.
The soap was strong yet weak so
it wouldn't make her complexion crack.
Then I started at the top of her,
scrubbing the roof of the Ford Galaxie,
my Uncle Frank's cruising machine.

When he trusted me, he watched me
from afar. Then he let me go alone,
having given me a tenet of his wisdom—
a black man gotta make his car shine.

I knew how to hold the water hose,
spray it so it came out in a shower.
I chased the bubbles away and over her,
until the white was like a star's smile,
and the black seemed to pull me into it.
Through the rolled up windows, I checked
the preliminaries, the interior,
an intimate space of hushed conversations,
smiles, and hands on thighs in corners
after the bars closed, of lipstick,
of the black woman's accoutrements.
I checked to see if it was clean enough
to hail a woman's aloof eyes and lips.
Uncle Frank told me what women wanted—
a black man gotta look like money.

The tires were the last, but I saved
a tough energy for them. In motion,
a car's wheels are the signals of the way
its soul hisses, sucks in its breath.
It breathes air like that spring air
of purple and yellow when I washed
the first car I ever drove, as Uncle Frank
let me turn it around in the alley.
I dreamed of romancing girls with a machine
that could play music and smell like evergreens.
I dreamed of the hunt and being in the cut.
Uncle Frank threw in professionalism
to keep me out of Baltimore's apocalypse—
a black man gotta wear suits and ties.

A black man gotta have a private world.

Michael S. Weaver

Blind Solo

after A Love Supreme

A young poet comes to me
in the silence of my office,
a Jewish woman with brown hair
so thick it would roll in my fingers.
She tells me, leaning slightly,
"I like to experiment." I rub
my head where I once had an afro,
pull at the insurgent gray
that tears down the black wool
of youth. I worry myself back
to Saturday nights when I sprayed
and combed and puffed my hair.
In the sixties, listening to Motown,
I chased brown-black-yellow girls
with hair nappy as mine or straight.
I studied myself in mirrors, as
now I suspect this poet wants
to know the bronze kinetic.
She whirls her hair back
in a fluff of brown strands.
I can smell the whiff of air
in the midst of her whirling,
as if I am there, in her dream.
A single strand is on her tongue.
It reminds me of how my mother
pulled the hair back from the faces
of her customers in our basement.
WSID Radio played morning gospels,
while she did the heads of old women
and young women, pressing Africa
until it was waxen and glossy.
She worked their hair into a lather
and dried it until it was like cotton.
She greased it and put the hot comb
to what America called "ugly."
They gossiped and smiled deep smiles.

In front of me, this poet smiles
a curious smile, as if to wonder
what will he want to do with me?
I imagine one piece of fruit
between our lips as we kiss in a bed
where we are naked down to our ages.
I dream an affair with this young
poet. I am a predictable mentor.
In the dream she presses her brown hair
to my chest, panting. We caress.
Somewhere I remember the lie
of my glory, her glory. Our skin
reminds us of its treatise. I awaken
from the daydream, see her blinking.
My back aches as I see her braces
on her teeth, and I dismiss her, kindly.
She shuffles to the door with a backpack,
to take her beauty back into New York,
which has been listening to our silences
and understands we are prisoners of
what we cannot say. Her eyes gleam, ask,
but I was beautiful, wasn't I?

Michael S. Weaver

Mafioso

Frank Costello eating spaghetti in a cell at San Quentin,
Lucky Luciano mixing up a mess of bullets and
calling for parmesan cheese,
Al Capone baking a sawed-off shotgun into a
huge lasagna—

          are you my uncles, my
only uncles?

      Mafiosi,
bad uncles of the barren
cliffs of Sicily—was it only you
that they transported in barrels

like pure olive oil
across the Atlantic?

               Was it only you
who got out at Ellis Island with
black scarves on your heads and cheap cigars
and no English and a dozen children?

No carts were waiting, gallant with paint,
no little donkeys plumed like the dreams of peacocks.
Only the evil eyes of a thousand buildings
stared across at the echoing debarcation center,
making it seem so much smaller than a piazza,

only a half dozen Puritan millionaires stood on the wharf,
in the wind colder than the impossible snows of the Abruzzi,
ready with country clubs and dynamos

to grind the organs out of you.

                           Sandra Mortola Gilbert

Digging in the
Streets of Gold

My parents were fish.
They came from Europe, swimming.

This was before Hitler was invented,
when a wheelbarrow of money
got you a loaf of bread.

Twice, they voted for Stevenson,
and he dropped dead on the streets of London.

Mamie was drunk. McCarthy mad.

They did their jobs.
They didn't weep over the Rosenbergs.

They tried to buy their way
out of history.
The rising elevator was their armor.
The wolf at the door the family crest.

Two weeks before he died, my father smiled wisely
over murdered Kennedy, and lifted his shovel
and bent his back,
and went to dig in the streets of gold.

                                                                 Barry Seiler

Matinee

Two o'clock on a Saturday afternoon in November,
your father drops you off near the worn steps
of the Manor movie house, the marquee
blinking in a relay of hot lights and foot-high
letters you are too young to read. You clutch
your silver quarter tight in your small hand
as your father reaches past you and pushes open
the car door, nudges you out with his smile
to where other children crowd up to the box
office, screaming and yelling in their bright coats.
You remember the phrase "Let's pretend" that the new
girl on your street taught you through the summer,
always wanting you to play hateful "house," to pretend
tameness when your own blood ran wild with foxes
and invisible deer. Still, you fell in love with the word—
pretend, now, you are a Sleeping Beauty glittering
your way through an ancient war of rough bodies until
you reach the theater's magical cave, hunch down
in a torn seat in the first row, lifting your face
to the safety of the blank screen. You drift among smells
of hot balls, jujubes and cherry dots, hotness and sweetness
on a hundred tongues, savor salty popcorn from a cardboard
carnival box. In the musty shadows the screen swells with
Hollywood technicolor, cowboys-and-Indians, Indians swooping
down on painted ponies, scalping innocent whites, raising
even your hair as you sit, petrified, by war whoops

and swirling hatchet blades, and brown faces webbed
with black. Like the other children, you cheer,
throw popcorn when the good cowboys kill every Indian
at movie's end, and the hero in his white hat points out,
"The only good Indian is a dead one." You stumble
outdoors, wedged in the crowd. A dark-eyed boy pulls
your long hair, and just as you get ready to kill him
you spot your father waiting for you in his old car.
You climb in and tell him how horrible Indians are.
He listens as the first snow of the year starts to fall,
turns on the windshield wipers as you both yield in silence
to their measured slaps, ice crystals melting inward
on the window glass. Christmas bulbs strung along bare wires
over Main Street shimmer, blue green red, in the snow dusk.
"Your grandfather was Indian," your father says at last.
"You're part Indian. Indians were here first, like the first snow."
You cross your arms as he backs out into a cloud of smoke.
The snow drops into the lights of town like feathers from a vast
and wounded bird. Pretend, *pretend*. You glitter as you fall.

Susan Clements

Deer Cloud

The Mohawk lover who told her he stripped all his clothes
off when they asked, "What is wrong with you?," boasted
once after a joint field trip to his shrink's office
that he could pinpoint a psychiatrist's success by how many
aboriginal arts and crafts covered up his otherwise bland walls.
Now she has her own shrink to visit for bi-monthly maintenance,
fifteen minutes to obtain a prescription for Ativan, to count
the number of times Dr. Rothenberg uses the words "reason"
and "rational." Sure enough, the walls she faces behind his face
prove a cover-up, R. C. Gorman originals, Indian women with bowed
heads and still, rounded bodies flowing, harmonious, into fluorescent
desert. Mohawk herself, she informs the doctor the paintings
put her at ease. The minute she speaks, the thought shifts into lie,
the framed women look trapped and tranquilized. But she, a polite
Indian on tranquilizers, doesn't mention it. Her shrink, a polite
Jew, possibly on tranquilizers, doesn't mention how

with bowed head she used to cry, and why
he never asks her why.

Behind her back on the far wall hangs a grand painting, a Sioux
woman on a galloping horse, all freedom and wind. She only sees it
when she walks in, and out, again, but today's glimpse makes her
brave enough to say she had a dream last night, when her shrink
    wonders
does she sleep well? "I sleep well, I dream well, last night
I dreamed an old Indian man approached me in the dark wood
and gave me his name." Her tired-eyed shrink admits he hardly recalls
his dreams, just gray fragments. Had he been raised in a sane
family like hers, dream-telling each day, he would have needed
to invent dreams for the telling. He doesn't ask her
her new name, begins scrawling out her prescription so she
can wear chemical branks for another two months, so she
won't ask, "Am I nothing to you but a biochemical imbalance,
blood floating around with no spirit, no real reason
to cry, to hurt, to scream rage? Where are the ghosts of your
people, Dr. Rational Rothenberg? Where are the ghosts of mine?"
Behind her, the Sioux woman gallops between her shoulder blades.
She knows a medicine woman her successful shrink could go to,
maybe help him dream. But she is a polite Indian hooked
on tranquilizers, and doesn't mention it.

                                                    Susan Clements

Can't Tell

When World War II was declared
on the morning radio,
we glued our ears, widened our eyes.
Our bodies shivered.

A voice said
Japan was the enemy,
Pearl Harbor a shambles
and in our grocery store
in Berkeley, we were suspended

next to the meat market
where voices hummed,
valises, pots and pans packed,
no more hot dogs, baloney,
pork kidneys.

We children huddled on wooden planks
and my parents whispered:
We are Chinese, we are Chinese.
Safety pins anchored,
our loins ached.

Shortly our Japanese neighbors vanished
and my parents continued to whisper:
We are Chinese, we are Chinese.

We wore black arm bands,
put up a sign
in bold letters.

Nellie Wong

Amazone

Blond-haired, green-eyed, Italian girl,
The first of your "type" to enter the wasp
World of advertising, 1943: you were
Young, healthy, and eager to be French.

(Red-headed grandfather be blessed for
Lightening things up a bit, but our people
Lived too far South and vowel-ending surnames
Darkened our hopes for approval.)

You didn't have a daughter to teach you
How to become ethnic, and my niecehood
Was spent revering your silence, your
Permanence, the *parfum* on your dresser.

■ ■ ■

I like now to imagine the irony of
Dressing rituals: when you swathed yourself
In Frenchness and fetched your married sister
For the opera, singing Italian arias along
The way.

Mary Jo Bona

Blonde White Women

They choke cities like snowstorms.

On the morning train, I flip through my *Ebony*,
marveling at the bargain basement prices
for reams of straightened hair
and bleaches for the skin. Next to me,
skinny pink fingers rest upon a briefcase,
shiver a bit under my scrutiny.
Leaving the tunnel, we hurtle into hurting sun.
An icy brush paints the buildings
with shine, fat spirals of snow
become blankets, and Boston stops breathing.

It is my habit to count them. So I search
the damp, chilled length of the train car
and look for their candle flames of hair,
the circles of blood at their cheeks,
that curt dismissing glare
reserved for the common, the wrinkled, the black.

I remember striving for that breathlessness,
toddling my five-year-old black butt around
with a dull gray mophead covering my
nappy hair, wishing myself golden.
Pressing down hard with my
carnation pink Crayola, I filled faces

in coloring books, rubbed the waxy stick
across the back of my hand until the skin broke.

When my mop hair became an annoyance
to my mother, who always seemed to be mopping,
I hid beneath my father's white shirt,
the sleeves hanging down on either side of my head,
the coolest white light pigtails.
I practiced kissing, because to be blonde and white
meant to be kissed, and my fat lips slimmed
around words like "delightful" and "darling."
I hurt myself with my own beauty.

When I was white, my name was Donna.
My teeth were perfect; I was always out of breath.

In first grade, my blonde teacher
hugged me to her because I was the first
in my class to read, and I thought the rush
would kill me. I wanted her to swallow
me, to be my mother, to be the first fire
moving in my breast. But when she pried
me away, her cool blue eyes shining with
righteousness and too much touch,
I saw how much she wanted to wash.

She was not my mother,
the singing Alabama woman
who shook me to sleep
and fed me from her fingers.
I could not have been blacker
than I was at that moment.
My name is Patricia Ann.

Even crayons fail me now—
I can find no color darker,
more beautiful, than I am.
This train car grows tense with me.
I pulse, steady my eyes,
shake the snow from my short black hair,
and suddenly I am surrounded by snarling madonnas

demanding that I explain
my treachery.

Patricia Smith

Cincinnati

Freedom at last
in this town aimless
I walked against the rush
hour traffic
My first day
in a real city
where

no one knew me.

No one except one
hissing voice that said
dirty jap
warm spittle on my right cheek.
I turned and faced
the shop window
and my spittled face
spilled onto a hill
of books.
Words on display.

In Government Square
people criss-crossed
the street
like the spokes of
a giant wheel.

I lifted my right hand
but it would not obey me.
My other hand fumbled
for a hankie.

My tears would not
wash it. They stopped
and parted.
My hankie brushed
the forked
tears and spittle
together.
I edged toward the curb
loosened my fisthold
and the bleached laced
mother-ironed hankie blossomed in
the gutter atop teeth marked
gum wads and heeled candy wrappers.

Everyone knew me.

Mitsuye Yamada

American Son

I
When I was ten
I rolled my hair in rags
for Shirley Temple ringlets
polished my teeth white
for a Pepsodent smile
clattered about in slick
tap shoes
so my father
sent me away
to his mother in Japan
who took me in
because I was hers,

a piece of an only son sent
home like dirty laundry to be
washed and pressed
then returned to America less
tomboy American more
ladylike Japanese

a daily reminder of him
who only yesterday
crossed that river
on a swinging narrow bridge
to school

a thin-boned body like his
that worked years ago
in the teeming rice fields
until dark.

II
Satokaeri
returning
to one's origins
wherever that may be
a tradition in Japan
caring for grandmothers
and great-grandmothers
my father said
do this
for me.

Satokaeri
returning
and turning
for an absentee son
whose memories of boyhood
days hardened like
frosting on an uneaten cake.

III
I came unformed
took sliding runs on polished corridors
never closed *shojis* behind me
never stopped asking
questions
about Grandmother's curly hair
she unrolled daily and ironed
straight with a rod
warmed on coals,
never stopped being frightened

by Great-Grandmother's smile
showing black teeth
she dyed with a wad of cotton
dipped in berry juice
like the *grandes dames*
in old Japanese movies.

My grandmother answered
only questions I never asked
"Yes, your papa is my son
Yes, my landlord my son
comes home only twice
in twenty-three years
once to build this house.
He was a good son.
What good
is a son
in America?"

Mitsuye Yamada

Why I Don't Speak Italian

God knows, teaching the Renaissance I could use it.

Every Sunday and national holiday
during World War II
my Italian grandfather raised the American flag
up the pole planted in our front lawn.

My Aunt Clara told childhood stories
about being called *dago* and *guinea*,
hurt by friends' juvenile jokes:
"when Italian tires become flat
dago wop, wop, wop, wop."
Once, when I was four,
to console my swarthy aunt I told her
she was almost as beautiful
                    as a blonde.

In wartime movies my buddies and I saw
white-skinned Germans stand firm and doomed
while a tan Italian surrendered in the Sahara to Bogart,
sang *Aïda,* and fixed the stalled American tank.

The teenaged girls who flourished on Bay Ridge Avenue
passing by our whistles and wisecracks
giggled and flashed back in English only.

To visit Rome, Venice, and Florence,
where I could identify Da Vinci's drawings
by their left-handed strokes,
I bought a recorded language course.
The first disc was cracked, skipped and repeated.

Oh I know enough, when teaching sonnets,
to explain why Teutonic English is rime-poor
compared to vowel-rich, mellifluous Italian.
I even recite Dante's Ulysses:
    Considerate la vostra semenza
fatti non foste a viver come bruti
ma per sequir virtute e conoscenza.

Too old to gape on corners anymore,
at times, when I see a stunning
fair-skinned and magnificent blonde,
I also know how my dark, civilized
Roman ancestors felt
when they crossed the Rhine
and gazed,
speechless,
upon the giant, golden-haloed barbarians.

                                        Arthur L. Clements

The First

Mrs. Conti was the first
blonde Italian I ever knew
she didn't have any children

she was the first
who had a husband
with a mistress
Mr. Conti was the first man
with money enough
to have a mistress
whiskey money
he bootlegged whiskey once
and now, a czar in Trenton,
his wife could drive a car
Mrs. Conti was
the first one of our friends
with free time and her own car
she'd visit our house on Thursdays
"Poor Veronica"
my parents would say—poor Veronica
she had purses of every color and size
purses were no problem for Mrs. Conti
she gave me all the old ones
smelling of tobacco and perfume
Veronica was the only woman
I'd ever seen
smoke a cigarette
at least in those days
except in the movies
the black patent-leather purse
was my favorite
a gold satin lining
shiny and fine
kept in tissue by my paper dolls
filling the room with a mysterious scent
once I put my Sonja Henie doll inside
she came out covered with smoke
adultery, sadness
and lust
beautiful Sonja
her strong muscles
her upraised arms
her tiny sparkling skirts
smooth legs
strong knees
a skater who could cut figures with the angels

a natural blonde
clean and able
a champion
she could drive a car anywhere she wanted
she didn't have to fill her time on Thursdays.

Grace Cavalieri

Brain on Ice

The El Train Poem

There's a seat right next to me
On the Milwaukee el
Obviously vacant,
Awaiting some Loop-bound occupant.
Riders from Ukrainian Village,
Or maybe Warsaw,
Rush past me in righteous,
But ignorant horror.
Not calmed by my Givenchy tie
Or Bass Boy penny loafers.
Apparently not reassured
By my literary look.
Unmoved by my perusal of the
New York Review of Books.
To them I am Cabrini Green
Strapped to an attaché case,
And for instilled fear
Of being robbed, stabbed, raped
Or worse
Conversed with incoherently,
They dare not sit next to me.

I am the Color Purple
In a navy blue overcoat.
I am Bigger Thomas on his way to work.
I may be Nat Turner on urbanized revolt.
I am Mandingo

With a big   thick   black
Toshiba laptop.
I am Super Fly with Oxford collar
And Harvard law degree.
An invisible do-rag hovers above
My missing Malcolm X shades,
There is a bulge in my pocket
And it just might be a blade.
I am the stereotypical cause-effect
That masochistically strikes them blind.
I am the charred rope with which
They hang their consciousness
During terrorized imprisonment
In Hollywood formatted blackness.

It is an undefiled seat
Adjacent to the door
Opening at the same Loop stall
Outside the deco-art marble plantation
In which we all
Are hourly enslaved.

                                        Michael Warr

Malcolm Is 'Bout
More Than Wearing a Cap

The problem is not the letter X.
It is not the myriad of emblazoned caps,
even when worn backward by whiteboys.
This is not a damnation of hats.
But when Arsenio sports a rhinestone-
studded X to match his Armani suit,
I see Malcolm emasculated by fashion.
As if X symbolized a new NBA team to
challenge the Pistons, Cavs, and Bulls,
the X on their jerseys blinking "Buy American"
with every slam dunk for McDonald's

cause of the week. Then a sandwich is
named Sandwich X. And a four-wheeler
is named Bronco X. Until the substance
of X is xed out.

Soon Sesame Street will teach the letter X
with a militant horn-rimmed Malcolm
Muppet as a visual teaching aid.
Bert irritating Ernie by any means necessary.
And a dollar for every X on a cap
can either make a millionaire,
or hopefully help pay for a revolution.
A word we hear these days
almost as much as we see Xs.
In America where all is commodified.

Will X stand for change
or changing what America wears?
As ruling designers alienate
the Malcolm from the X.
Separate the meaning of Malcolm
from the punctuated power of X.
To Malcolm is to do.
I mean your cap is mean
but Malcolm is 'bout more
than wearing a cap.
Your horn-rims are clean,
but Malcolm is 'bout true vision.
Your T-shirt is down,
but Malcolm is 'bout taking over.
Your enemy will also wear the X,
sell the X, sex the X, film the X,
praise the X, record the X, raise the X.
paint the X, fraternize and buy the X.
But the enemy will never Malcolm the X.
Only we can Malcolm the X.

Michael Warr

American Dream: First Report

First nobody liked us; they said we smelled
and looked too short and dark.
Then the TV proposed marriage, and we said yes.
Momma and sisters kept the commercials going,
to prove we were married in the palaces of soap.

Who would have guessed that the end
of those voyages, the agony of steerage,
insults from the Yankees, the tenement rooms
without windows, like fish cans,
the penny pinching and fear of the bosses
would end this way, as well-dressed citizens
devoted to the disinfection of our carpets,
as the culminating dream of Grandpa
(who liked to spit on floors while he talked)?

Joseph Papaleo

Behaving Like a Jew

When I got there the dead opossum looked like
an enormous baby sleeping on the road.
It took me only a few seconds—just
seeing him there—with the hole in his back
and the wind blowing through his hair
to get back again into my animal sorrow.
I am sick of the country, the bloodstained
bumpers, the stiff hairs sticking out of the grilles,
the slimy highways, the heavy birds
refusing to move;
I am sick of the spirit of Lindbergh over everything,
that joy in death, that philosophical
understanding of carnage, that
concentration on the species.
—I am going to be unappeased at the opossum's death.
I am going to behave like a Jew

and touch his face, and stare into his eyes,
and pull him off the road.
I am not going to stand in a wet ditch
with the Toyotas and the Chevies passing over me
at sixty miles an hour
and praise the beauty and the balance
and lose myself in the immortal lifestream
when my hands are still a little shaky
from his stiffness and his bulk
and my eyes are still weak and misty
from his round belly and his curved fingers
and his black whiskers and his little dancing feet.

Gerald Stern

The Mary Morelle Show

My Aunt Maria
had a show
a talk show
it was big
in the midwest
a huge success
she interviewed the Beatles,
the Stones, Lucille Ball,
Kennedy himself
on Plains TV
in North Plains, Ohio.

She was the eighth
of ten kids
and given the name
Maria Amelia Earhart Morelle.
Her parents, born in Italy,
immigrated here
and it was thought they
had a passion for naming
their kids after famous Americans
but it wasn't that.

The United States
took their own
Italian names
and spit them out
in shortened versions.
Giovanni became Jonny became Jon
Cavacini became Cacini became Caci (Casey).
The pressure to assimilate
performed miraculous mutations.
Alfonsina became Alfy became Al
Letinoni became Letino became Leto became Leto (Lido).
What was Italian became no one
what was American became everyone.
To be both was to be someone else.
Brief, clipped endings
were survival.

Whole words got chewed up
and swallowed
and regurgitated
into a perfect
ethnic-free mold.
No, it wasn't that they *liked* it
my grandparents knew too much
how better to feed the hungry dog
of assimilation
than with its own meat.
So they picked
long, tedious "American" names
cultural icons.
The youngest son's
full name
was Franklin Delano Roosevelt Morelle
but everyone
just called him Del.

She started out in radio
where her nose
didn't matter
but later on
it did.

Television, they say,
makes a big nose
even bigger.
So she got a new one
a little, slightly upturned
less Italian one.
They say
it helped her career
though she never changed her name
but somehow
over the years
the last vowel
got silenced.
Morelle to Morellé
and we all know
once the nose goes
the last vowel will follow.

Theater began to take
an interest in her
she could sing and act
she played Auntie Mame
starred in *Applause, Applause*
played Charlie Chaplin.
She was a hit
and the pressure grew.
Release took the shape
of the bottle.
She liked dry martinis
red wine
and a long hot
game of cards.
She cussed
expertly
when she lost
and when she won.
I remember
mixing her martinis
when I was a kid.
I always got
the olive.

They used to
suggest she wear
certain colors
on camera
to ease the tone
of her olive skin.
Yellows and pinks were out
earth tones
and basic black and white
were in.
She dressed elegantly
and expensively.
Her sisters and brothers
never got used to the celebrity
they felt exposed
to the scrutiny
of this world
but fiercely proud nonetheless.
Her Momma and Poppa wept
and prayed for their daughter
for they knew too much
of this world already.
And all the family
were left wondering
just how she did it.

How did she do it.
This was the 50s and 60s
she never married
she worked
day and night
she trimmed her nose
she got drunk
she worked
day and night
she learned everything
there was to know
and then learned more.
She worked
day and night
she was a tough
intelligent, talented woman

ahead of her time.
Italian people stared at her
the clothes
the success
the different ways
sometimes in awe
sometimes in fear.
Other people stared at her
sometimes in envy
almost always in disgust.
Rumors flew
she caught them
with a raw fist.
How did she do it.

She pretended not to be Italian
on TV
and when she was off the air
she kept the company of Italians
ate Italian food
played Italian games
spoke mainly Italian
uttered the long liquid Italian names
over and over again
stayed close to the old neighborhood.

My Aunt Maria
had a show
a famous show
the Mary Morelle Show
she was a star
she knew everyone
that was anyone
and it was all crisp business
and shiny cars.
They drove her around
gave her many compliments
enjoyed her *spunk*
they never came to her home
afraid they might slip and ask
why, at 40, did she still live with her Momma

My Aunt Maria
had a show
the Mary Morelle Show.
She knew everyone
that was anyone
but did anyone
really know
her.

Denise Nico Leto

To H.N.

It is always easy to sentimentalize old lovers. They are distant
and distance, we have heard, increases desire.
You live now a few miles down the freeway, and years ago.
How I wish there were rice fields, an ocean, between us,
a hedge of foxgloves, rows of sweet peas, cedar forests, canyons, deserts,
and a story of plane wheels screeching on the tarmac
or helicopters lifting above a city, tiny figures, stick-like, like those a
    child draws,
hanging from the landing rim, falling to the sea.
It would have been history then, not me, who failed you.
My guilt would be greater and, therefore, more easy.

I recall your father, who still sews in a store I sometimes pass.
And your mother who served me steaming bowls, riddled with cori-
    ander, globes of oil,
a pepper that stung my eyes to tears. And your sisters, each younger,
more fluent than you. And one, more beautiful. (In those days
there was little I refused.) And your brothers who, with sticks on
    strings,
fought on the streets, in school corridors, the shouts of chink and gook,
claiming a fierceness that surprised their larger white opponents.
Twelve of you in a three-bedroom flat. I sat at the table
and read with you through Fitzgerald, O'Connor's story of the Bible
    salesman
who steals the crippled girl's wooden leg, leaves her stranded in the
    hayloft
in a cracker Georgia. You were eighteen. Your mother thought

I was teaching you English. Seeing in your family my father's
a half century before, I almost believed that. Sometimes
we went roller-skating, to a movie, disobeying your parents.
I went home afterwards to the woman I was living with. Who became
    my wife.

What else? You'd lived in Vientiane, spoke Laotian, Vietnamese.
I recall moments in a car, on my couch, in my bed.
And still can't stop. Won't make amends.
A cousin of yours was among the bones they dug up
in Hue. You got used to our winters, their icy winds.
I flunked out of grad school. You graduated one May.

And what it all adds up to I can't tell.
An accident of history? Something sordid, brief, betrayed?
You were beautiful. The only Asian woman I've ever touched, reaching
beyond the mirror of my own self-hatred, propelled by my lust.
And there was this night, at the top of the tallest building in town,
looking down at the lights and car beams shuttling towards the horizon,
when you bent by a candle-flame, said you would never forget this night.

But somehow I suspect that for you, as for me, that memory now means
    little.
You're probably indifferent. Which is just as well.

                                                        David Mura

My Rich Uncle,
Whom I Only Met Three Times

We were never invited to his house.
We went there once while they were all in Hawaii,
climbed steps from which someone had shoveled
the snow, not him, to the wide terrace.
Yellow brick, the house peered into fir and juniper.
It was too large for me to imagine what it held
but I was sure every one of them, four girls
and bony wife, each had a room of her own.

He had been a magician and on those rare
nights he had to stay at the Detroit Statler
downtown, he would summon us for supper
in the hotel restaurant. Mother would put on
and take off every dress in her closet, all six,
climb in the swaybacked brown Hudson muttering shame.
He would do tricks with his napkin and pull
quarters from my ears and spoons from his sleeves.

He had been a clumsy acrobat, he had failed at comedy
and vaudeville; he was entertaining for a party
when he met a widow with four girls and an inheritance.
He waltzed right out of her romantic movie dreams
and he strolled into her house and she had him redone.
He learned to talk almost like her dead husband.
He learned to wear suits, order dinners and give orders
to servants. His name changed, his background rebuilt,
his religion painted over, he almost fit in.

Of my uncles, only he was unreal, arriving by plane
to stay on the fanciest street in downtown Detroit.
The waiter brought a phone to the table, his broker
calling. I imagined a cowboy breaking horses.
He made knives disappear. He made a napkin vanish.
He was like an animated suit, no flesh, no emotions
bubbling the blood and steaming the windows as
my other uncles and aunts did. Only the discrete
Persian leather smell of money droned in my nose.

His longest trick was to render himself invisible.
Then one night after the guests had left, he went down
to the basement in the latest multi-level glass vast
whatnot shelf of house and hanged himself by the furnace.
They did not want his family at the funeral. She had
no idea, his wife said, why would he be depressed?
I remember his laugh like a cough and his varnished
face, buffed till the silverware shone in his eyes.
His last trick was to vanish himself forever.

Marge Piercy

Untitled Blues

after a photograph by Yevgeni Yevtushenko

I catch myself trying
to look into the eyes
of the photo, at a black boy
behind a laughing white mask
he's painted on. I
could've been that boy
years ago.
Sure, I could say
everything's copacetic,
listen to a Buddy Bolden cornet
cry from one of those coffin-
shaped houses called
shotgun. We could
meet in Storyville,
famous for quadroons,
with drunks discussing God
around a honky-tonk piano.
We could pretend we can't
see the kitchen help
under a cloud of steam.
Other lurid snow jobs:
night & day, the city
clothed in her see-through
French lace, as pigeons
coo like a beggar chorus
among makeshift studios
on wheels—Vieux Carré
belles having portraits painted
twenty years younger.
We could hand jive
down on Bourbon & Conti
where tap dancers hold
to their last steps,
mammy dolls frozen
in glass cages. The boy
locked inside your camera,

perhaps he's lucky—
he knows how to steal
laughs in a place
where your skin
is your passport.

                    Yusef Komunyakaa

Second Class Citizen

FOR MOM

we laughed
calling it latent wop syndrome
the compulsive addiction
that triggered your spending
week after week
using layers of i. magnin clothes
t-birds and two hundred dollar a pair shoes
to eradicate the shabby shame of
growing up foreign and poor
being born to farm laborer parents
in a contractor's shack
using bank books to balance
your cheated childhood
that scrawny immigrant's kid
who still squirms uneasily around
behind the elegant vogue dressed façade
scared that someday this
middle-class masquerade
will crack down the middle and fall away
letting a squatty italian fishwife with a
broken womb in black
wearing fat nun's shoes
climb through and escape
you with one foot planted
on the skidding skateboard
of near country club status
the other nailed
back there on ellis island

stuck in quarantine
and waiting official permission
to be let off the boat

Jennifer Lagier

Three Gypsies

FOR MY MOTHER

Balancing on Oriental spike heels,
these three Zhou daughters squint
from the Kodak print, their silk
dresses shaping their bodies
with cloth hips and cardboard collars.
They lean forward, maybe to talk
or stay upright. Gold gypsy beads,
plastic roses and pearl brooches
draw down their flat bosoms, line
their necks and sun-stroked arms.
Serious in their dressed-up beauty,
they are unaware that the silk dyes
and embroidery do not mix with
the Kansas browns of the lawn,
or the wood A-frames of houses
in construction behind them.
Carolyn smiles through zippered brows,
her blue silk skirt puddled
around her ankles like cast-off clothes.
She cannot be taller than four feet.
Daiyan holds her coral skirt out
like bat wings, chest puffed out,
a belt hula-hooped around her American
jumper. Hands taped flat on her thighs
to show off the ten cent rings
on each finger, Sonya stands with her toes
pointing inward. Her earrings do not
match: one springs outward, a locked
pendulum, while the other droops
like the water of a sprinkler behind them.

There are patches of green, a calico
of browns, tans and leaf. In this
tapestry, a boy bikes past with a Federal
Way News bag on his shoulder.
He turns to watch this parade of gypsies.

Shalin Hai-Jew

from Sweet Daddy

So Motown taught me all about men. Men worshipped
women. Men couldn't live without women. The men who
wailed beneath my phonograph needle were always begging you
not to go, whining because you'd left after they'd begged you
not to go, or praying out loud that you'd come on home so they
could beg you not to go before you left them again.

But I remember my mother coming home from the taverns,
dressed in sequins and Chanel, crying because the blues had bro-
ken through and touched bone, because she couldn't threaten
to leave a man she didn't have.

I remember my friend Debra, her eleven-year-old belly tight
with the child of her mother's lover. She'd listened to the songs
too, and waited along with me for the mindless drone of
romance. She remembered him saying "I love you, I love you,
really baby, I love you," and that's the way it was supposed to
be, wasn't it, even in the movies wasn't it all sweet pain and
shivering?

Debra told me she wasn't scared because babies just slipped
out of your body while you were sleeping.

No men seemed to be begging my mother and Debra for
anything. But I was still awkward, still skinny-legged, still wild
by the head, still gawky and uncertain, still a stone fox when no
one was around. I wanted so much to believe in the music.

So while the women I knew teetered, fell and crumbled in
need of a beating heart, I kept waiting for a man to beg me for
something.

It's not like I was asking for much
I didn't wanna be Diana, I just wanted to be Florence
the exact crooner in the background, the one with the hips

the one men winked at while shaking Diana's hand
the one who was so filled with heat and music
that one day her heart just burst instead of broke
I just wanted to be her

■   ■   ■

There was a time I would have given a fine, light-skinned boy
with curly hair several million dollars to simply look like he was
about to think about thinking about asking me to dance.

That's what it was all about, a man who looked the way
Motown sounded. He'd have the slickest edges. I only got to
dance with the ones who sang a wet game in my ear or crooned
off key into the side of my face, messing up the lyrics and wet-
ting up my earlobes.

Those fine, "high yella" guys always made my body feel
stupid. Lord, I'd see one of them every once in a while and I'd
gaze at him like he was *all* the answers. But the closest I'd
come to dancing with one was when he stepped on my toe on
the way to somebody else.

If you say Motown didn't teach you to slow dance, you're
lying, pure and simple. Oh, you paler types may have done the
tea parlor routine to Frankie Valli and the Four Seasons when
your folks were around, but I know that as soon as they left you
screwed the red bulb into the basement lamp and gave Smokey
the rights to your body.

It was easy to pretend I was dancing with a boy everyone
else wanted. All I had to do was put on "Ooh, Baby, Baby,"
wrap my hands around a pillow, bury my lips in it and move my
feet real slow.

But pretty soon I had to realize that if I was sixteen and waiting
to dance, with my legs all greased up and my hair growing nappy
under the hot lights, a real cute boy would be off somewhere
else, breaking a more beautiful heart.

Patricia Smith

What It's Like to Be a Black Girl
(For Those of You Who Aren't)

first of all, it's being nine years old and
feeling like you're not finished, like your
edges are wild, like there's something,
everything, wrong. it's dropping food coloring
in your eyes to make them blue and suffering
their burn in silence. it's popping a bleached
white mophead over the kinks of your hair and
primping in front of mirrors that deny your
reflection. it's finding a space between your
legs, a disturbance at your chest, and not knowing
what to do with the whistles. it's jumping
double dutch until your legs pop, it's sweat
and vaseline and bullets, it's growing tall and
wearing a lot of white, it's smelling blood in
your breakfast, it's learning to say fuck with
grace but learning to fuck without it, it's
flame and fists and life according to motown,
it's finally having a man reach out for you
then caving in
around his fingers.

■ ■ ■

A thin layer of Vaseline and a thick pair of sweatsocks made
your legs look bigger, made the muscles of your calves bulge. So
when you jumped rope or when you just *walked*, the boys all
came around, they sniffed at you like hot, hungry dogs, their
pelvises just wouldn't sit still.

And you always had to make your hair look like more hair
than it was. First you crammed the pores of your scalp with
grease, then you flattened your hair with a pressing comb until it
lay flat and black upside your head like ink. I was always trying
to work a couple of rubberbands up on my little bit of hair, and
the result could have been called pigtails—until the rubberbands
popped off, that is.

If you lived on the west side of Chicago in the '60s and

your hair was long and wavy and your skin was cream and your
legs shone like glass, your ticket was as good as written.

But if you were truly bone black and your hair practically
choked on its kinks, you waited for the music to give you a shape.

The Marvelettes made me pretty, Smokey wailed for just a
little bit of me, and the Temptations taught me to wait, wait,
wait for that perfect love.

Every two weeks, a new 45 hit the streets, but I already
knew it, crying in my room under the weight of an imaginary
lover, breathing steam onto mirrors, pretend slow dancing in the
arms of a seriously fine young thang who rubbed at the small of
my back with a sweet tenor.

In the real world the boys avoided me like creamed corn—
but I was the supreme mistress of Motown, wise in the ways of
love, pretending I knew why my blue jeans had begun to burn.

Those devils from Detroit were broiling my blood with the
beat. They were teaching me that wanting meant waiting. They
were teaching me what it meant to be a black girl.

Patricia Smith

Starlight Haven

Susie Wong was at the Starlight Haven,
the Good Times Bar and Sailors' Home.
It was always dark at noon—
you had to blink three times before
you could see Susie standing by
the washed chutney jar half filled
with ten- and twenty-cent coins.
When the bar was empty her eyes were sad,
and she'd mop the Formica tables,
dry a row of tall Anchor Pilsner
glasses. The wet cloth slapped-slapped
like Susie's Japanese slippers
over the dirty floor.
                    Then the swing doors
bang and the darkness is full of white
uniforms, full of cold Tigers
sweating in warm air-conditioning.

I think of the flutter in Susie's pulse—
Buy a drink, Tommy boy! G.I. Joe!
Yankee Doodle! Howdy Doody! Romeo!—
and suddenly Johnny Mathis
like black magic is crooning "Chances Are."
Her girlish voice is soft and happy,
soft like a tubby belly after
six babies and ten years of beat-up
marriage, happy as only Singapore
Susie Wongs can be, when Johnny
and Ray are rocking the bottles
and their tops pop off and the chutney
jar is singing chink, chink.
The red-faced brawny men are laughing
at her voice. Quack, quack, they laugh
so hard they spill Tigers over
the plastic counter. Quack, quack, fuck, fuck.
Susie looks at the bar-man who makes
his coolie eyes dumb black stones
and wipes up the yellow puddles
without a grunt.   Thirty years later
I hear mother singing "In the sweet
by and by." She is a Jesus woman
grown up from bar-girl. Sailors and Tommies
have disappeared from her Memory Lane.
I still keep the bracelet mother gave me,
gold saved from beer spilled on the clean
tables, her clean lap. I savor the taste
of that golden promise, never to love men
in white who laugh, quack, quack, fuck, fuck.

                    Shirley Geok-lin Lim

Black and White

Why is it in my middle-aged dream
I talk to my younger father
openly, affectionately,

as I had never talked to him
when he was alive? He's his usual pale
self, thinner than I remember
when he was a man and I a child.
He's now a figure in a snapshot
taken at the zoo in Guangdong,
himself a specimen of cancer.
I turn to listen to the news
on television so I don't
have to remember my dream,
his mortal life. But it persists.
He is vulnerable, come alive
from the black and white as if
I had moved into a twelve-inch
screen of the sixties, falling asleep
on the cool linoleum before
the flashing images. He would watch
American shows—John Wayne, Bill Haley,
the American Bandstand—saying,
look, meaning, the young kids rocking
and rolling, they're just like you,
suddenly seeming to understand
who I was, that girl doing the twist,
the cha-cha, all night in tight blue jeans
and give-away lipstick, moving
to the drums of the conga. That heavy
Malacca night I fell asleep in front
of his black and white television,
knowing, in my sleepiness, I was
not one of those swirling skirts, clean
bobbed hair and rolled down socks.
My body grew black earth. Rubbing
my elbow creases made small dirt
balls appear like opium shit. My hair
frizzed, dipped in permanent chemicals,
refused to bloom. Between my legs
a dangerous charm I never showed
my father, a feather talisman,
an inkling of my future. So he thought
me black and white, like an American,
his *Peranakan* daughter, who has tamed

her dancing body, till in my dreams
she is only a child, open,
affectionate, talking to her father
about love—his power to hold
his children in his power. No secrets
about my love for him now, who
in my memory is disappearing,
pound by pound, into the photograph
of a man, emaciated, hardly
middle-aged, with his good-bye smile,
and I want to weep, to hold his body
for once, as a woman holds a child,
that her caring can be cleansed.

Peranakan: native-born

Shirley Geok-lin Lim

Barrio Beateo

Woke up to one of those cold
    burnt tamales left on the
    skillet mornings
Opening the plain window of my
    so empty mind to the Mersey Beat
Brought to me long distance by
    Murray the K
The barrio was quiet I was not
Murray the K was not British
    he just was
What every Fabian bored teenager wanted
It was "I Want to Hold Your Hand"
    or "I Saw Her Standing There"
    excellent sounds good dancing
"El Tomatae" in their Sunny and the
    Sunglows face didn't understand
My mode, my change "El Beateo" they pointed
Why wasn't I typical
    thug, *pachuco*, gringo ass kicker,

greaser, onion peeler, taco vendor
Pos que tiene este muchacho,
   está loco? (What's wrong with this boy,
   is he crazy?)
The radio so alive would hypnotize me into
   a Brit zombie
On a ferry across the Mersey
With the Stones, Dave Clark 5, Manfred Mann,
   Honey Combs, Billy J. Kramer and the Dakotas,
   the Kinks, the Yardbirds, Gerry and the
   Pacemakers
Brilliant clothes very Mod, smashing haircuts
   fancy that for a Chicano
The Mersey Beat now forgotten in a library
Murray the K dead like Beatle wigs, no more
   ski pants or funny hats, now somewhere
   in grave
Thanks Murray, Babe
I love you

El Tomatae was a Chicano gang.

Jesse F. García

Welcome

         When I was little and brown
          The humming plane stopped
        Midway Field was there
   And I was proud of my blue shorts
White shirt
Blue socks
White shoes
True Puerto
Rican proud.
Excited by Colgate smiles
Like the ads nailed
To my town's walls.
So I was confused
And shivered

When the December
Chicago wind
Slapped my face.

David Hernandez

Tee

a bic lighter
cranked to the max

the tear-shaped flame
sparks a pipe

whose smoke surges
like young brothers

entering a theater
to watch john wayne

eliminate entire tribes
with a single bullet

before the box of raisinets
opens like your eyes

when the pusher comes

Reuben Jackson

Big Chill Variations

he gives me a handshake
more complicated than logarithms,

tells me my black english
has fallen on hard times,

and how he was serving molotov cocktails
to white america

while i was chasing its daughters in vermont.

a disgrace
he calls me,
a disgrace.

but still somehow
worth dinner,

a ride in his bmw,

which he swears is an acronym for
"black male warrior."

"you are the first poet
ever to dine in this club, reuben,"

"that fork is for the watercress salad."

his treat—

paid with an american express card.

gold,
but with black trim.

Reuben Jackson

Albert James

albert james was black long before me
and the rest of the fellas; he was black
when black was worse than poor.

i'm talking hair that gave the finger to drugstore
pomade,
eyes red as georgia's famed clay hills.

it was 1960.
we were children.

still, his
presence in our homes was tantamount
to treason in our parents' eyes.

albert, forgive us.
we did not know about lumumba and miles davis;

neither knew nor loved any shade below
northern negro tan.

albert james was black
before nationalists
praised his shade

and extolled the benefits of fire.

i saw the flophouse where you
od'ed
likewise turn to ghost.

                              Reuben Jackson

A Daddy Poem

My father is a hand-
some guy.

Looks like
a cross between
Clark Gable & Ernest Hemingway.
If you don't believe me,
I got proof:
Once a white woman
(at one of those
    parties)
said to my father,
"You're good looking
for a colored man."

                    William J. Harris

Song No. 3

(for 2nd & 3rd grade sisters)

cain't nobody tell me any different
i'm ugly and you know it too
you just smiling to make me feel better
but i see how you stare when nobody's watching you.

i know i'm short black and skinny
and my nose stopped growin fo it wuz 'posed to
i know my hair's short, legs and face ashy
and my clothes have holes that run right through to you.

so i sit all day long just by myself
so i jump the sidewalk cracks knowin i cain't fall
cuz who would want to catch someone who looks like me
who ain't even cute or even just a little tall.

cain't nobody tell me any different
i'm ugly anybody with sense can see.
but, one day i hope somebody will stop me and say
looka here, a pretty little black girl lookin' just like me.

Sonia Sanchez

Song at Midnight

. . . do not
send me out
among strangers
        —Sonia Sanchez

brothers,
this big woman
carries much sweetness
in the folds of her flesh.

her hair
is white with wonderful.
she is
rounder than the moon
and far more faithful.
brothers,
who will hold her,
who will find her beautiful
if you do not?

                    Lucille Clifton

Junior High Dance

No one wanted to dance with us
in 8th grade, to glide across
the shiny expanse of gym floor,
choosing us from among
the awkward and shy girls,
the boys loud and pushing instead,
uncouth to everyone but chaperones.
I had on the ugliest pantsuit—
matching orange and blue—
homemade by my mother before
she really learned to sew,
before she dazzled us with
cotton and corduroy.
My best friend had an earache,
but stayed anyway, swaying
to the music, letting it
carry her heavy body
a little forward, away
from the wall, back.
The speakers didn't wail
the way I wanted them to,
their volume respectable,
although you could still hear
Diana Ross singing—*I'm coming out*—
her anthem of disco liberation.

We watched the other kids dance,
lithe Hispanic girls who always
seemed to know when to turn,
how to bow and shimmy, or smile.
Watched the older black girls
who, self-satisfied and worldly wise,
knew all the latest steps,
and the variations on the latest
steps, so when I dared once before
to venture on the dance floor,
they hooted at me, said *that's old*,
with surety they had about nothing
else. April and I hung back,
sassy wallflowers joking about
our teachers—their whiteness,
their lack of street savvy.
They still thought Diana Ross
was a Supreme, that she still sang
You Can't Hurry Love with Flo and Mary,
that Motown was still Hitsville, U.S.A.
No one could convince us
we had something to learn
from them, no one could tell us
they were anything more than old
as they blew up balloons,
made sure the lights stayed on.
And we had our corner,
our tiny bit of that place,
where we listened to that garish
seventies music, not letting
our bodies stray far, staying
right there, no matter how funky
the beat, no matter how delicious.

Allison Joseph

What Would I Do White?

What would I do white?
What would I do clearly full
of not exactly beans nor
pearls my nose a manicure
my eyes a picture of your wall?

I would disturb the streets by
, passing by so pretty kids
on stolen petty cash would look
at me like foreign
writing in the sky

I would forget my furs on any chair.
I would ignore the doormen at the knob
the social sanskrit of my life
unwilling to disclose my cosmetology,
I would forget.

Over my wine I would acquire
I would inspire big returns to equity
the equity of capital I am
accustomed to accept

like wintertime.

I would do nothing.
That would be enough.

June Jordan

So Mexicans Are Taking Jobs from Americans

O Yes? Do they come on horses
with rifles, and say,

        Ese, gringo, gimmee your job?
And do you, gringo, take off your ring,
drop your wallet into a blanket
spread over the ground, and walk away?

I hear Mexicans are taking your jobs away.
Do they sneak into town at night,
and as you're walking home with a whore,
do they mug you, a knife at your throat,
saying, I want your job?

Even on TV, an asthmatic leader
crawls turtle heavy, leaning on an assistant,
and from a nest of wrinkles on his face,
a tongue paddles through flashing waves
of lightbulbs, of cameramen, rasping,
"They're taking our jobs away."

Well, I've gone about trying to find them,
asking just where the hell are these fighters.

The rifles I hear sound in the night
are white farmers shooting blacks and browns
whose ribs I see jutting out
and starving children,
I see the poor marching for a little work,
I see small white farmers selling out
to clean-suited farmers living in New York,
who've never been on a farm,
don't know the look of a hoof or the smell
of a woman's body bending all day long in fields.

I see this, and I hear only a few people
got all the money in this world, the rest
count their pennies to buy bread and butter.

Below that cool green sea of money,
millions and millions of people fight to live,
search for pearls in the darkest depths
of their dreams, hold their breath for years
trying to cross poverty to just having something.

The children are dead already. We are killing them,
that is what American should be saying;
on TV, in the streets, in offices, should be saying,
    "We aren't giving the children a chance to live."

Mexicans are taking our jobs, they say instead.
What they really say is, let them die,
and the children too.

                                        Jimmy Santiago Baca

Poet: What Ever
Happened to Luther?

he was strange weather, this luther. he read books, mainly poetry
and sometimes long books about people in foreign places. for a
young man he was too serious, he never did smile, and the family
still don't know if he had good teeth. he liked music too, even
tried to play the trumpet until he heard the young miles davis. he
then said that he'd try writing. the family didn't believe him
because there ain't never been no writers in this family, and
everybody knows that whatever you end up doing, it's gotta be in
your blood. it's like loving women, it's in the blood, arteries and
brains. this family don't even write letters, they call everybody.
that's why the phone is off 6 months out of a year. then again, his
brother willie t. use to write long, long letters from prison about
the books he was reading by malcolm x, frantz fanon, george
jackson, richard wright and others. luther, unlike his brother,
didn't smoke or drink and he'd always be doing odd jobs to get
money. even his closest friends clyde and t. bone didn't fully
understand him. while they be partying all weekend, luther would
be traveling. he would take his little money with a bag full of

food, mainly fruit, and a change of underwear and get on the
greyhound bus and go. he said he be visiting cities. yet, the real
funny thing about luther was his ideas. he was always talking
about afrika and black people. he was into that black stuff and he
was as light skin as a piece of golden corn on the cob. he'd be
calling himself black and afrikan and upsetting everybody,
especially white people. they be calling him crazy but not to his
face. anyway the family, mainly the educated side, just left him
alone. they would just be polite to him, and every child of god
knows that when family members act polite, that means that they
don't want to be around you. it didn't matter much because after
his mother died he left the city and went into the army. the last
time we heard from him was in 1963. he got put out the army for
rioting. he disappeared somewhere between mississippi and
chicago. a third cousin, who family was also polite to, appeared
one day and said that luther had grown a beard, changed his
name and stopped eating meat. she said that he had been to
afrika and now lived in chicago doing what he wanted to do,
writing books, she also said that he smiles a lot and kinda got
good teeth.

Haki R. Madhubuti

That Great Wingless Bird

FOR DAVID REEVE

I was thrashing on the couch
trying to meditate with my dogs
sprawled across the worn linoleum
when the automatic shots rang out.
First, I thought it was a car backfiring
on the street, or the neighbor kids
getting an early start on the 4th of July
but it was only bad actors on the television
running amok, shooting up a prop world with Uzis.
Relieved and then bored by this violent movie
on a cable channel, I dozed dreaming
of some dope-infested, gang-fighting,
third or last world where women were screaming.

The pop-pop-poppa of small arms fire tingled
my ears once more and I think I awoke
to ear reaming cop sirens.
Disgusted with violence, I shut off the tube
and dry-humped the couch.
Twinkling stars danced lewdly
outside my cheap-curtained windows.

In the morning when I let my dogs out,
they ran to the hard clay driveway
I share with my welfare neighbors and danced
in a large pool of slow syrup blood.
When they began to lick it, I ran
after them, picked up some empty
shell casings and threw them
at their crazy asses. Vampire dogs!
Later that morning I answered a letter
from a university professor a world away
from this land of dead eagles and wild dogs.

"*Dear Sir*: (I began)

In answer to your letter regarding
changing cultural patterns among
the indigenous Amerinds of the Great Plains,
well, here be what it is:

Our now culture is a nuthouse shell
covering varied worlds of denial.
Sometimes, we strip buck naked
and superglue chicken feathers to our butts
and prance around in circles.
We tell each other this is what our elders wanted.
What they wanted to preserve
before they exited their own generations
having failed at most things
except the ability
to procreate.

However, yes, we can and will
still do this prairie chicken, butt-shaking
traditional hoe-down whenever we get the urge

but first we must each eat an Indian taco.
Then, we get in a circle and hop,
propelled by taco gas and prize money.
Later, we hock our commodes
and let our kids go wild and hungry
as we drink, bingo, and drive endlessly
looking for hints of feathered warriors
and hoping for beauty,
that great empty word.
Yes, hoping for beauty,
that great wingless bird."

                                        Adrian C. Louis

Immigrants

wrap their babies in the American flag,
feed them mashed hot dogs and apple pie,
name them Bill and Daisy,
buy them blonde dolls that blink blue
eyes or a football and tiny cleats
before the baby can even walk,
speak to them in thick English,
      hallo, babee, hallo,
whisper in Spanish or Polish
when the babies sleep, whisper
in a dark parent bed, that dark
parent fear, "Will they like
our boy, our girl, our fine American
boy, our fine American girl?"

                                        Pat Mora

Depression Days

I buy the dark with my last fifteen cents.
Reel after reel, I hide on the decks with men
who fill their chests with salt air of the high seas,
who sing, "Red Sails in the Sunset."

I try not to think of the men who climbed
on the cold truck with me this morning,
stomachs screechy as gears. We were hungry
for paychecks. I try not to think

of last night on my cot, my private reel,
me a border kid, smelling Colorado, gripping an ax,
slicing that cold pine smell, playing CCC lumberjack
in a house dark from my father's death.

Our skin puckered this morning, shrank from the desert
wind that slid into the wooden barracks herding us
around the stove's warm belly, my joke to the doc,
"Am I alive?" limp as the clothes bags around our necks.

I try not to think of the sergeant spitting, *"Delgado,"*
and I step from the line, his glare at my dumbness.
"I said Delgado," me saying, "I am Delgado."
The twitch of his lips. The wind.

Then his "See me later," later trying not to hear
his brand of kindness, "You don't look Mexican, Delgado.
Just change your name and you've got a job."
My father eyeing me.

So I buy the dark with my last fifteen cents.
I try not to think of the bare ice box, my mother's
always sad eyes, of my father who never understood
this country, of the price of eggs and names and skin.

Pat Mora

A Note on My Son's Face

I
Tonight, I look, thunderstruck
at the gold head of my grandchild.

Almost asleep, he buries his feet
between my thighs;
his little straw eyes
close in the near dark.
I smell the warmth of his raw
slightly foul breath, the new death
waiting to rot inside him.
Our breaths equalize our heartbeats;
every muscle of the chest uncoils,
the arm bones loosen in the nest
of nerves. I think of the peace
of walking through the house,
pointing to the name of this, the name of that,
an educator of a new man.

Mother. Grandmother. Wise
Snake-woman who will show the way;
Spider-woman whose black tentacles
hold him precious. Or will tear off his head,
her teeth over the little husband,
the small fist clotted in trust at her breast.

This morning, looking at the face of his father,
I remembered how, an infant, his face was too dark,
nose too broad, mouth too wide.
I did not look in that mirror
and see the face that could save me
from my own darkness.
Did he, looking in my eye, see
what I turned from:
my own dark grandmother
bending over gladioli in the field,
her shaking black hand defenseless
at the shining cock of flower?

I wanted that face to die,
to be reborn in the face of a white child.

I wanted the soul to stay the same,
for I loved to death,
to damnation and God-death,
the soul that broke out of me.

I crowed: My Son! My Beautiful!
But when I peeked in the basket,
I saw the face of a black man.

Did I bend over his nose
and straighten it with my fingers
like a vine growing the wrong way?
Did he feel my hand in malice?

Generations we prayed and fucked
for this light child,
the shining god of the second coming;
we bow down in shame
and carry the children of the past
in our wallets, begging forgiveness.

II
A picture in a book,
a lynching.
The bland faces of men who watch
a Christ go up in flames, smiling,
as if he were a hooked
fish, a felled antelope, some
wild thing tied to boards and burned.
His charring body
gives off light—a halo
burns out of him.
His face scorched featureless;
the hair matted to the scalp
like feathers.
One man stands with his hand on his hip,
another with his arm
slung over the shoulder of a friend,
as if this moment were large enough
to hold affection.

III
How can we wake
from a dream
we are born into,
that shines around us,
the terrible bright air?

Having awakened,
having seen our own bloody hands,
how can we ask forgiveness,
bring before our children the real
monster of their nightmares?

The worst is true.
Everything you did not want to know.

Toi Derricotte

Blackbottom

When relatives came from out of town,
we would drive down to Blackbottom,
drive slowly down the congested main streets
   —Beubian and Hastings—
trapped in the mesh of Saturday night.
Freshly escaped, black middle class,
we snickered, and were proud;
the louder the streets, the prouder.
We laughed at the bright clothes of a prostitute,
a man sitting on a curb with a bottle in his hand.
We smelled barbecue cooking in dented washtubs,
   and our mouths watered.
As much as we wanted it we couldn't take the chance.

Rhythm and blues came from the windows, the throaty voice of
   a woman lost in the bass, in the drums, in the dirty down
   and out, the grind.
"I love to see a funeral, then I know it ain't mine."
We rolled our windows down so that the waves rolled over us
   like blood.
We hoped to pass invisibly, knowing on Monday we would
   return safely to our jobs, the post office and classroom.
We wanted our sufferings to be offered up as tender meat,
and our triumphs to be belted out in raucous song.
We had lost our voice in the suburbs, in Conant Gardens,
   where each brick house delineated a fence of silence;
we had lost the right to sing in the street and damn creation.

We returned to wash our hands of them,
to smell them
whose very existence
tore us down to the human.

Toi Derricotte

Lost Name Woman

Mississippi China woman,
why do you wear blue jeans in the city?
Are you looking for the rich ghost
to buy you a ticket to the West?

San Francisco China woman,
you will drink only Coca-Cola.
You stir it with a long straw,
sip ss-ss like it's a rare elixir.

Massachusetts China woman,
you've cut your hair and frizzed it.
Bangs hide your stubborn brow, eyes
shine, hurricane lamps in a storm.

Arizona China woman,
now you are in Gold Mountain Country,
you speak English like the radio,
but will it let you forget your father?

Woman with the lost name,
who will feed you when you die?

Shirley Geok-lin Lim

Coca-Cola and Coco Frio

On his first visit to Puerto Rico,
island of family folklore,
the fat boy wandered

from table to table
with his mouth open.
At every table, some great-aunt
would steer him with cool spotted hands
to a glass of Coca-Cola.
One even sang to him, in all the English
she could remember, a Coca-Cola jingle
from the forties. He drank obediently, though
he was bored with this potion, familiar
from candy stores in Brooklyn.

Then, at a roadside stand off the beach, the fat boy
opened his mouth to coco frio, a coconut
chilled, then scalped by a machete
so that a straw could inhale the clear milk.
The boy tilted the green shell overhead
and drooled coconut milk down his chin;
suddenly, Puerto Rico was not Coca-Cola
or Brooklyn, and neither was he.

For years afterward, the boy marveled at an island
where the people drank Coca-Cola
and sang jingles from World War II
in a language they did not speak,
while so many coconuts in the trees
sagged heavy with milk, swollen
and unsuckled.

Martín Espada

Naming

■   ■   ■

Unilateral conceptions of American identity encourage people to abandon their culture and change their names. Racist slurs and labeling have a powerful impact on the way people imagine the world and their culture. At the same time, while exploring the colonizing effects of language, *naming* also considers the possibilities of rejecting racist stereotypes and voicing denied experiences. In "But My Blood," Rose Romano describes her instinctive need to protect her definition of herself that includes, rather than denies, her Italian heritage:

> What does it mean to be American?
> It doesn't mean anything to me.
> It's only a place—but I have
> blood, red and warm. I was Italian
> when they called us wops. Now
> they like us so they assure us
> we no longer need to suffer as
> Italian—now, we're just as
> American as anyone. But my blood
> will not change.

Señora X No More

Straight as a nun I sit.
My fingers foolish before paper and pen
hide in my palms. I hear the slow, accented echo
    How are yu? I ahm fine. How are yu?
of the other women who clutch notebooks
and blush at their stiff lips resisting
sounds that float gracefully as
bubbles from their children's mouths.
My teacher bends over me, gently squeezes
my shoulders, the squeeze I give my sons,
hands louder than words.
She slides her arms around me:
a warm shawl, lifts my left arm
onto the cold, lined paper.
"*Señora*, don't let it slip away," she says
and opens the ugly, soap-wrinkled fingers
of my right hand with a pen like I pry open
the lips of a stubborn grandchild.
My hand cramps around the thin hardness.
"Let it breathe," says this woman who knows
my hand and tongue knot, but she guides
and I dig the tip of my pen into that white.
I carve my crooked name, and again at night
until my hand and arm are sore,
I carve my crooked name,
my name.

Pat Mora

Dying with the Wrong Name

Three parts of an unfinished poem

DEDICATED TO ALL THE IMMIGRANTS
WHO LOST THEIR NAMES AT
ELLIS ISLAND

I
These men died with the wrong names,
Na'aim Jazeeny, from the beautiful valley
of Jezzine, died as Nephew Sam,
Sine Hussin died without relatives and
because they cut away his last name
at Ellis Island, there was no way to trace
him back even to Lebanon, and Im'a Brahim
had no other name than mother of Brahim,
even my own father lost his, went from
Hussein Hamode Subh' to Sam Hamod.
There is something lost in the blood,
something lost down to the bone
in these small changes. A man in a
dark blue suit at Ellis Island says, with
tiredness and authority, "You only need two
names in America" and suddenly—as cleanly
as the air, you've lost
your name.   At first, it's hardly
even noticeable—and it's easier, you move
about as an American—but looking back
the loss of your name
cuts away some other part,
something unspeakable is lost.

And you know, these were not small
men, each was severe, though part
comic, as we will be remembered as well—but
Nephew Sam ran a cigar store in Michigan City, and
in the back room a poker game with chips and
bills often past 30,000; in his middle years,
Sine Hussin lifted the rear end of a 1939 Ford
so they could change a tire, and my father went

from Lebanon to the packinghouses in Sioux Falls
and Sioux City to the steel mills in Gary, from
nothing to houses and apartments worth more than
a million—in each sweaty day in Sioux City, down
to the boarding houses and small stores, in each drop
of movement at 5:30 and 5 a.m. cooking food for gandy
dancers and millworkers to nights working in the tavern
selling scotch while B. B. King and T. Bone Walker hustled
blues, each dollar another day mixing names and money.
And these were men who opened the world
with a gesture of the hand,
a nod and things moved, houses were built
for each new immigrant, apartment buildings bought
and sold—given as wedding presents
mayors and congressmen were made and broken—these men live
now on the edge of myth—each other under
a stone carved in English, the Arabic of Hussein Hamod Subh,
Na'aim Jazeeny, Sine Hussin
lost
each one sealed away
with the wrong name
except in this poem, and a poem
goes out to so few
but we trust as we can

II
Sine Hussin is still sitting in that
old chair, upholstered in brushed maroon wool,
he sits with his back to the window
at an angle, an old crystal lamp rests
on the ornate mahogany table, Im'a Brahim
sits in the companion chair, crocheting, her
legs full, veined and old, managing to walk, a
short Osman of no more than 4'8" or so,
but obviously before her first child
the cameo shape of her face was more delicate, and
you know the smell of this room, meat and fried onions,
fresh garlic on the salad, tartness of lemon
twists into the air, and an ease toward evening
as you walk in
all the silence splits into hellos and hugs

while the world comes together
in the small room

III
Even now, it's hard for me to
fully understand what this old couple meant
to my father—
his own father had died before my father came
to America in 1914, his mother still in Lebanon,
unseen for decades. My father is 39 or 40 now, I
am 4 or 5, we are constantly carrying groceries
to this old house, the old couple always says "no"
but then they take them, but only after we have
some *fatiyah* and coffee, eat some fruit, talk
(I'm usually impatient to go), then we climb back
into the car and go home. My father, a man I came to know
as so secretive, yet so generous, a man alone; now I know
this was part of that other reality, where his name, that
language, Hussein, Sine Hussin, Im'a Brahim, *Asalamu Aleikum*,
all of these sounds were part of his name, this was that other
edge of Lebanon he carried with him, that home, that same
good food of the rich smells, it had to be in these moments,
    these things
were not lost, but were alive and living in this room,
in this house, in these people, in this moment.

                                        Hamod (Sam)

Leaves

FOR SALLY

Tonight, Sally and I are making stuffed
grapeleaves, we get out a package, it's
drying out, I've been saving it in the freezer, it's
one of the last things my father ever picked in this
life—they're over five years old
and up till now
we just kept finding packages of them in the
freezer, as if he were still picking them

somewhere   packing them
carefully to send to us
making sure they didn't break into pieces.

■ ■ ■

"To my Dar Garnchildn
Davd and Lura
from Thr Jido"
twisted on tablet paper
between the lines
in this English lettering
hard for him even to print,
I keep this small torn record,
this piece of paper stays in the upstairs storage,
one of the few pieces of American
my father ever wrote.   We find his Arabic letters
all over the place, even in the files we find
letters to him in English, one I found from Charles Atlas
telling him, in 1932,
"Of course, Mr. Hamod, you too can build
your muscles like mine . . ."

■ ■ ■

Last week my mother told me, when I was
asking why I became a poet, "But don't you remember,
your father made up poems, don't you remember him
singing in the car as we drove—those were poems."
Even now, at night, I sometimes
get out the Arabic grammar book
though it seems so late.

                                        Hamod (Sam)

How I Got That Name

An Essay on Assimilation

I am Marilyn Mei Ling Chin.
Oh, how I love the resoluteness
of that first person singular
followed by that stalwart indicative
of "be," without the uncertain i-n-g
of "becoming." Of course,
the name had been changed
somewhere between Angel Island and the sea,
when my father the paper son
in the late 1950s
obsessed with some bombshell blonde
transliterated "Mei Ling" to "Marilyn."
And nobody dared question
his initial impulse—for we all know
lust drove men to greatness,
not goodness, not decency.
And there I was, a wayward pink baby,
named after some tragic
white woman, swollen with gin and Nembutal.
My mother couldn't pronounce the "r."
She dubbed me "Numba one female offshoot"
for brevity: henceforth, she will live and die
in sublime ignorance, flanked
by loving children and the "kitchen deity."
While my father dithers,
a tomcat in Hong Kong trash—
a gambler, a petty thug,
who bought a chain of chopsuey joints
in Piss River, Oregon,
with bootlegged Gucci cash.
Nobody dared question his integrity given
his nice, devout daughters
and his bright, industrious sons.
As if filial piety were the standard
with which all earthly men were measured.

Oh, how trustworthy our daughters,
how thrifty our sons!
How we've managed to fool the experts
in education, statistics and demography—
We're not very creative but not adverse to rote-learning.
Indeed, they can *use* us.
But the "Model Minority" is a tease.
We know you are watching now,
so we refuse to give you any!
Oh, bamboo shoots, bamboo shoots!
The further west we go, we'll hit east;
The deeper down we dig, we'll find China.
History has turned its stomach
on a black, polluted beach—
where life doesn't hinge
on that red, red wheelbarrow,
but whether or not our new lover
in the final episode of "Santa Barbara"
will lean over a scented candle
and call us a "bitch."
Oh God, where have we gone wrong?
We have no inner resources!

Then, one redolent spring morning
the Great Patriarch Chin
peered down from his kiosk in heaven
and saw that his descendants were ugly.
One had a squarish head and a nose without a bridge.
Another's profile—long and knobbed as a gourd.
A third, the sad, brutish one
may never, never marry.
And I, his least favorite—
"not quite boiled, not quite cooked,"
a plump pomfret simmering in my juices—
too listless to fight for my people's destiny.
"To kill without resistance is not slaughter"
says the proverb. So, I wait for imminent death.
The fact that this death is also metaphorical
is testament to my lethargy.

So, here lies Marilyn Mei Ling Chin,
married once, twice to so-and-so, a Lee and a Wong,

granddaughter of Jack "the patriarch" Chin
and the brooding Suilin Fong,
daughter of the virtuous Yuet Kuen Wong
and G.G. Chin the infamous,
sister of a dozen, cousin of a million,
survived by everybody and forgotten by all.
She was neither black nor white,
neither cherished nor vanquished,
just another squatter in her own bamboo grove
minding her poetry—
when one day heaven was unmerciful,
and a chasm opened where she then stood.
Like the jowls of a mighty white whale,
or the jaws of a metaphysical Godzilla,
it swallowed her whole.
She did not flinch nor writhe,
nor fret about the afterlife,
but stayed! Solid as wood, happily
a little gnawed, tattered, mesmerized
by all that was lavished upon her
and all that was taken away!

Marilyn Chin

Elegy for Chloe Nguyen

(1955–1988)

Chloe's father is a professor of linguistics.
Mine runs a quick-you-do-it laundromat in Chinatown.
If not pretty, at least I'm clean.

Bipedal in five months, trilingual in a year;
at eleven she had her first lover.

Here's a photo of Chloe's mother in the kitchen
making petits fours, petits fours that are very pretty.
Here's my mother picking pears, picking pears
for a self-made millionaire grower.

The night when Chloe died, her father sighed,
"Chloe was my heart; Chloe was my life!"

One day under an earthen-black sky
and the breeze brushing our adolescent pinafores,
a star fell—or was it a satellite
exploding into a bonfire at the horizon?
Chloe said, "This is how I want to die,
with a bang and not with a flicker."

Oh, Chloe, eternally sophomore and soporific!
Friend of remote moribund languages!
Chloe read Serbo-Croatian, the Latin of Horace.
She understood Egyptian hieroglyphics, the writing of the tombs.
The tongues of the living, the slangs of the dead—
in learning she had no rival.

Then came the lovers of many languages
to quell her hunger, her despair.
Each night they whispered, "Chloe, you are beautiful."
Then, left her with an empty sky in the morning.

Chloe, can you hear me? Is it better in heaven?
Are you happier in hell? This week I don't understand the lesson
being a slow learner—except for the one about survival.
And Death, I know him well . . .

He followed my grandfather as a puff of opium,
my father as a brand-new car.
Rowed the boat with my grandmother,
blowing gales into my mother's ear.
Wrapped his arms around my asthmatic sister,
but his comforting never won us over.

Yes, Death is a beautiful man,
and the poor don't need dowries to court him.
His grassy hand, his caliph—you thought you could master.

Chloe, we are finally Americans now. Chloe, we are here!

Marilyn Chin

Niggerlips

Niggerlips was the high school name
for me.
So called by Douglas
the car mechanic, with green tattoos
on each forearm,
and the choir of round pink faces
that grinned deliciously
from the back row of classrooms,
droned over by teachers
checking attendance too slowly.

Douglas would brag
about cruising his car
near sidewalks of black children
to point an unloaded gun,
to scare niggers
like crows off a tree,
he'd say.

My great-grandfather Luis
was un negrito too,
a shoemaker in the coffee hills
of Puerto Rico, 1900.
The family called him a secret
and kept no photograph.
My father remembers
the childhood white powder
that failed to bleach
his stubborn copper skin,
and the family says
he is still a fly in milk.

Martín Espada

From an
Island You Cannot Name

Thirty years ago,
your linen-gowned father stood
in the dayroom of the VA hospital,
grabbing at the plastic
identification bracelet
marked Negro,
shouting "I'm not!
Take it off!
I'm Other!"

The army photograph
pinned to your mirror
says he was,
black, Negro,
dark as West Indian rum.

And this morning,
daughter of a man
from an island you cannot name,
you gasp tears
trying to explain
that you're Other,
that you're not.

Martín Espada

Mama, Come Back

Mama, come back.
Why did you leave
now that I am learning you?
The landlady next door
how she apologizes
for my rough brown skin

to her tenant from Hong Kong
as if I were her daughter,
as if she were you.

How do I say I miss you
your scolding
your presence
your roast loin of pork
more succulent, more tender
than any hotel chef's?

The fur coat you wanted
making you look like a polar bear
and the mink-trimmed coat
I once surprised you
on Christmas morning.

Mama, how you said "importment"
for important,
your gold tooth flashing
an insecurity you dared not bare,
wanting recognition
simply as eating noodles
and riding in a motor car
to the supermarket
the movie theater
adorned in your gold and jade
as if all your jewelry
confirmed your identity
a Chinese woman in America.

How you said "you better"
always your last words
glazed through your dark eyes
following me fast as you could
one November evening in New York City
how I thought "Hello, Dolly!"
showed you an America
you never saw.

How your fear of being alone
kept me dutiful in body

resentful in mind.
How my fear of being single
kept me
from moving out.

How I begged your forgiveness
after that one big fight
how I wasn't wrong
but needed you to love me
as warmly as you hugged strangers.

Nellie Wong

On the Road to
Damascus, Maryland

On the road to Damascus, Maryland,
between the trailer camps and rosebushes
I had a vision
in the back seat
of my parents' car.

Once again,
it was happening.
I felt myself turning
into someone else.
I wasn't sure who, yet.

My parents were worried.
Next week I'd be 35
and I still didn't seem
to know who I was.

At other times
I'd already been:
a New York Jew,
a radical teacher,
an Ethical Culturist,
a barefoot breadbaker,

a nice girl
in knee socks.

I was relieved
when they changed the subject
to where we'd eat lunch
in Damascus.

I sat in the back seat
dreamily
making a list
of new names.

Enid Dame

How I Changed My Name, Felice

In Italy a man's name, here a woman's,
transliterated so I went to school
for seven years, and no one told me different.
The teachers hardly cared, and in the class
Italian boys who knew me said Felice,
although outside they called me feh-LEE-tchay.

I might have lived, my noun so neutralized,
another seven years, except one day
I broke a window like nobody's girl,
and the old lady called a cop, whose sass
was wonderful when all the neighbors smiled
and said that there was no boy named Felice.
And then it was it came on me, my shame,
and I stepped up, and told him, and he grinned.

My father paid a quarter for my sin,
called me inside to look up in a book
that Felix was American for me.
A Roman name, I read. And what he said
was that no Roman broke a widow's glass,
and fanned my little Neapolitan ass.

Felix Stefanile

Jade

The woman insisted
my name must be Jade.
Your name's not Jade?
Well, it should be.
It suits you, jewel of the orient.

I knew a young hooker
called Jade.
She had red dyed hair
and yellow teeth
bucked around a perpetual candy bar.
They called her Jade
because she was Clyde's
jewel of the orient.
Her real name was Sumiko . . .
Hardy or Johnson or Smith.
She was from Concord.
Boring, she said,
and kept running away
from home. Her father
would come looking for her,
beat her again,
drag her home
while her mother
babbled and bawled in Japanese.
Concord was boring.
Jade kept running away,
Clyde's jewel of the orient.
He took care of her well,
and she couldn't wait
to see him, her hunger
like locusts in drought,
to put the cold needle to her vein;
blood blossoming in the
dropper like bougainvillea
pushing the heroin through,
her eyes exploding with green lights,
the cold encasing
each corpuscle,

rushing through
heart to the spine,
a freeze settling in each
vertebra until
she's as cold as stone,
metabolism at zero degrees,
speech center numbed
and life as still as icicles.
Pain, boredom, loneliness
like a frosty pillow
where she lays her nodding
head.
                    I wanted to tell
                    the woman who kept
                    insisting my name was Jade
about Jade.
who od'ed. Her jaundiced body
found on her cold floor
mattress,
roaches crawling in her ears,
her dead eyes, glassy
as jewels.

                              Janice Mirikitani

Being Jewish in a Small Town

Someone writes kike on
the blackboard and the
"k's" pull thru the
chalk   stick in my

plump pale thighs
even after the high
school burns down the
word is written in

the ashes   my under
pants elastic snaps

on Main St because
I can't go to

Pilgrim Fellowship
I'm the one Jewish girl
in town but the 4
Cohen brothers

want blond hair
blowing from their
car   they don't know
my black braids

smell of almond
I wear my clothes
loose so no one
dreams who I am

will never know
Hebrew   keep a
Christmas tree in
my drawer   in

the dark   my fingers
could be the menorah
that pulls you toward
honey in the snow

Lyn Lifshin

We Exist

FOR BETH BRANT

Indians must be the loneliest people on Earth—
lonely from our histories,
our losses,
even those things we cannot name
which are inside us.
Our writers try to counteract the history

which says we are a dead, a conquered People.
But our words are like a shout in a blizzard.

In snow one December,
those at Wounded Knee lay dying,
dead, their mouths frozen open.
Soldiers dug a ditch
for the bodies.
Then prairie soil crumbled over the People,
and their hearts fed on roots and stones.
Their mouths filled with dust.

At sunrise the daughter lies on her bed,
legs drawn up, fist in her mouth.
I am poisoned, she thinks, beneath my heart.
This is what it means to be Indian.
My mother is not here.
They mined her for her grief,
following each vein, invading
every space, removing, they said,
the last vestige of pain.

At dawn, this time of prayer, the daughter
in a voice mined from a sickness of soul,
tries to name the words
which say we exist.

Janice Gould

Jacket Notes

Being a colored poet
Is like going over
Niagara Falls in a
Barrel

An 8 year old can do what
You do unaided

The barrel maker doesn't
Think you can cut it

The gawkers on the bridge
Hope you fall on your
Face

The tourist bus full of
Paying customers broke-down
Just out of Buffalo

Some would rather dig
The postcards than
Catch your act

A mile from the brink
It begins to storm

But what really hurts is
You're bigger than the
Barrel

Ishmael Reed

Having the Wrong Name
for Mr. Wright

"Pietrofesso," I'd repeat to Mr. Wright, the science teacher in
Junior High
        (or to Miss Fiske, English; Miss Conan, History)
        "P-i-e-t-r-o-f-e-s-s-o," I'd spell out, mortified,
        "Stefana with an f, Pietrofesso"
Staff is what they called me, my last name slurring into Peterface-oh.
Later I was known as Petrify.

What I felt could only be known
by the other wrong names in my class:
Sophie Fjilarski, the skinny pale and pimply girl whose father
was an apartment building janitor,
or Ángel Saxenian with hair on her arms,
or Gennaro, wiry and dark-eyed, a fast-thinking kid
whose last name twisted like sparklers into Cacciacavallo.

Gennaro didn't give a damn about grades
as did the good boys, plodding Wasps,
who were already talking about colleges.
Now I wonder what happened to Gennaro . . .
in middle age did he have second thoughts
about those Warehams and Fullers and Barths
who became lawyers and executives
while he, mercurial, quick, a brilliant
flame of intelligence in Mr. Wright's classes,
was out of school and working by age seventeen?
We were signaled alien—Sophie, Angel, Gennaro and I—
as Mr. Wright grimaced and garbled our names in roll-call
                    . . . maybe we should have apologized.

That was a time when,
at school or at the Y or on camp applications,
the forms to be filled always had a blank for
        "Nationality."
I never knew what to put down.
I was born where I went to school and so were my parents,
but I didn't recognize myself as American.
        Should I just write "foreign"?
After all, those foreign-type people I saw at weddings or at Christmas,
the ones who talked funny and looked wrong,
—they were my relatives,
faces like masks of perpetual bewilderment, grim and lined with old
    worries.
They were not the comely and jolly Americans
of Saturday Evening Post covers.
Fifty years in America and my grandparents had not English
enough to speak to my brothers and me.

It was hard to think of myself as American,
yet it seemed not right to put Italian in the Nationality blank

(I had never seen Italy, didn't know its language)
       yet that is what I wrote.
       No teacher ever corrected me.

Helen Barolini

Taking It Back

Hand-tinted, creamy olive skin,
green eyes, ripe and innocent
both, and clear as holy water
she dips into at High Mass,
Bella, my Spanish grandma
smiled across the hall

at Grandma Winnie, pale
as bleached muslin,
as white-washed Southern porches
built by French and English
Protestants, though her eyes
sparked like Indian flint.

■ ■ ■

Like fugitives, or outlaws
on the lam, we moved away,
changed the spelling
of our last name, the one
on the I.D. bracelet
I had never taken off before,

the one that studded my roller-skate case.
With my brother's pen knife
I pried off the letters
and left white scars
where the Spanish name had been.

■ ■ ■

"What is she?" his mother asked,
perplexed, I could tell, by
the neutral skin tones and hybrid name.
"She's a mutt," he laughed
ruffling my hair backwards
as if waiting for me to lick his hand.

Marriage could solve this,
I thought, this dilemma
of spellings and explanations
that spelled out shame.
But taking his name meant more
than just giving mine away.

■ ■ ■

When the fingertip veil
fell like a white curtain
between layers of history,
I signed the new name
easily, the crisp, one syllable,
so Germanic, so acceptable.

On the inside cover
of the Little Golden Books I find
in a trunk, on each there is
a dark, scumbled spot
where the old spelling is gouged
out, leaving an open wound.

■ ■ ■

Other . . .
I always check "other"
after reading through the choices,
Puerto Rican, Chinese, Eskimo,
White, Hispanic; because nothing
fits, but "other" also fits nothing.

In a black, marble room
lit by one overhead bulb,
in slow-dancing dream time,

I float from slab to slab
lift the white sheets, and shake
my head, leaving each body,
so familiar, still unidentified.

■ ■ ■

It is the same girl
who dressed in musty, moth-bitten
mink and clomping high heels,
also known as Dolores, or Della Street,
who looks back at me,
laminated for the DMV, spelled

backwards through time,
like a ghost girl, passing
through different bodies,
to come here, to take back
what never belonged to anyone,
what still splits off in the wind.

                              Dixie Salazar

Piñon Nuts

We begged him to teach us Spanish
but he wouldn't. Here in the heart
of America, skin tones
and tongues were homogeneous
as milk, from pure-bred cows.

We heard Spanish once a year
on visits to Colorado, where Grandpa
sold used cars at the Rainbow Garage
after the Depression wiped out
a city block of his stores,

and left him bitter as the juice
of venison strips he gnawed,
escaping into his camper

with its false bottom
for hiding deer, shot out of season.

Ignoring postal regulations,
he mailed us deer meat once,
bleeding in a bed of piñon nuts,
telling Bella, "*¿Qué tiene Ud?*"
then, "Shut up" in English.

Bella went off to Mass
in their newest Chevy
and a velvet dish hat
chosen from over a hundred,
one for every fight they had.

His father died with the sheep
in a blizzard, Grandpa was saved
by stuffing his feet in a foxhole.
My father, his namesake, got whipped
he says, every time Grandpa saw him.

In '59, he was 73. Snowdrifts piled
high as frozen waves. Forced to turn back,
two miles past timberline, they found
Grandpa's name carved on a tree, the date
of the day before—his last deer.

After Bella died, he slept
on the broken spine of the back porch,
wouldn't eat or take his insulin,
telling her photograph, or anyone
who'd listen, how much he loved her.

Each letter began with
"*Corazón de mi corazón,*" a courtship
in a graveyard; he poured out the words
he only found again later, for her picture.
In between were all those hats.

Rainbow trout swimming in bacon fat,
empañadas, flaky and spiced, a bowl
of piñon nuts, Grandma making faces

behind his back. "*Montaña, huevos, ventana,*"
the bits of Spanish she taught us, these

and a swish of hats on my wall
are all that's left. In Spanish class
today, I learned "piñon" meant pine.
I rolled the word in my Anglo mouth,
like a sweet, round nut.

                              Dixie Salazar

The Hula Skirt, 1959

FOR D

Before my fourth birthday my father
and (what I didn't know) my pregnant mother and I
flew through clouds and over silos and barns
to Disneyland and a motel
where I locked a restaurant bathroom stall
and crawled out under the door for fun
and chose the Peter Pan ride the only ride I recall
I recall as a yellow seat and closed eyes
then flew to Honolulu then Maui
where we drove between the cane plantations
that I would later watch burn in harvesting
its sweet pithy wrist
to my grandmother drying her hands and opening her arms
to meet my almost Japanese face,
the chickens clucking to get in the way it seemed,
and I felt shy around grandfather's wheelchair
and empty mouth. A baby's grin.
Then it was my birthday that I'd waited for since my third one
and mom brought out a store-bought cake
(Mama, too hot to bake, she insisted)
that was pink and I had many packages
including a brown-skinned doll wearing a muu-muu
and in the last funny-shaped one
an orchid-print bra and hula skirt.
They wrapped it around my tiny, pale waist

adjusted the top and said, smile Kimi,
for this snapshot of banana trees and me.
Two pack-rats, this hula skirt has survived these thirty years
to land in my even smaller New York apartment
where my daughter will take it for show-and-tell
and sing something my mother taught her that begins with
    aloha
and is about the humuhumu nukunuku apua that go
    swimming by.
That much I remember.

                                        Kimiko Hahn

Song of the Third Generation

I learned to read in the dark,
in the car, wherever the light
moved, shifted. My mother believed
I would burn my eyes out.
Between the breath and the text
my birth and hers kept happening
in the late night
in the daily horoscopes
in the 4:30 Movie
and the huge picture books filled with Hollywood stars.
My Ava Gardner died, my mother says.
My mother learned how to read the text of a life
as her mother learned to translate *Il Progresso*:
by reading a little bit of headline,
any little bit.
They could both predict disasters—my mother's
in American English: divorce, drug addiction
and insane asylums. Nonna's in rich Calabrian dialect:
earthquakes, earthquakes, and food shortages.
Somewhere between our mouths
and what we said is what we learned.
Somewhere in the old country

we breathed text
without knowing how to read.
I learned in the old way too—
in a corner of the kitchen
watching my mother pour the batter
of flour and zucchini blossoms
into bright spattering oil,
or in the cool basement at the edge of the ironing board,
the lint speckling her dark sweater,
at her elbow as she whipped the cloth
beneath the needle of her industrial Singer.
No other record, no other text
exists but the buzzing and this way of learning
in the old way, which is any way
that we can.

Julia Lisella

Ka 'Ba

A closed window looks down
on a dirty courtyard, and black people
call across or scream across or walk across
defying physics in the stream of their will

Our world is full of sound
Our world is more lovely than anyone's
tho we suffer, and kill each other
and sometimes fail to walk the air

We are beautiful people
with African imaginations
full of masks and dances and swelling chants
with African eyes, and noses, and arms,
though we sprawl in gray chains in a place
full of winters, when what we want is sun.

We have been captured,
brothers. And we labor

to make our getaway, into
the ancient image, into a new

correspondence with ourselves
and our black family. We need magic
now we need the spells, to raise up
return, destroy, and create. What will be

the sacred words?

                    Amiri Baraka

Funk Lore

We are the blues
   ourselves
   our favorite
    color
    Where we been, half here
              half gone

We are the blues
   our selves
   the actual
    Guineas
   the original
    Jews
   the 1st
    Caucasians

That's why we are the blues
   ourselves
  that's why we
   are the
   actual
    song

   So dark & tragic
    So old &
       Magic

        that's why we are
                the Blues
                    our Selves

    In tribes of 12
      bars
    like the stripes
      of slavery
          on
      our flag
      of skin

    We are the blues
            the past the gone
            the energy   the
            cold the saw teeth
            hotness
            the smell above
            draining the wind
            through trees
            the blue
            leaves us
            black
            the earth
            the sun
            the slowly disappearing
            the fire pushing to become
            our hearts

& now black again we are the
whole of night
with sparkling eyes staring
down
like jets
        to push
        evenings
        ascension
        that's why we are the blues
        the train whistle
        the rumble across
        the invisible coming
        drumming and screaming

that's why we are the
blues
& work & sing & leave
tales & is with spirit
that's why we are
    the blues
    black & alive
    & so we show our motion
          our breathing
          we moon
          reflected soul

that's why our spirit
  make us

  the blues

we is ourselves

the blues

Amiri Baraka

American Sonnets
for My Father

I
You died in spring, father, and now the autumn dies.
Bright with ripe youth, dulled by time,
plums of feeling leaked red juices from your eyes,
pools of blood hemorrhaged in your quivering mind.

At forty, I climb Point Pinnacle, today,
thinking of you gone forever from me.
In this russet November, woods of Millay,
I wear your old hat, dear Italian patriarch, to see
if I can think you out of your American grave

to sing your unwritten song with me.
Your poetry, love's value, I carry with your spirit.
I take off your old black hat and sniff at it
to smell the still living vapor of your sweat.

II
You worked too hard, an oldest child of too many,
a lame thin boy in ragged knickers,
you limped all through the 1920s up city steps,
door to door with your loads of night and daily
newspapers, each worth a cheap
labored penny of your family's keep.
You wore your heart and soles sore.
At forty, not climbing autumn hills like me,
strapped down with pain and morphine, you lay
        with lung disease,
hearing your breath rattle in your throat like keys
at the gates of hell. Your body was always a weak fiend
perplexing your masculine will.
You filled me with pride and immigrant tenacity.
Slave to filial duty, weaver of all our dreams,
you couldn't be free to sing. So be it.
You are done, unfulfilled by song except in me.
If your dreams are mine, live again, breath in me and be.

III
You never understood America's scheme.
The wound of your lost dream,
father, will never heal, your spirit mourns forever
in me, aches with childhood memory,
sighs for my own mortality
in you, which I, at last, accept
more completely than ever when we
laughed together and seemed we'd go on forever—
even though we always knew
you would die much sooner than I
who am your spirit come from you.
"Remember, a father lost, lost his!" you told us,
preparing us with Shakespearean quotation
and operatic feeling for your inevitable death.

IV
Good night, go gently, tired immigrant father
full of pride and propriety. We, your
three daughters, all grew
to be healthier, stronger, more American than you.
Sensitive father, I offer you this toast,
no empty boast, "I've never known a man braver!"
The wound that will not heal in me
is the ache of dead beauty.
Once full of history, philosophy, poetry,
physics, astronomy, your bright, high flying psyche
is now dispersed, set free from your tormented body,
but the theme you offered, often forlorn,
sheer luminescent soul, glistened with enough light
to carry us all full grown.

Daniela Gioseffi

Pigeons

Pigeons are the spiks of Birdland.
   They are survivors of blood, fire and stone.
      They can't afford to fly south
         or a Florida winter home.
Most everybody passing up a pigeon pack
tries to bread it up because they move funny
and seem to be dancing like young street thugs
with an 18-foot, 10-speaker Sanyo boom box radio
on a 2-foot red shoulder strap.
                        Pigeons have feathers of a different color.
                        They are too bright to be dull
                        and too dull to be bright
                           so they are not accepted anywhere.

               Nobody wants to give pigeons a job.
               Parakeets, canaries and parrots
               have the market sewn up as far as that goes.
               They live in fancy cages, get 3 meals a day
               for a song and dance routine.
               When was the last time you saw a pigeon

in someone's home?
Unless they bleach their feathers white
and try to pass off as doves,
you will never see pet pigeons.
Besides, their accents give them away
when they start cooing.

Once in a while, some creature will treat them decent.
    They are known as pigeon ladies, renegades,
        or bleeding-heart Liberals.
                        What they do is build these wooden cages
                    on rooftops that look like huge
                pigeon housing projects
            where they freeze during the winters
        and get their little claws stuck in tar
    on hot summer days.
No wonder they are pigeon-toed.
I tell you,
        Pigeons are the spiks of Birdland.

David Hernandez

A Poem about Intelligence for My Brothers and Sisters

A few years back and they told me Black
means a hole where other folks
got brain/it was like the cells in the heads
of Black children was out to every hour on the hour naps
Scientists called the phenomenon the Notorious
Jensen Lapse, remember?
Anyway I was thinking
about how to devise
a test for the wise
like a Stanford-Binet
for the C.I.A.
you know?
Take Einstein

being the most the unquestionable the outstanding
the maximal mind of the century
right?
And I'm struggling against this lapse leftover
from my Black childhood to fathom why
anybody should say so:
$E = mc$ *squared*?
I try that on this old lady live on my block:
She sweeping away Saturday night from the stoop
and mad as can be because some absolute
jackass have left a kingsize mattress where
she have to sweep around it stains and all she
don't want to know nothing about in the first place
"Mrs. Johnson!" I say, leaning on the gate
between us: "What you think about somebody come up
with an E equals M C 2?"
"How you doin," she answer me, sideways, like she don't
want to let on she know I ain
combed my hair yet and here it is
Sunday morning but still I have the nerve
to be bothering serious work with these crazy
questions about
"E equals what you say again, dear?"
Then I tell her, "Well
also this same guy? I think
he was undisputed Father of the Atom Bomb!"
"That right." She mumbles or grumbles, not too politely
"And dint remember to wear socks when he put on
his shoes!" I add on (getting desperate)
at which point Mrs. Johnson take herself and her broom
a very big step down the stoop away from me
"And never did nothing for nobody in particular
lessen it was a committee
and
used to say, 'What time is it?'
and
you'd say, 'Six o'clock.'
and
he'd say, 'Day or night?'
and
and he never made nobody a cup a tea

in his whole brilliant life!"
"and
(my voice rises slightly)
and
he dint never boogie neither: never!"

"Well," say Mrs. Johnson, "Well, honey,
I do guess
that's genius for you."

June Jordan

For Talking

Saint Didacus, 1968

in catholic school
they teach you
about sinfulness & holiness
& our imagined sins
were their imagined holiness

> Sherry Sianaca & I giggling
> in the middle of a lecture on original sin
> Sister Mary David tapes my mouth shut
> with masking tape
> places me in a chair in front of the classroom
> to await the arrival of the monsignor
> who finally enters the room
> puts his face one inch from mine
> & asks, *"Have you learned your lesson?!"*
> the other kids giggle
> I wonder why their mouths are not taped shut

no, I have never learned
my lesson, Father Higgins,
the muffled sounds are louder now
& have turned into words

Angela Di Martini & I talking
Miss Philpot screams at us
to come to the front of the room
we do, shaking with fear
"Put your hands on the desk," she yells
we do, palms up
"No, turn them over!"
we do, slowly
Slam! She hits
the backs of our hands with a ruler
for talking

the words are talking now
falling out
like teeth

Sister James Marie
giving a geography lesson
I am day dreaming
am jarred to attention when I hear
"Mediterranean" & *"the boot"*
she points to Sandy Seavello & me
ushers us to the front of the class
"Italy," she says, *"that's where
the olive skinned people live. Like Denise & Sandy.
See how dirty they look?"*

I can hear many voices now
none of them mine

there is new dirt lurking everywhere
those dirty Italians
smell 'em a mile away
greasydagoguineawopwopwop

after school
I wash until
I have a shiny hue
next day I wake up
very clean
& still Italian
at school

Sandy & I
rub our hands together
we laugh
because we do not want to cry,
for talking
sometimes
takes years.

Denise Nico Leto

The Language of Great-Aunts

The great-aunts have a corner, and wrinkled skin
indistinguishable from their thick stockings,
and they invariably speak in the other language
of which we, as children, are able to recognize
only the commands, which are obvious, and the narrow
eyes, which make them law, drawn overly tight.

And their smiles are also long and tight,
black and without real teeth, scars on the skin
but only slight ones; red lips pressed, narrow,
their smiles are like the lines on their stockings,
which as two boys, at our height, we recognize
and wonder if these lines also speak some language.

And they do: theirs is the visible language
that when these women chew, only their mouths are tight
and immediately, because we are down there, we recognize
that, if they chewed harder, their wrinkled skin
would chew too, jiggling under their faces like the stockings
which are too big because their legs have grown too narrow.

But if we laugh, we get again the quick pin-narrow
eyes, who themselves speak a third language
more powerful than the line mouths of the stockings.
The eyes of the great-aunts disappear when drawn tight
and conspire somewhere under their spiderwebbed skin
made more webbed by attempts, not to warn, but to recognize.

We are never sure what exactly they are trying to recognize:
who we are, perhaps, or what we've done, and the narrow
amount of us they admit through the eyelids into that skin
is the part in us, inside, that makes us recognize
at these moments that our stomachs grow muscle-tight
and we change our big attentions fast from their stockings.

Because we are still too much children, their stockings
allow us to understand what others will not, to recognize
like commands what their eyes are really saying: how tight
their lives have grown, making their insides more narrow
than outside; words, black lines, eyes, all are one language,
saying *too tight now, too weak inside to hold up this skin.*

We watch their stockings grow larger, their legs more narrow.
We recognize by touch the verbs of this single language.
Later we stay tight, and pull in mirrors at our strong skin.

Alberto Alvaro Ríos

Nani

Sitting at her table, she serves
the sopa de arroz to me
instinctively, and I watch her,
the absolute *mamá*, and eat words
I might have had to say more
out of embarrassment. To speak,
now-foreign words I used to speak,
too, dribble down her mouth as she serves
me albondigas. No more
than a third are easy to me.
By the stove she does something with words
and looks at me only with her
back. I am full. I tell her
I taste the mint, and watch her speak
smiles at the stove. All my words
make her smile. Nani never serves
herself, she only watches me
with her skin, her hair. I ask for more.

I watch the *mamá* warming more
tortillas for me. I watch her
fingers in the flame for me.
Near her mouth, I see a wrinkle speak
of a man whose body serves
the ants like she serves me, then more words
from more wrinkles about children, words
about this and that, flowing more
easily from these other mouths. Each serves
as a tremendous string around her,
holding her together. They speak
nani was this and that to me
and I wonder just how much of me
will die with her, what were the words
I could have been, was. Her insides speak
through a hundred wrinkles, now, more
than she can bear, steel around her,
shouting, then, What is this thing she serves?

She asks me if I want more.
I own no words to stop her.
Even before I speak, she serves.

Alberto Alvaro Ríos

Espresso

Lemon rind rubbed on the rim
of the demitasse cups.
Black Japanese china
with pink-gold roses.

The smell of the wet grounds
like dirt from the garden
after rain
because—
they always took *espresso*
in the garden
after rain.

Mrs. Mannini or
Aunt Rose or
"cumadda Fran"
would be in the kitchen
(I was twenty-one before I learned
how to spell the word *comare*,
saved for second mothers).
Or if we were lucky
Nana would be there
looking through bargain-basement curtains
out as if to call in light
of a southern slant
we had never known
for a girlchild we could help
her remember. There would be *pignoli* nuts
and almonds that would appear
from the folds of her apron
and we would chase 'round the table
to see who could be her favorite.

While she flipped the pot upside down
we watched the quick stream of water
slip out the steam hole
and we listened to the water drizzle
over black grounds.

"Mary, get the spoons,"
and my cousin would let me help
place the napkins, the *biscotti*,
the plates with lush scenes:
women with one breast exposed,
men laboring their lovesongs—
themes I thought I never heard
until my first grand opera,
the Met, of course, and I knew:
I have always been hearing these songs.
Then, lemon on the tray
peel curling, such a sweet
bite to the tongue.
Tiny silver spoons:
one with an enameled crest,

two from the set that matched,
one from *Nana*.

We could hear the words from
the men in the garden
and the feet of the children young enough
to be free from kitchen chores
as they hop-scotched on the patio tiles.
My cousin Andrea would scream
whenever she came into
nana's kitchen:
the Protestant boy told her
"your grandmother has a witch
in her kitchen."
Did we ever know
how much the little *Befana*—
this ancient mother of gifts—
ah, how she loved her little ones?

And I would stand and squint my eyes
to fight the pain
when "gran-papa" would pinch
the flesh of my cheeks
the tears trickling over his thumb
("*bella figlia, bella figlia*")
I could only tremble
to the waves of sounds
I could not speak:
somehow I knew
this was the cutting language of love.

                  There was an aluminum pot for everyday
the kind one can always find in department stores
and there was the lush copper one
brought here from Reggio:
long and tubular
articulate in the curve of its spout.
That came out on holidays.

It sat on the credenza
even in May

behind the Virgin Mary statue
between the lilacs from Mrs. Prosky
and my mother's Sharon roses.

When we moved
(*Nana* died and we
were headed up in the world—
"a real suburb,")
the aunts stopped serving *espresso*
even on holidays.

Somehow
though *Nana* swore
she had no favorites
I have the copper pot.
The spout of water
elegant in its graceful arc
burns my hand.

                                        Carol Lee Saffioti

Secret Love

My father's back
heaves toward the sea,

and the stripes of his shirt
pull toward his right wrist,

which clerked mail into the boxes
and carried coffee for the bosses.

Now he needs a firm pillow to rest
the ache against as he reads

in his loveseat, summer and winter,
the lamp by his good shoulder.

Yet watch him bend at night to lock
the stick of Judah in the terrace door

or hear his tenor soar against the president
and injustice to the poor.

He is secure on his pension. He does not
use a cane at 84 or face the floor.

This is the back I lay beside in secret peace
during the dark daytimes after my

humiliation at school and before his invisible
war of work. He sleeps well still in flannel.

Thanks, Pop, and I touch his silky back. Then he
dresses to go out. We worry a bit more.

Today, my mother thought to reassure
and said, You'll live to be a hundred.

I will if you will, he said.
They shook on it.

                                        Milton Kessler

Good Grease

The hunters went out with guns
at dawn.
We had no meat in the village,
no food for the tribe and the dogs.
No caribou in the caches.

All day we waited.
At last!
As darkness hung at the river
we children saw them far away.
Yes! They were carrying caribou!
We jumped and shouted!

By the fires that night
we feasted.

The old ones clucked,
sucking and smacking,
sopping the juices with sourdough bread.
The grease would warm us
when hungry winter howled.

Grease was beautiful
oozing,
dripping and running down our chins,
brown hands shining with grease.
We talk of it
when we see each other
far from home.

Remember the marrow
sweet in the bones?
We grabbed for them like candy.
Good.
Gooooood.

Good grease.

Mary TallMountain

6th Grade—
Our Lady of Pompeii

6th grade—our lady of pompeii
the nun said
you're living in america
                now
write your name with a C
            the american way
when i argued
had to write it
        100 times
        with a C
my americanized classmates snickered

after school
seeing my face
hearing my story
mama told the nun off
mia noma e Vittoria
                    2 T's   no C

                    Vittoria repetto

Mama

I. RICE CHILD
She is the lady
who microwaves tea.
She serves *nishi me*
on paper plates,
picks caterpillars
off cherry tomatoes
with wooden chopsticks,
and places a cup
of coffee
in front of her husband's
picture.

She is the bind that holds
the Kishis and Kageyamas together.
Her name is Tamai Kumagai.
Friends call her Obasan.
She is my Obaachan, my grandmother.
I call her Mama.

On Fridays,
I followed her
to Save & Save
where we picked up
packages of rice tea.

At night
through my window
under a cucumber moon,

she sang me songs
about Cowpatch and Mortar,
how they saved the crab's children,
and about Momotaro,
"Momotaro, Momotaro,
is hiding and waiting," she said,
"in the center of your peach."

I repeated her stories to the sky,
where I learned new lessons.

I am the child
she wrapped in a kimono.
My feet adorned in bamboo shoes.
My hair braided in plastic chopsticks.
I wore her wedding dress
on Halloween.
I was third born,
the last child to taste her rice candy.

II. THE MARRIAGE
Her marriage was arranged
by the Tsurus and Kumagais.
She was the daughter
willing to leave Japan.

In 1924, she sailed on the U.S.S. *Jackson*,
the last ship which brought Asians
to Seattle after Coolidge passed
the Immigration Act.

Her brother-in-law married a woman
by signing a photograph.
He divorced her the day she arrived;
threw her picture in the trash
and demanded a new wife.

III. FAMILY
She and her husband moved
to Medicine Bow, Wyoming.

He worked in the coal mines,
and later became head foreman
for Union Pacific Railroad.

She combed lice
out of her children's hair,
shampooed them with kerosene,
and boiled their bath water
on a gas stove.

She collected foil
from cigarette wrappers,
pressed it together
into mercury balls,
and mailed them to Japan.
Her relatives melted
those bundles into weapons.

The night World War II broke out,
her husband lost his job.
They lit a bonfire
of wood and garbage,
dropped in letters and flags.

IV. HER WISH
During the Fifties,
she moved to L.A.
and spent her days
mixing chocolate and butter
in a kitchen of cockroaches.

Once in a car,
between Olympic and Sawtelle,
she tried to jump out
of the passenger window.
Her husband held her back,
as she cried, "I want to die."

V. HER GIFT
In September
I became a woman.

She started to sew me
a black dress
with a peplum skirt,
saying, "I want you
to wear this to my funeral."
She handed me a silk box
with a pearl necklace
she had been saving
for nineteen years.

Pouring me
a cup of rice tea
she told me
Kumagai means
"Bad bear";
Kageyama means "Behind
in the shade of a mountain."

She is the lady
who microwaves tea.
She is my Obaachan.

Claire Kageyama

Preparations for Seder

"Therefore, even if all of us were wise, all of us people of understanding,
all of us learned in Torah, it would still be our obligation to tell the story
of the exodus from Egypt, for redemption is not yet complete."
                                                    —*The Haggadah*

Preparing schmaltz for matzoh balls,
I peel the skin off chickens, scrape yellow fat
from pink meat, think of my father: how he stood
at the elbow of his mother, eating the "cracklings"
she'd hand down from the stove, morsels of meat
fried free of the fat, as she rendered schmaltz
years ago, in Boston.

Today, preparing for Seder, I think of Grandmother
as I salvage these tasty cracklings, relish them
for myself, hand them to my children as I cut more
and more fat from the chicken: how much harder
for her, hot before the wood stove, peeling bits
of fat from the muscle of chickens that ran
free in the yard.

Now the fat is plentiful, preserved with chemicals.
The echo of my father's voice calls out warnings
of carcinogens in the fat of animals and I wonder
what I am doing to myself, my children. But this
is the eve of Passover. I am making matzoh balls.
My knife plunges under the skin for more fat.
I will not forsake the traditions of my ancestors.

At the Seder meal, we sip the chicken broth,
then cut into the matzoh balls, savory
with marrow and garlic, parsley and schmaltz,
remembering forty years in the desert, the freedom
of the promised land, succulent and dangerous,
bobbing before us like these matzoh balls we relish
and eat and praise the taste of, wanting more.

Michael S. Glaser

Changing Address Books

I
This is a project as overwrought
with emotion as falling in love,
writing a will, moving, or
getting divorced.

This is a history book, filled with
stories and forgotten memories.
It is a slice of life's iceberg,
a garden with roots that became tangled,
branches that fell off or never grew.

This is an alphabet of associations,
a genealogy of birthdays and anniversaries,
a lost and found, a place of reconnection
and return to sender, a yearbook of friendships,
a keepsake, coin of our own personal realm.

II
There are different ways of saying a thing,
of naming its name. Rhyme and reason have
their claims, though both can ease us
away from what is not being said

the fact, for example, that some of these
names are the names of people who are dead:
Grandpa Glaser, Uncle Bernie, Uncle Juke,
Corise, Lisa, Tom, Chava. . . .

Seeing them here with addresses and phone
numbers still attached is more than
a reminder of what has passed. It is a
remembrance, a yahrtzeit, a flame that stops
me when I'm about to pass them by—
there, say, under "G" for my family,
or S and Z and B and S again.

III
Changing address books pushes
the past against the present
where there is little time or
place for the dead, though

my mind harkens back to the prayers
we said in temple when I was young,
about how the dead live on in the minds
of those who cherish their memories,
and how we prayed that their names
might be inscribed for a blessing
in the book of life. . . .

This old address book is like a Kaddish,
a prayer, a reminder of love that was

and still sustains. It is a voice
that calls us away from other lists
to remember again the lives of these
particular people, who were real,
who were loved, who are missed.

Michael S. Glaser

Crazy Horse Monument

Hailstones falling like sharp blue sky chips
howling winds the brown grass bends, while
buffalo paw and stamp and blow billowing steam,
and prairie wolves chorus the moon in morning.

The spotted snake of a village on the move
a silent file of horses rounding hills,
in a robe of gray, the sky chief clutches thunder
and winter seeks to find the strongest men.

> Crazy Horse rides the circle of his people's sleep,
>   from Little Big Horn to Wounded Knee,
> Black Hills, their shadows are his only robe
>   dark breast feathers of a future storm.

Those of broken bodies piled in death,
of frozen blood upon the white of snow,
yours is now the sky chant of spirit making,
pacing the rhythm of Crazy Horse's mount.

And he would cry in anger of a single death,
and dare the guns of mounted soldiers blue,
for his was the blood and pulse of rivers,
and mountains and plains taken in sacred trust.

> Crazy Horse rides the circle of his people's sleep,
>   from Little Big Horn to Wounded Knee,
> Black Hills, their shadows are his only robe
>   dark breast feathers of a future storm.

And what would he think of the cold steel chisel,
and of dynamite blasting a mountain's face,
what value the crumbled glories of Greece and Rome,
to a people made cold and hungry?

To capture in stone the essence of a man's spirit,
to portray the love and respect of children and elders,
fashion instead the point of a hunting arrow sharp,
and leave to the elements the wearing-down of time.

Crazy Horse rides the circle of his people's sleep,
    from Little Big Horn to Wounded Knee,
Black Hills, their shadows are his only robe
    dark breast feathers of a future storm.

Peter Blue Cloud

from Prose Poems

Edith B——— and her mother on a Sunday afternoon. The ancient mother, ill, about to have a biopsy tomorrow, falling asleep in her chair but plays piano like a brilliant young girl. There's a portrait of her in 1908 just before her "European Tour." She is wearing a blue dress with lace fichu. How gnarled but light her hands are, a snapping light in her blue eyes.

Mother and daughter play a two-handed duet—one thin and lithe, the other broad and bumptious, both wearing paisley print blouses and navy stretch pants, chunky brown shoes. The poodle with his bowed legs lies asleep on the orange plaid blanket on the floor, a Sunday afternoon silence, the clock with domino pieces for numbers, map of the U.S. made of a quilt of United States stamps. The lonely daughter with her chopped-off hair, her anti-Semitism, arcane references, fretfulness and snobbery. Her bitterness about Leonard Bernstein, "how the Jews buy up concerts"—she warms to her subject. Stands like a woeful child at the door as we leave, saying in her stilted voice, "I hope I shall know you." But we are Jews and she never will.

■ ■ ■

My Jewish mother. Stuffing coat pockets full of secret gifts—tiny bottles of cologne, pumpkin seeds, recipes, clean socks and underwear. I drag these burdens around forever, wherever I go, like a curse: where will you ever find this much love? and a blessing: never settle for less.

■ ■ ■

Jews in the courtyard. Around the holy candles, intense, their faces ghostly in prayer. Skinny Jewish porters carrying the soldiers like human taxi cabs. The Jew's-head lamp giving off an eternal radiance and a damp, sour smell in Argentina. Jews on the subway, suspicious and alert. The Jew in love with a small blonde woman. Jews praying together, dovening like the waves of the sea. Jewish fashion plates in silk blouses and jeans. Jews praying in the aisles at Bloomingdale's.

Jews at the back of the bus, bending over the forbidden water fountain. Marching into the ovens—a few stumbling. Jews refusing to believe this is paradise. Buried under the American railroads, side by side with Chinese. Jews run off the cliffs with the buffalo, paraded in bloody scorn beneath the Arc de Triomphe, hung by the neck in Washington Square Park till dead, sitting shiva on boxes, raving, dying their hair yellow or red and fitting in. And yet always the Jews—if not these Jews, then some other Jews.

Liz Rosenberg

In Answer to Their Questions

Italian
is where I'm understood, loved, and included,
where aglio e olio
is Neapolitan
for soul food.

Italian
means my living habits
are not quirks
but ceremonies, mostly invisible

to the non-Italian eye.
My skin color is olive, not "white"
and the hair spreading down my arms and legs and over
the top of my lip
is a dense garden
cultivated for centuries
by Neapolitan peasants
digging, dropping their sweat
into the soil
like seeds, passing down their genes
breaking their backs to subsist
resisting their own extinction
down there nel mezzogiorno,
the land of the forgotten,
they clung like cockroaches to life.

Italian
means the boat
from the boot-shaped country
the immigrants teeming like lentil beans
in New York Harbor
exhausted and sick, crammed in thick below the deck
shoved into steerage like cattle
they made a three-week passage
over icy water,
watched their dead family members heaved overboard
by authorities who altered passenger lists
removing Italian lives
like lint
from old clothing.

Italian
meant my Neapolitan grandparents
losing their families one by one
to hunger and disease
forced to leave
one by one, eldest sons
first in line for a boat
that would deliver them
to a land where the streets
are paved with silver and gold.

Italian
meant my grandfathers Dominic and Donato
supporting their wives and children
by sweeping the streets of New York
the custodians, but never the beneficiaries
of that wealth.

But Italian meant
you do what you must to survive
You keep your mouth shut
celebrate what you got
and be thankful
you're alive.

It meant one generation later
five kids draped on couch and chairs
t.v. blares, Sinatra sings while the phone rings.

Italian American
meant whole neighborhoods
laid out like a village in Naples:
Ambrosio, Iovino, Capone, Barone, Nardone, Cerbone,
Luisi, Marconi, Mastrianni, Bonavitacola,
"the Americans" living side by side
with "those ginzos straight off the boat."

Italian
meant Sunday morning sausage and meatballs
foaming in oil,
a pot of pasta water set to boil
and the hollow tap of a wooden spoon

Italian
meant the old men playing bocce ball
in Hartley Park,
Mr. Bonavitacola roasting peppers
in his backyard,
and every nose in the neighborhood
inhaling the aroma.

Italian
was the sound of my cousin Anthony's accordion

as he practiced upstairs
squeezing the air
into deep hums and festival sounds,
the accordion strapped to his back
the sun glinting off chrome and black keys,
a taste of the Festa de San Antonio all year long.

Italian
meant the yellow patties of polenta
frying in a pan,
a pot full of escarole greens
and Ma spreading the lentil beans
on the kitchen table,
talking to me after a day at school
sorting the good from the bad,
the good from the bad
at the kitchen table.

Or my sister Lisa
sitting the kids down,
pouring salt crystals onto a plate on the kitchen table,
telling us: "Here's the white people,"
& pouring pepper over them, "And here's the black people,"
& pouring olive oil over them, "And here come the Italians!"
and us squealing with laughter as the oil bubbles slithered
and slid over the salt and pepper,
retaining their distinct
and voluptuous identity.

But Italian
also means those garlic breath bastards
dirty dago wops with greasy skin
ginzos straight off the boat
slick-haired, like vermin they bring disease

Italian
means the entire Mafia looking over my shoulder
whenever I cash a check.
"Capone? She's from Chicago!"
and their laughter
because they associate my Italianness
with a killer and hardened criminal.

But second generation Italian American
means I do what I must
to survive,
means I won't keep my mouth shut,
won't shrink to fit
someone else's definition of our lives.

Italian American
means my living habits
are cultural ceremonies, not quirks.
My skin color is olive
And the hair spreading down my arms and legs and over
the top of my lip
grows thicker and thicker
the more I resist,
the more I insist
on possessing
entirely who I am.

Giovanna (Janet) Capone

All I Want

All I want is the bread to turn out like hers just once
        brown crust
        soft, airy insides
        rich and round
that is all.
So I ask her: How many cups?
        Ah yaa ah, she says,
        tossing flour and salt into a large, silver bowl.
        I don't measure with cups.
        I just know by my hands,
        just a little like this is right, see?
        You young people always ask
        those kinds of questions,
        she says,
thrusting her arms into the dough
and turning it over and over again.
The table trembles with her movements.

I watch silently and this coffee is good,
                              strong and fresh.
        Outside, her son is chopping wood,
        his body an intense arc.
        The dull rhythm of winter
        is the swinging of the axe
        and the noise of children squeezing in
        with the small sighs of wind
        through the edges of the windows.

She pats and tosses it furiously
shaping balls of warm, soft dough.
        There, we'll let it rise,
        she says, sitting down now.
        We drink coffee and there is nothing
        like the warm smell of bread rising
        on windy, woodchopping afternoons.

                                   Luci Tapahonso

Two Grandmas

One grandma
I knew;
the other
I didn't.

This one shopped on
Belmont and
Blake Avenues
from pushcarts.
Took me with her
to the chicken market
where they plucked
and burned their feathers,
took out the whole eggs
and, sometimes,
the *eiyele*
for the chicken soup
filled with necks

and legs
and onions and parsley.
Oh, the *griebines*
fired in the pan—the scent floating
around the kitchen
throughout the rooms
of our railroad flat
over the furniture store
on Sutter Avenue.

Grandma, forever cooking:
jarring blueberry jam,
boiling apples for sauce,
spicing herring,
chopping pike and carp
for *gefilte* fish.

We were always hungry,
anxious to devour
the scents,
the bits and pieces
of chicken with onions,
the *shmaltz*
on fresh rye bread.

Grandma stirred
and filled
our hunger.

Even now,
as I remember
her shopping,
cooking, singing:
"Alein, alein—
alles far meine kinder."

Stanley H. Barkan

South Bronx Testimonial

I
We live amidst hills of desolate
buildings, rows of despair crowded
together in a chain of lifeless
shells. Every five minutes the echoing roar
of racing elevated trains sears through
the atmosphere low over the horizon.

But at every moment like magic the shells
breathe, and take on appearances of second
cousins, sometimes even look like old retired
ladies who have nothing more to do but ride
empty subways from stop to stop.
At night, hidden from the city, youngbloods
invade trainyards laden with colors
of dreams crying for existence on the empty walls
of desolation's subway cars, for old ladies
to read on and on . . .

II
The I.R.T. is hot and humid
on August 9th. Two Chinese men sit
side by side on their way
to Woodlawn, steel clubs to putt
on green. One Black man dressed in
black, reads the *Daily News*
from back to front, I read the pictures
from across the aisle sitting next to
pregnant señora, husband and child.

Already the universe has grown with these
people, I want to know more, but we
must all exit at the next stop.
My curiosity and I will never know
how the lady concluded her episode
on the mass transit. Did she have
natural childbirth, or was she
one of the victims too?

III
We were all insane, the eternal
dance, drinking a polluted
nectar, breathing a poisoned air, humming
a disjointed tune in disoriented
melody. We create chaos, wallow
in it, market it, the way
the food is tampered.

We are all hopelessly, blindly, incurably
insane. Staring at each other from
pseudo façades, pretending to be immune
to the plague of lunacy, yelling
irrelevant incoherences at our selves.

We have lost our freedoms: to walk
barefoot over the earth without
stepping on some dubiously "manufactured chemical"
guaranteed to produce plastic lawn, or dip
in the ocean without catching
slime, sing from the mountain, watching
sun without seeing one rooftop
antenna, wanting to play outdoors, not worried
about getting kidnapped
or molested, the list
goes on.

IV
In our wagon, oysters are treasured, their
hard shells clapping against each other, words
that crash into our ears. We cushion them, cup
them gently in our hands. We kiss and
suck the delicate juice, sculpturing flowers
from the stone skin. We wash them
in the river by moonlight with offerings
of songs. And after the meal
we wear them in our hair, and
in our eyes.

Sandra María Esteves

Grandma in the Shower

puckered breasts like Leiberman's
salamis hanging behind the riot
of seeded ryes, bagels, those round
mahogany loaves, solid as riverstone.

      Grandma's
vay-a-zmeres chasing dybbuks and strokes
of ill-fortune from our kitchen
her incense of onions and garlic
her vaporous *shu shu shu*

        And her shoe in the door
when father arrived
home from the city
crushed olive-green fedora
in one hand, folded *Tribune*, a map
to the new world in the other; father

already wizened at 40
by new possibilities—his
generation
of assimilated, degreed
and quasi-pedigreed immigrants

        who Sundays
packed their Nash Ramblers
a day in the country
and on the look-out for
some place not defined
by native tongues
or smells—green and one hundred
percent American,

but Grandma
held fast
spit in the soup
for good luck
before the meat left her bones

the upstairs bedroom
her private domain, safe haven

            where Grandma,
Queen of the Sparrows,
sat solidly in her flowered chintz chair
whistling out the window,
Kiev's songstress, luring the birds,

her salmon-colored undies dancing the wash-line:
Grandma, older than anyone I ever knew.
Grandma's moustache. Grandma's teeth in the glass.

                                    Dale M. Kushner

Haciendo Apenas la Recolección

For weeks now
I have not been able
to liberate me from my name.
Always I am history I must wake to.
In idiot defeat I trace my routes
across a half-forgotten map of Texas.
I smooth out the folds stubborn
as the memory.

Let me see: I would start from San Marcos,
moving northward,
bored beyond recognition
in the stale air of a '52 Chevy:
to my left, the youngest of uncles
steadies the car;
to my right, Grandfather finds humor
in the same joke.
I am hauled among family
extended across the back seat,
as the towns bury themselves forever
in my eyes: Austin, Lampasas, Brownwood,
past Abilene, Sweetwater,
along

the Panhandle's alien tallness.
There it is: Lubbock sounding harsh as ever.
I press its dark letters,
and dust on my fingertips is so alive
it startles them
as once did sand.
Then west, 10,000 acres and a finger's breadth,
is Levelland
where a thin house once stood,
keeping watch over me and my baseball glove
when the wrath of winds cleared the earth
of stooping folk.
There's Ropesville, where in fifth grade
I didn't make a friend.
My arm is taut by now and terrified.
It slackens,
begins falling back into place,
while the years are gathering slowly
along still roads and hill country,
downward
to where it all began—500 McKie Street.
I am home, and although the stars
are at rest tonight,
my strength is flowing.

Weep no more, my common hands;
you shall not again
pick cotton.

                                        Tino Villanueva

On Alabama Ave., Paterson, NJ, 1954

At seven I dreamed again and again
of plummeting down the narrow stairs
into the arms of Mario the greenhorn

with his curly black hair. Old
Mrs. Pepe cleaned scungilli outside
on the porch. I watched her big hands
go in and out of the pot and thought
about her son Mario wishing he were
my pop. In the tiny flat on the third
floor, Pop was already bald and bellowing
rage. Mamma bit her tongue into silence
she never stopped wishing on me.

When Mamma's five sisters came over
she was happy. They talked dirty
in Calabrian and laughed loud. They
smacked each other on the back or
grabbed hands, smoked cigarettes and
ate the whole time, coffee cake, macaroni,
meatballs, biscotti, and fruit. Little
apricots sweet and delicate and yellow,
and tossed the smooth brown pits
on a blue plate, where they clattered
like dice.

                                    Rachel Guido deVries

From Okra to Greens /

A Different Love Poem / We Need a Change

i haveta turn my television down sometimes cuz
i cant stand to have white people / shout at me /
sometimes i turn it off
cuz i cant look at em in my bedroom either /
being so white /
that's why i like / greens /
they cdnt even smell you / wdnt know what you taste like
without sneakin / got no
idea you shd be tingled wit hot sauce & showered wit vinegar
yr pot liquor spread on hot rolls

i gotta turn the tv off cuz the white people
keep playing games / & followin presidents on vacation at the war
there's too much of a odor problem on the tv too / which
brings me back to greens

i remember my grandma at the market pickin turnips
collards kale & mustards / to mix-em up / drop a ½ a strick a lean
in there wit some ham hock & oh my whatta life /
i lived in her kitchen / wit greens i cd recollect
yes the very root of myself
    the dirt & lil bugs i looked for in the fresh collards /
    turnin each leaf way so slow / under the spicket / watchin
    lil mounds of dirt fall down the drain
i done a good job
grandma tol me / got them greens just ready for the pot
& you know / wdnt no white man on the tv /
talkin loud n formal make no sense of the miracle
a good pot a greens on a friday nite cd make to me
that's the only reason i turn em off the tv
cant stand they gossipin abt the news / sides they dont
never like the criminals & enemies i like anyway
that's why i like GREENS / i know how to cook em
& i sure can dream gd / soppin up the pot liquor
& them peppers /

Ntozake Shange

But My Blood

I'm beginning to talk to myself.
No one else will listen.
I don't fit into my place.
There are things I know and
will not change. Do they seriously
expect me to rearrange reality
until I happen to find a pattern
that suits their convenience?
Yeah, they do.

They all know what it means
to be insane, or else why would
they be so quick to see reality
through the eyes of those with
power? Any power—government,
literary community, Hollywood, world's
foremost authority, demands of the
rich, frustrations of the poor, resentments
of the working class.

What does it mean to be American?
It doesn't mean anything to me.
It's only a place—but I have
blood, red and warm. I was Italian
when they called us wops. Now
they like us so they assure us
we no longer need to suffer as
Italian—now, we're just as
American as anyone. But my blood
will not change.

                              Rose Romano

So I Lost My Temper

Another one was coming toward me
yelling and wagging his finger
in my face. So I lost my temper.
I yelled louder than he could.
I backed him into a corner. His wife
tried to console him. It's an Italian
trait, she explained. I went out
and bought a votive candle and
a little glass cup to put it in. Then
I went home and made a big pot
of spaghetti.

Another one said he didn't believe
I could be that way, that Italian women

are much too sexual to be like
that, that he was sure I knew
how to make a man feel appreciated.
I went out and bought some tomato
seeds and a small clay pot. Then I
went home and lit the votive candle,
planted the tomato seeds, and made
a big pot of spaghetti.

Another one assured me that all women's
bars are owned and operated by the
Mafia, that the women who signed
the papers, redecorated the place,
stand behind the bar every night,
serve the drinks, sweep up at
closing time, and count the money,
are just a front. I went out and bought
a statue of the Sacred Heart of Mary.
Then I went home and put her on my
dresser, lit the votive candle in front
of her, watered the tomatoes, and made
a big pot of spaghetti.

I'm walking down the street
and I hear the words—*garlic eater*.
I tuck holy cards into the corners
of the mirror over my dresser.
I hear the word—*greaseball*.
I staple a tiny palm cross on
the door frame in my bedroom.
Dago—I put a red and white
checked tablecloth on the little
round table in my kitchen.
Guinea—I re-do my bathroom in
green, white and red.
Wop—I stop shaving the little
black hairs growing out of my chin.

If this trend continues,
when I'm eighty years old
I'll wear black shapeless dresses,
black stockings, black chunky shoes,

and my hair in a bun at the back
of my neck.

Now I'm thinking maybe
this is how Italian women
become grandmothers.

Now I'm thinking maybe
this is how Italian grandmothers
last long enough to become
boss of the family:
they lose their temper.

                                        Rose Romano

For My Great-Grandfather:
A Message Long Overdue

You with the beard as red as Barbarossa's
uncut from its first sprouting to the hour
they tucked it in your belt and closed your eyes,
you with the bright brass water pipe, a surefire
plaything under the neighbors' children's noses
for you to puff and them to idolize

—the pipe you'd packed up out of somewhere
in Bohemia, along with the praying shawl
and the pair of little leather praying boxes—
Great-Grandfather, old blue-eyed fox of foxes,
I have three pages of you. That is all.

1895. A three-page letter
from Newport News, Virginia, written
on your bleached-out bills of sale under the stern
heading: ROSENBERG THE TAILOR, DEBTOR,
A FULL LINE OF GOODS OF ALL THE LATEST IN
SUITING AND PANTS. My mother has just been born.

You write to thank your daughter for the picture
of that sixth grandchild. There are six more to come.
"My heart's tenderest tendrils" is your style.
"God bless you even as He blessed Jacob." Meanwhile
you stitch the year away in Christendom.

Meanwhile it seems you've lost your wife, remarried
a girl your daughter's age and caused distress.
"It was a cold relentless hand of Death
that scattered us abroad," you write, "robbing us
of Wife and Mother." Grieving for that one buried
you send new wedding pictures now herewith
and close with *mazel* and *brocha*, words that bless.

The second bride lived on in one long study
of pleats and puckers to the age of ninety-two,
smoked cigarettes, crocheted and spoke of you
to keep our kinship threaded up and tidy.

Was that the message—the erratic ways
the little lore that has been handed on
suffers, but sticks it out in the translation?
I tell you to my children, who forget,
are brimful of themselves, and anyway
might have preferred a farmer or a sailor,
but you and I are buttoned, flap to pocket.
Welcome, ancestor, Rosenberg the Tailor!
I choose to be a lifetime in your debt.

                                        Maxine Kumin

Bulosan Listens to a Recording of Robert Johnson

You sing a hard blues,
black man. You too have been driven:
a tumbleweed in strong wind.

I close my eyes, your voice rolls
out of the delta, sliding
over flashy chords
that clang like railroad tracks.

Gotta keep movin'
Gotta keep movin'
Hellbound on my trail

One summer
I worked the *wash-lye*
section of a cannery up north,
scrubbed schools of headless fish,
breathed ammonia fumes so fierce
I almost floated off
like the arm of a friend,
chopped clean at the elbow
by a cutter's machine.

Gotta keep movin'
Gotta keep movin'

We are the blue men, *Cabayan*,
our pockets empty of promise.
Mississippi, California—
bad luck conspires against us,
cheap wine stings in our veins.
We reel, drunk and bitter,
under the white, legal sun.
Robert Johnson/Carlos Bulosan—
our names so different,
our song the same.

Alfred Encarnacion

Miss Clement's Second Grade

They sat in even rows
like new chocolates in a long box,
quiet enough to hear pencils

trying uneven letters.
On those days Maria stared
at clean blue-lined paper
while boiler heat sifted
through thumping registers
by Anthony Lombardo's desk.
As Maria shaped vowels,
she wished to be a Smith
so she could hand out crayons
like Evelyn Brown,
have her papers on display.
During quiet writing,
when everyone seemed the same,
she almost forgot
the hours locked in the teacher's closet,
missing how to take two from eight.
Every day Miss Clement wore a navy dress,
tied her blond hair in a circular braid.
Every night Maria laughed
with Wilbur and Charlotte.
They didn't mind her Italian name.

Maryfrances Cusumano Wagner

Recognized Futures

Turning to you, my name—
this necklace of gold, these letters
in script I cannot read,
this part of myself I long
to recognize—falls forward
into my mouth.

You call my daily name, *Lisa*,
the name I've finally declared
my own, claiming a heritage
half mine: corn fields golden

in ripening haze, green music
of crickets, summer light sloping
to dusk on the Iowa farm.

This other name fills my mouth,
a taste faintly metallic, blunt
edges around which my tongue
moves tentatively: *Suhair*,
an old-fashioned name, *little star*
in the night. The second girl,
small light on a distanced horizon.

Throughout childhood this rending split:
continents moving slowly apart,
rift widening beneath taut limbs.
A contested name, a constant
longing, evening star rising mute
through the Palestine night.
Tongue cleft by impossible languages,
fragments of narrative fractured
to loss, homelands splintered
beyond bridgeless rivers,
oceans of salt.

■ ■ ■

From these fragments I feel
a stirring, almost imperceptible.
In the morning light these torn
lives merge: a name on your lips,
on mine, softly murmured,
mutely scripted, both real
and familiar, till I cannot
distinguish between your voice
and my silence, my words
and this wordless knowledge,
morning star rising
through lightening sky,
some music I can't quite
hear, a distant melody,
flute-like, *nai* through

the olives, a cardinal calling,
some possible language
all our tongues can sing.

Nai: Arabic flute

Lisa Suhair Majaj

The Left Bank Jazz Society

"Can anybody here keep time?"

Freddie Hubbard's music
is an hour late. We pick
at our lunch packed at home
and brought to Baltimore's
gem of a jazz club.
A grandmotherly baker
sells homemade cakes and pies
in the back. The Left Bank
is like an old cabaret
or a hall of Father Divine
in New York feeding the soul,
but we are waiting for jazz.
We are waiting for Hubbard
to let a constellation pop out
of that trumpet of his
with our liquor and laughter,
with our quiet expectation.

My buddy, "the Duck,"
holds court with his humor.
He teases me about Mable,
reticent and sweet. He
punches me and smiles
his wisdom smile. Then Freddie
strides in with his trumpet,
explains he is worth waiting for.
Duck smiles because he knows
the trumpet, its tension,
the way it tightens your face

until a laser shoots from
between your eyes to the horn.
It is black people's pain
turning sweet, becoming music.

Duck died in Florida,
but he left me a few proverbs—
black music moves the black soul,
c.p. time is black resistance,
we wait for a melody of justice.

Play it, Mable, vigilant and able,
black and black-sweet . . .

Michael S. Weaver

Blood

"A true Arab knows how to catch a fly in his hands,"
my father would say. And he'd prove it,
cupping the buzzer instantly
while the host with the swatter stared.

In the spring our palms peeled like snakes.
True Arabs believed watermelon could heal fifty ways.
I changed these to fit the occasion.

Years before, a girl knocked,
wanted to see the Arab.
I said we didn't have one.
After that, my father told me who he was,
"Shihab"— "shooting star"—
a good name, borrowed from the sky.
Once I said, "When we die, we give it back?"
He said that's what a true Arab would say.

Today the headlines clot in my blood.
A little Palestinian dangles a truck on the front page.
Homeless fig, this tragedy with a terrible root
is too big for us. What flag can we wave?

I wave the flag of stone and seed,
table mat stitched in blue.

I call my father, we talk around the news.
It is too much for him,
neither of his two languages can reach it.
I drive into the country to find sheep, cows,
to plead with the air:
Who calls anyone *civilized*?
Where can the crying heart graze?
What does a true Arab do now?

Naomi Shihab Nye

Mnemonic

I was tired. So I lay down.
My lids grew heavy. So I slept.
Slender memory, stay with me.

I was cold once. So my father took off his blue sweater.
He wrapped me in it, and I never gave it back.
It is the sweater he wore to America,
this one, which I've grown into, whose sleeves are too long,
whose elbows have thinned, who outlives its rightful owner.
Flamboyant blue in daylight, poor blue by daylight,
it is black in the folds.

A serious man who devised complex systems of numbers and rhymes
to aid him in remembering, a man who forgot nothing, my father
would be ashamed of me.
Not because I'm forgetful,
but because there is no order
to my memory, a heap
of details, uncatalogued, illogical.
For instance:
God was lonely. So he made me.
My father loved me. So he spanked me.
It hurt him to do so. He did it daily.

The earth is flat. Those who fall off don't return.
The earth is round. All things reveal themselves to men only gradually.

I won't last. Memory is sweet.
Even when it's painful, memory is sweet.

Once, I was cold. So my father took off his blue sweater.

                                                    Li-Young Lee

The Gift

To pull the metal splinter from my palm
my father recited a story in a low voice.
I watched his lovely face and not the blade.
Before the story ended, he'd removed
the iron sliver I thought I'd die from.

I can't remember the tale,
but hear his voice still, a well
of dark water, a prayer.
And I recall his hands,
two measures of tenderness
he laid against my face,
the flames of discipline
he raised above my head.

Had you entered that afternoon
you would have thought you saw a man
planting something in a boy's palm,
a silver tear, a tiny flame.
Had you followed that boy
you would have arrived here,
where I bend over my wife's right hand.

Look how I shave her thumbnail down
so carefully she feels no pain.
Watch as I lift the splinter out.
I was seven when my father
took my hand like this,

and I did not hold that shard
between my fingers and think,
Metal that will bury me,
christen it Little Assassin,
Ore Going Deep for My Heart.
And I did not lift up my wound and cry,
Death visited here!
I did what a child does
when he's given something to keep.
I kissed my father.

Li-Young Lee

Nikki-Rosa

childhood remembrances are always a drag
if you're Black
you always remember things like living in Woodlawn
with no inside toilet
and if you become famous or something
they never talk about how happy you were to have
your mother
all to yourself and
how good the water felt when you got your bath
from one of those
big tubs that folk in chicago barbecue in
and somehow when you talk about home
it never gets across how much you
understood their feelings
as the whole family attended meetings about Hollydale
and even though you remember
your biographers never understand
your father's pain as he sells his stock
and another dream goes
And though you're poor it isn't poverty that
concerns you
and though they fought a lot
it isn't your father's drinking that makes any difference
but only that everybody is together and you
and your sister have happy birthdays and very good

Christmases
and I really hope no white person ever has cause
to write about me
because they never understand
Black love is Black wealth and they'll
probably talk about my hard childhood
and never understand that
all the while I was quite happy

Nikki Giovanni

Legacies

her grandmother called her from the playground
    "yes, ma'am"
    "i want chu to learn how to make rolls," said the old
woman proudly
but the little girl didn't want
to learn how because she knew
even if she couldn't say it that
that would mean when the old one died she would be less
dependent on her spirit so
she said
    "i don't want to know how to make no rolls"
with her lips poked out
and the old woman wiped her hands on
her apron saying "lord
    these children"
and neither of them ever
said what they meant
and i guess nobody ever does

Nikki Giovanni

Because of My Father's Job

Spring hailstones would drive us
into the garage. I'd explain away
the smell of my father's tsukemono crock
with its rock-weight,
saying he needed his cabbage
like Popeye's spinach. I'd divert attention
to the moonsnail shell,
carried across the mountains from Puget Sound
by my sister. We'd shake off cobwebs,
listen to the dancing surf.

I still use the smell of cabbage,
like kelp & fishbone, as an anchor
although I have no memories of father
scooping butter clams
out of the gravel at Point-of-Arches
near Shi Shi Beach. Nothing
to connect him to the wind
on the headland at Strawberry Point,
the breakers unfolding a story
of poetry, edges & days
that don't always balance.

I have no memories of father
naming me
after Jimmy Osler of Skykomish,
who worked in the depot
and laughed so easily.
Who didn't change his friendship in '41.

I have copied the moustache
we shaved off my father once
when he was drunk. Last December
I sat at a motel kitchen table,
on the Oregon coast,
writing poems by candlelight.
My shadow fluttered on the walls & ceiling
as white waves

thundered & slid toward the cabin.
Turning to a mirror
I found his thick biceps
flexing themselves.
It doesn't matter now that he drank too much,
embarrassed the moon with his curses & songs.

James Masao Mitsui

Yuba City School

From the black trunk I shake out
my one American skirt, blue serge
that smells of mothballs. Again today
Neeraj came crying from school. All week
the teacher has made him sit
in the last row, next to the fat boy
who drools and mumbles,
picks at the spotted milk-blue
skin of his face, but knows
to pinch, sudden-sharp,
when she is not looking.

The books are full of black curves,
dots like the eggs the boll-weevil laid
each monsoon in the furniture-cracks
in Ludhiana. Far up in front
the teacher makes word-sounds
Neeraj does not know. They float
from her mouth-cave, he says,
in discs, each a different color.

Chitra Banerjee Divakaruni

How I Learned English

It was in an empty lot
Ringed by elms and fir and honeysuckle.
Bill Corson was pitching in his buckskin jacket,
Chuck Keller, fat even as a boy, was on first,
His t-shirt riding up over his gut,
Ron O'Neill, Jim, Dennis, were talking it up
In the field, a blue sky above them
Tipped with cirrus.
                              And there I was,
Just off the plane and plopped in the middle
Of Williamsport, Pa., and a neighborhood game,
Unnatural and without any moves,
My notions of baseball and America
Growing fuzzier each time I whiffed.

So it was not impossible that I,
Banished to the outfield and daydreaming
Of water, or a hotel in the mountains,
Would suddenly find myself in the path
Of a ball stung by Joe Barone.
I watched it closing in
Clean and untouched, transfixed
By its easy arc before it hit
My forehead with a thud.
                              I fell back,
Dazed, clutching my brow,
Groaning, "Oh my shin, oh my shin,"
And everybody peeled away from me
And dropped from laughter, and there we were,
All of us writhing on the ground for one reason
Or another.
                    Someone said "shin" again,
There was a wild stamping of hands on the ground,
A kicking of feet, and the fit
Of laughter overtook me too,
And that was important, as important
As Joe Barone asking me how I was
Through his tears, picking me up

And dusting me off with hands like swatters,
And though my head felt heavy,
I played on till dusk
Missing flies and pop-ups and grounders
And calling out in desperation things like
"Yours" and "take it," but doing all right,
Tugging at my cap in just the right way,
Crouching low, my feet set,
"Hum baby" sweetly on my lips.

Gregory Djanikian

Negotiating

∎ ∎ ∎

People positioned among several different cultures, languages, and identities are constantly reminded of their difference. This position as both American and unAmerican causes disorientation and suffering. Often, as Shirley Geok-lin Lim implies in "Modern Secrets," people cannot reconcile their positions among these borders, and slip into the spaces between worlds:

> Last night I dreamt in Chinese.
> Eating Yankee shredded wheat
> I said it in English
> To a friend who answered
> In monosyllables:
> All of which I understood.
>
> The dream shrank to its fiction.
> I had understood its end
> Many years ago. The sallow child
> Ate rice from its ricebowl
> And hides still in the cupboard
> With the china and tea-leaves.

In the Elementary School Choir

I had never seen a cornfield in my life,
I had never been to Oklahoma,
But I was singing as loud as anyone,
"Oh what a beautiful morning . . . The corn
Is as high as an elephant's eye,"
Though I knew something about elephants I thought,
Coming from the same continent as they did,
And they being more like camels than anything else.

And when we sang from *Meet Me in St. Louis*,
"Clang, clang, clang went the trolley,"
I remembered the ride from Ramleh Station
In the heart of Alexandria
All the way to Roushdy where my grandmother lived,
The autos on the roadway vying
With mule carts and bicycles,
The Mediterranean half a mile off on the left,
The air smelling sharply of diesel and salt.

It was a problem which had dogged me
For a few years, this confusion of places,
And when in 5th grade geography I had pronounced
"Des Moines" as though it were a village in France,
Mr. Kephart led me to the map on the front wall,
And so I'd know where I was,
Pressed my forehead squarely against Iowa.
Des Moines, he'd said. Rhymes with coins.

Now we were singing "zippidy-doo-dah, zippidy-ay,"
And every song we'd sung had in it
Either sun or bluebirds, fair weather
Or fancy fringe, O beautiful America!
And one tier below me,
There was Linda Deemer with her amber waves
And lovely fruited plains,
And she was part of America too
Along with sun and spacious sky

Though untouchable, and as distant
As purple mountains of majesty.

"This is my country," we sang,
And a few years ago there would have been
A scent of figs in the air, mangoes,
And someone playing the oud along a clear stream.

But now it was "My country 'tis of thee"
And I sang it out with all my heart
And now with Linda Deemer in mind.
"Land where my fathers died," I bellowed,
And it was not too hard to imagine
A host of my great uncles and -grandfathers
Stunned from their graves in the Turkish interior
And finding themselves suddenly
On a rock among maize and poultry
And Squanto shaking their hands.

How could anyone not think America
Was exotic when it had Massachusetts
And the long tables of thanksgiving?
And how could it not be home
If it were the place where love first struck?

We had finished singing.
The sun was shining through large windows
On the beatified faces of all
Who had sung well and with feeling.
We were ready to file out and march back
To our room where Mr. Kephart was waiting.
Already Linda Deemer had disappeared
Into the high society of the hallway.
One day I was going to tell her something.
Des Moines, I was saying to myself,
Baton Rouge. Terre Haute. Boise.

                                        Gregory Djanikian

When I First Saw Snow

Tarrytown, N.Y.

Bing Crosby was singing "White Christmas"
        on the radio, we were staying at my aunt's house
        waiting for papers, my father was looking for a job.
We had trimmed the tree the night before,
        sap had run on my fingers and for the first time
        I was smelling pine wherever I went.
Anais, my cousin, was upstairs in her room
        listening to Danny and the Juniors.
Haigo was playing Monopoly with Lucy, his sister,
        Buzzy, the boy next door, had eyes for her
        and there was a rattle of dice, a shuffling
        of Boardwalk, Park Place, Marvin Gardens.
There were red bows on the Christmas tree.
It had snowed all night.
My boot buckles were clinking like small bells
        as I thumped to the door and out
        onto the gray planks of the porch dusted with snow.
The world was immaculate, new,
        even the trees had changed color,
        and when I touched the snow on the railing
        I didn't know what I had touched, ice or fire.
I heard, "I'm dreaming . . ."
I heard, "At the hop, hop, hop . . . oh, baby."
I heard "B & O" and the train in my imagination
        was whistling through the great plains.
And I was stepping off,
I was falling deeply into America.

                                        Gregory Djanikian

Black Hair

At eight I was brilliant with my body.
In July, that ring of heat
We all jumped through, I sat in the bleachers

Of Romain Playground, in the lengthening
Shade that rose from our dirty feet.
The game before us was more than baseball.
It was a figure—Hector Moreno
Quick and hard with turned muscles,
His crouch the one I assumed before an altar
Of worn baseball cards, in my room.

I came here because I was Mexican, a stick
Of brown light in love with those
Who could do it—the triple and hard slide,
The gloves eating balls into double plays.
What could I do with 50 pounds, my shyness,
My black torch of hair, about to go out?
Father was dead, his face no longer
Hanging over the table or our sleep,
And mother was the terror of mouths
Twisting hurt by butter knives.

In the bleachers I was brilliant with my body,
Waving players in and stomping my feet,
Growing sweaty in the presence of white shirts.
I chewed sunflower seeds. I drank water
And bit my arm through the late innings.
When Hector lined balls into deep
Center, in my mind I rounded the bases
With him, my face flared, my hair lifting
Beautifully, because we were coming home
To the arms of brown people.

Gary Soto

The Elements of San Joaquin

Field

The wind sprays pale dirt into my mouth
The small, almost invisible scars
On my hands.

The pores in my throat and elbows
Have taken in a seed of dirt of their own.

After a day in the grape fields near Rolinda
A fine silt, washed by sweat,
Has settled into the lines
On my wrists and palms.

Already I am becoming the valley,
A soil that sprouts nothing
For any of us.

Gary Soto

Behind Grandma's House

At ten I wanted fame. I had a comb
And two Coke bottles, a tube of Bryl-creem.
I borrowed a dog, one with
Mismatched eyes and a happy tongue,
And wanted to prove I was tough
In the alley, kicking over trash cans,
A dull chime of tuna cans falling.
I hurled light bulbs like grenades
And men teachers held their heads,
Fingers of blood lengthening
On the ground. I flicked rocks at cats,
Their goofy faces spurred with foxtails.
I kicked fences. I shooed pigeons.
I broke a branch from a flowering peach
And frightened ants with a stream of piss.
I said "Shit," "Fuck you," and "No way
Daddy-O" to an imaginary priest
Until grandma came into the alley,
Her apron flapping in a breeze,
Her hair mussed, and said, "Let me help you,"
And punched me between the eyes.

Gary Soto

Always Running

All night vigil.
My two-and-a-half-year-old boy
and his 10-month-old sister
lay on the same bed,
facing opposite ends;
their feet touching.
They looked soft, peaceful,
bundled there in strands of blankets.
I brushed away roaches that meandered
across their faces,
but not even that could wake them.
Outside, the dark cover of night tore
as daybreak bloomed like a rose
on a stem of thorns.
I sat down on the backsteps,
gazing across the yellowed yard.
A 1954 Chevy Bel-Air stared back.
It was my favorite possession.
I hated it just then.
It didn't start when I tried to get it going
earlier that night. It had a bad solenoid.
I held a 12-gauge shotgun across my lap.
I expected trouble from the Paragons gang
of the west Lynwood *barrio*.
Somebody said I drove the car
that dudes from *Colonia Watts* used
to shoot up the Paragons' neighborhood.
But I got more than trouble that night.
My wife had left around 10 p.m.
to take a friend of mine home.
She didn't come back.
I wanted to kill somebody.
At moments, it had nothing to do
with the Paragons.
It had to do with a woman I loved.
But who to kill? Not her—
sweet allure wrapped in a black skirt.

I'd kill myself first.
Kill me first?
But she was the one who quit!
Kill her? No, think, man! I was hurt, angry . . .
but to kill her? To kill a Paragon?
To kill anybody?
I went into the house
and put the gun away.

Later that morning, my wife came for her things:
some clothes, the babies . . . their toys.
A radio, broken TV, and some dishes remained.
I didn't stop her.
There was nothing to say that my face
didn't explain already.
Nothing to do . . . but run.

So I drove the long haul to Downey
and parked near an enclosed area
alongside the Los Angeles River.
I got out of the car,
climbed over the fence
and stumbled down the slopes.
A small line of water rippled in the middle.
On rainy days this place flooded and flowed,
but most of the time it was dry
with dumped garbage and dismembered furniture.
Since a child, the river and its veins of canals
were places for me to think. Places to heal.
Once on the river's bed, I began to cleanse.
I ran.

I ran into the mist of morning,
carrying the heat of emotion
through sun's rays;
I ran past the factories
that lay smack in the middle
of somebody's backyard.
I ran past alleys with overturned trashcans
and mounds of tires.
Debris lay underfoot. Overgrown weeds

scraped my leg as I streamed past;
recalling the song of bullets
that whirred in the wind.

I ran across bridges, beneath overhead passes,
and then back alongside the infested walls
of the concrete river;
splashing rainwater as I threaded,
my heels colliding against the pavement.
So much energy propelled my legs
and, just like the river,
it went on for miles.

When all was gone,
the concrete river
was always there
and me, always running.

                          Luis J. Rodriguez

Fire

FOR EDUARDO GALEANO

I
It seems our days are shaped by conflagration.
Felice, a poet from Chicago, recalls
the sugar canes of Santo Domingo—
black, acrid taste, in the Caribbean sun.

I remember Oaxaca where flames swirled
around a row of carved beef heads, eyes boiling,
as an Indian hand tears off
muscle and meat for tacos.

And then also Managua where tires
kindle, arousing an odor akin to acid,
to protest Contra raids
or another injustice.

African drums. Indigenous flutes
and feathers. Chants and prayers.
Gypsies and a deep song, their rhythms
rise like steam, fueled by an earth *enlumbrada*.

Fire follows us like family,
like the rivers of revolt
In San Salvador, León and Morelos,
forever traced in mind.

II
In Chicago, Latino neighborhoods
are dotted with vacant lots like missing
teeth in an old man's mouth as buildings
are torched for insurance claims.

Consuming blaze once stormed through a three-flat
in the barrio of Pilsen.
Men / women / children, poured out doors,
jumped out windows, some with clothes clinging on flesh.

They accounted for all the occupants except
a 12-year-old boy; a father paced frantic
as firefighters drenched a collapsing roof.
For three days, crews scoured the scorch.

Neighbors held a vigil, as soaked and charred
walls crumbled in the search. And every
morning the alderman waited outside,
his own little girl in arms.

When finally city workers pulled
the boy out of the ruins, hundreds hushed
as he appeared among them, this *mestizaje*
devoured by the hell-spawn that never ceases

to stir us, to smolder in our breasts,
as fire becomes the luminous dawn,
the squeeze of skin, this memory
called our history.

Luis J. Rodriguez

The Dancing

In all these rotten shops, in all this broken furniture
and wrinkled ties and baseball trophies and coffee pots
I have never seen a post-war Philco
with the automatic eye
nor heard Ravel's "Bolero" the way I did
in 1945 in that tiny living room
on Beechwood Boulevard, nor danced as I did
then, my knives all flashing, my hair all streaming,
my mother red with laughter, my father cupping
his left hand under his armpit, doing the dance
of old Ukraine, the sound of his skin half drum,
half fart, the world at last a meadow,
the three of us whirling and singing, the three of us
screaming and falling, as if we were dying,
as if we could never stop—in 1945—
in Pittsburgh, beautiful filthy Pittsburgh, home
of the evil Mellons, 5,000 miles away
from the other dancing—in Poland and Germany—
oh God of mercy, oh wild God.

                                        Gerald Stern

In Memory We Are Walking

In memory we are walking
single file, up Goffle Road.

We are carrying an old red blanket
and tin buckets
that clang against each other
as we move.

We have been walking for more than an hour.
At last, we stop, sit for a moment

on grass and drink the lemonade
my mother made before we left home.

Then with my mother shouting commands
like a general, we spread out the blanket
under a mulberry tree, each of us taking
a corner, my father shaking the limbs
of the tree.

We laugh and capture mulberries
until the blanket sags with the weight.
Delicately, my mother scoops the fruit
into our buckets, gives us each
some to eat.

We walk along the brook,
watch the water rush
over rocks, and follow
the brook toward home.
I am ten years old.
I have seldom been out of Paterson.

The houses we pass,
squat, middle-class bungalows,
seem to be the houses
of the wealthy when seen through
my eyes, accustomed as I am
to mill-workers' houses,
built quickly and cheaply.

On the way back, my brother is tired;
he drags behind, until my father
puts him on his shoulders. My legs hurt,
but I would not say it.
I am happy. I do not know
that in the houses neighboring the park
people have watched us. They hate
our dark skin, our immigrant clothes.

My father tells us that a few years before,
he walked all the way to Passaic and back,

following the railroad tracks
because he heard there was a job open.
He did not have five cents for the train.

When he got to Passaic, the foreman
told him there were no jobs. The workers
turned to watch him leave,
their eyes strong as hands on his back.
"You stupid Dago bastard," one called.
"Go back where you come from.
We don't want your kind here."

                         Maria Mazziotti Gillan

I Remember Haifa
Being Lovely But

there were snakes in the
tent, my mother was
strong but she never
slept, was afraid of
dreaming. In Auschwitz
there was a numbness,
lull of just staying
alive. Her two babies
gassed before her, Dr.
Mengele, you know who
he is? She kept her
young sister alive
only to have her die
in her arms the night
of liberation. My mother
is big boned, but she
weighed under 80 lbs.
It was hot, I thought
the snakes lovely. No
drugs in Israel, no
food, I got pneumonia,

my mother knocked the
doctor to the floor
when they refused,
said I lost two in
the camp and if this
one dies I'll kill
myself in front of
you. I thought that
once you became a
mother, blue numbers
appeared mysteriously,
tattooed on your arm

Lyn Lifshin

A Black Man's Sonata

FOR JOHN DOWELL

Here in West Philadelphia,
one of my neighbors was
a black man just released from jail.
Home again, he imposed
a frigid order on his family.
He staked his territory,
crossing the street to threaten
a woman with his gun.
He tried his bravado in a bar,
and a man angrier than him
put a bullet in my neighbor's brain.
His house was hushed and solemn
as relatives came and went.
I think he wanted to die.
He threatened people and strutted
like a tiger because a bundle of hurt,
a mess of dangling threads, rags,
and curses had replaced his heart.

If I ever wonder where
America's heart is, I have only

to come to my neighborhood,
black homes of the poor and working poor.
The country radiates out from them
in history's circle where wealth
is built on poverty. If I ever
wonder whether to be poor
and black is to be exempt from evil,
I have only to watch the eyes
that watch me as I walk home.
They look for a weakness,
like tigers in the grass.
They look to see if I am a tiger, too.

The young boys, the hip hops,
are all about respect.
Respect me, and I'll respect you.
They were born after Aretha Franklin
sang out respect between man and woman.
The hip hops say, *don't dis me man.*
Many of them will not live
to be men, to go creaking along
in the streets with old bones.
Many of them will not know
the fear an old black man fears,
of death, of not seeing grandchildren.

I walk the streets slowly, heavily,
knowing my wife hates the streets,
praying the young will not devour us.
We sleep under the sun's needles,
our deep black stripes in a fire yellow.

Michael S. Weaver

Improvisation for Piano

after *Mood Indigo*

Freshly lit cigarette in his mouth,
his collar turned up in the cold,
his face turned wry, and the question,
the awful question hidden beneath.
It is so difficult to see the baby
I sent scooting over to my mother,
laughing out, "He can walk, see."
It is difficult to look in my arms and
remember how he once fit there, how
I could keep the world away from him
if it threatened to hurt him, to rob him.
When I admit that he has been hurt,
that he has been robbed and that I was helpless,
I wonder what register there is for pain.
He is leaving home, and I am sending
another black man into life's teeth and jaws.
All that I know about being black
is some kind of totem knotted with the prints
of my fists beating out a syncopated pain.
I can't begin to tell him how to carve.
I can cry. I can counsel other black men,
but love is its own resistance in
the eye a father shares with his son.

The storm window glass sticks to me
with its cold, and I watch him go under
the big tree up the street and away.
The night is some slow rendition of
Mood Indigo, and the blues takes me
away to some place and frightens the shit
out of me, as I think of how my son will live.
What life will he have without proper
attire, I wonder. I think to run after him,
catch him, and say, "Here, another sweater."
And I know the other sweater is the first time
I saw "nigger" in a white man's eyes.
I know he needs gloves, too, for his hands,

when they stiffen, as he wonders how
blackness colors his life. I close the door.
There is a silence like dead flesh
in the bedroom. My son has left home,
a big, black manchild. I pull my cold feet
under the comforter and swallow sleep medicine.

I slip away hoping there are angels.

Michael S. Weaver

Winnings

It's Gardena, late Saturday afternoon
on Vermont Avenue, near closing time
at the thrift store, and my father's
left me to rummage through trash bins
stuffed with used paperbacks, 25¢ a pound,
while he chases down some bets
at the card clubs across the street.

The register rings up its sales—$2.95,
$11.24, $26.48 for the reclaimed Frigidaire—
and a girl, maybe six or so, barefoot,
in a plaid dress, her hair braided
in tight cornrows, tugs at the strap
of her mother's purse, begging a few
nickels for the gumball machine.

She skips through the check-stand,
runs toward the electric exit, passing
a fleet of shopping carts, bundles
of used-up magazines (*Ebony* and *Jet*)
stacked in pyramids in the far aisle,
reaches the bright globe of the vendor,
fumbles for her coins, and works the knob.

My father comes in from the Rainbow
across the street, ten hands of Jacks

or Better, five draw, a winner
with a few dollars to peel away
from grocery money and money to fix
the washer, a dollar for me to buy
four pounds of Pocket Wisdoms, Bantams,
a Dell that says *Walt Whitman, Poet
of the Open Road*, and hands it to me,
saying "We won, *Boy-san*! We won!"
as the final blast of sunset kicks through
plate glass and stained air, firing through
the thicket of neon across the street,
consuming the store, the girl, the dollar bill,

even the Rainbow and the falling night
in a brief symphony of candied light.

Garrett Hongo

Susans

I

First day of kindergarten I slice my four-years' thumb
with a razor blade, blood beading thick, deep river curve
on my half-breed skin. Warned against playing with sharp
things, I forget why I picked up the blue blade that lay
flat by my mother's sewing machine with its needle stopped
in mid-air. Did the blade's edge glint in the morning sun,
pulling my entranced hand to its dangerous shine? My mother
screams, blood threatens to stain the dress of sun-yellow
she has sewn for me. I am the daughter she seduced my father
for, bleeding at this passage into a lost life, long
school years locked away from the woods behind our house,
from moss glowing pale-green on rotted logs, spring
beauties and trilliums, rare lady slippers, and in fall
mushrooms with their secret undersides of silken fans.
Soon the cut will heal into an accidental curve
of infinity, a scar that marks that time
when the brown-eyed deer still came five feet close.

II
In kindergarten class there is a second Susan, a Susan of blonde hair
and blue eyes, her ears small as moon snails beneath Hollywood curls
crowned with a pink bow. Her white skin scarless, she sings
in tune like an angel, "You are my sunshine," while we are led
out to the playground in double file. I think she could be
singing to me in my yellow dress. The teachers love her,
tell her how pretty she is, how bright. Ignored, I inch
away from her, my own skin brown and freckled,
my hair boy-short because it won't grow, my thumb feeling
as though it will again bleed. "Freckles," this second Susan
taunts me, "you have freckles." I race to the swings,
pumping myself high into the cooling air above the river,
closing my eyes, holding my hot face out to the wind,
betrayed by the voice of an angel possessing my name.
Back home I cry the way I didn't cry
when I cut my finger on the razor blade, inform my mother
how I was teased, tagged "freckles," how the teachers
favored the blue-eyed girl who sang in tune.

III
My mother explains the second Susan comes from a family
of doctors richer than we, in money. She has stories
to soothe all my wounds. When she was a girl she tried to cover
her freckles with white flour, ashamed of the sun's flung
kisses. Now she believes they are constellations on a sky
of skin, lovely as myth. She reminds me that I was named by her
after a Susan in a favorite poem, a wild girl who roamed outside
among rain and flowers.

IV
A grown woman sunning in solitude on a high hill, freckling
at leisure, I remember the girl who possessed my name, the years
she shunned me and others who were different or poor, the losers who
ran away with "carnies," or married "spics," or wrote silent poems.
She became first ice queen, then a doctor. I glimpse the old
scar on my thumb, long gleam reminding me how we all bear pain,
in that way we are all one—wonder if the girl
who sang in tune sings, "You are my sunshine," when her poorest
patients lie dying in hospital rooms white as her skin.

Susan Clements

The Reservation

You seldom talked about the Indian side
of the family, a thing of shame
after World War II, when the men came home, victorious,
the women herded back to houses isolated
as reservations. I can still see you
in an organdy apron, your black hair iridescent,
nearly blue as indigo bunting feathers
drawing down sunlight—how you tortured
that wild hair, and mine, each night with the stern
jabs of bobby pins into tight curls, attempting
tameness. "Be a lady," you said, "lower your voice,
sit with your knees together," as if you wanted
to pin my entire body into a single knot.
But nothing held. At the first hint of rain
your hair fell out soft and long to your shoulders
tired from pushing clothes through the old ringer washer,
stretching your still young flesh up towards the clothesline
where you hung your children's shirts and dresses,
ghosts flapping free from the small bodies
that clung to you all through the 'fifties.
You jerked the clothesline forward into empty air.
Sometimes after supper, when you washed dishes, I dried, you slipped
into storytelling, telling me about your Blackfoot father,
so handsome he should have been on the nickel,
shooting dice, shooting pistols in the air
that time he chose to ride a stolen horse
through town in love battle for his wife.
Did you know your words led me into a secret life
away from yours, I, "the savage," crawling around
in bushes, hiding out with birds, my hands
hugging the dark earth while other children
played silly games in the schoolyard?
Years later you told me you were a tomboy as a child.
How I loved you for that, your own secret life,
remembering the crying spells you had every spring
when you would take off your stiff apron, take me
by my dirt-blessed hand deep into the woods behind the house

where we sat in silence, mother and daughter,
among spring beauties and curled adder's tongue.

Susan Clements

English-Speaking Persons Will Find Translations

I
The train whistles punctual as a clock:
Mannheim, Stuttgart, Ulm, Augsburg.
And the flow of the rivers endures.

From the Bahnhof in Dachau to the concentration
camp is a short ride. At the newsstand people
buy *Der Spiegel*, *Zeitgeist* and *Playboy*.

I exchange glances with eine Frau, she smiles
shyly; I smile back and she looks away.
In the distance I see the camp.

Most of the buildings were razed,
but what remains are the only old
buildings in all of Dachau.

So many of us get off the bus;
we crowd each other on the way to the gate,
pushing to be first, not miss a thing.

II
In the museum, a sign tells of the catalogue
where "English-Speaking Persons Will Find
Translations of the Whole Exhibit."

I pay my ten marks, though it is not
translation I want. There is a movie,
24 minutes long. The narrator describes

the rise of the Nazis: "The hardest hit
were the Jews. The few who survived
have only the German armaments industry

to thank, for it lacked manpower."
He mentions the others: "The inhabitants
of the town of Dachau were not unfriendly.

Sometimes they would give prisoners
working outside a piece of bread
or at least a sympathetic look."

I wander from the theater into the strange,
quiet sunlight, listen to birds and tourists
chatter. I think of the translations,

so many words, like so many pieces of bread,
sympathetic looks—difficult to understand.

III
At the crematorium, caretakers brush
dust from the windows like German women
at their shutters. Behind the ovens,

small memorials top the ash graves,
rows of flowers, groomed. Their signs read:

"לא שכח" "Vergiss Nicht" "Do Not Forget"

Inside the crematorium the whitewashed walls
are guarded by signs in four languages:
"DO NOT WRITE ON THESE WALLS!"

The only old paint in the whole camp
is the word "Brausbad"—shower—
carefully untouched above a door

to the gas-chamber that here was never
—we are told repeatedly—never used.

My eyes linger over the whitewash, the paint,
the tons of silent rock that line the grounds.
I listen for the borders of others' lives,

hear conversations of home, requests
for pictures by the ovens, the ash graves.
Back home, Kodak will develop apparitions

—silent images silvered into negatives.

IV
Later, I travel backward on an air-conditioned
train following the fields, the trimmed hedges,
listening to the patter of foreign tongues.

At night, on television, an American movie,
uncut for foreign consumption, is dubbed
in German. I watch the pictures, watch

an Indian raise a white cloth with his war club,
see a white man shoot him in the face.
The cavalry charges, burns the village,

the tents curl up in smoke as one by one
soldiers hump the Indian women,
white asses beating the sky in victory

and then, with swords, they take off the heads
of the children. Later, the men receive medals.

After midnight, words from Dachau scatter
in my head, red and blue with smoke.
I dream of my college professor explaining

with numbers how many lives we saved
by the bombs on Hiroshima, Nagasaki.

V
I wake to watch the sun rise silent and red
over brown roofs, think of the silent trees
by the crematorium: an old chestnut, willows,

then recall my own silence as I watched parents
show young children the exhibits, posing them for
pictures by the ovens, smiles for the cameras.

I hail a cab back to the airport, think
of Vietnam, the marches, the words, until
the murders at Kent and Jackson State

when silence returned multiplying other,
later silences to my wife, my children,
myself—what we say and don't say—

the missiles that can silence us all.

"לא שכח" "Vergiss Nicht" "Do Not Forget"

What good is remembrance when words die
on my tongue, when I fear what others think?
What does it mean, to find words, to speak,

I wonder, as I hand my ticket to the stewardess
and board the DC-10, sleek and silver in the sun.
The gray-haired pilot is in his place, and I

take mine, listen intently as a voice tells us
to buckle our belts, then something about customs,
what we should do and what to declare when we land.

                                        Michael S. Glaser

Crazy Horse Speaks

I
I discovered the evidence
in a vault of the Mormon Church
3,000 skeletons of my cousins
in a silence so great
I built four walls around it
and gave it a name.
I called it Custer
and he came to me
again in a dream.
He forgave all my sins.

II
Little Big Horn.
Little Big Horn does not belong to me.
I was there
my horse exploded beneath me.
I searched for Long Hair
the man you call Custer
the man I call My Father.
But it wasn't me who killed him
it was ——————
who poked holes in Custer's ears
and left the body for proof.
I dream of him
and search doorways and alleys
for his grave.
General George Armstrong Custer
my heart is beating
survive   survive   survive.

III
I wear the color of my skin
like a brown paper bag
wrapped around a bottle.
Sleeping between
the pages of dictionaries
your language cuts
tears holes in my tongue
until I do not have strength
to use the word *Love*.
What could it mean
in this city where everyone is
Afraid-of-Horses?

IV
There are places I cannot leave.
Rooms without doors or windows
the eternal rib cage.
I sat across the fire
from Sitting Bull
shared smoke and eyes.
We both saw the same thing
our futures tight and small

an 8 × 10 dream
called the reservation.
We had no alternatives
but to fight again and again
live our lives on horseback.
After the Civil War
the number of Indian warriors
in the West doubled
tripled the number of soldiers
but Indians never have shared
the exact skin
never the same home.

V
I am the mirror
practicing masks
and definitions.
I have always wanted to be anonymous
instead of the crazy skin
who rode his horse backward
and lay down alone.
It was never easy
to be frightened
by the sound of a color.
I can still hear white
it is the sound
of glass shattering.

VI
I hear the verdict
in the museum in New York
where five Eskimo were flown in
to be a living exhibit.
Three died within days
lacking natural immunity
their hearts miles
and miles of thin ice.
The three dead Eskimo
were stuffed and mounted
hunched over a fishing hole
next to the two living
who held their thin hands

close to their chests
mortal and sinless.

VII
Whenever it all begins again
I will be waiting.

Sherman Alexie

Powwow Polaroid

We were fancydancing, you see.

Step-step, right foot, step-step, left foot, faster, twisting, turning, spinning, changing.

There are photographs taken but only one ever captured the change. It was a white tourist from Spokane. She was lucky, she was quick, maybe it was film developed by the CIA.

She took the picture, the flashbulb burned, and none of us could move. I was frozen between steps, my right foot three inches off the ground, my mouth open and waiting to finish the last sound.

The crowd panicked. Most fled the stands, left the dancers not dancing and afraid. The white woman with the camera raised her arms in triumph, crossed her legs at the ankle, tilted her head to one side.

My four-hundred-pound aunt wept into the public address system. My uncle held his great belly in his hands, walked among the fancydancers, said this:

forgiveness.

Sherman Alexie

Soul Make a Path
Through Shouting

FOR ELIZABETH ECKFORD
LITTLE ROCK, ARKANSAS, 1957

Thick at the schoolgate are the ones
Rage has twisted
Into minotaurs, harpies
Relentlessly swift;
So you must walk past the pincers,
The swaying horns,
Sister, sister,
Straight through the gusts
Of fear and fury,
Straight through:
Where are you going?
I'm just going to school.

Here we go to meet
The hydra-headed day,
Here we go to meet
The maelstrom—

Can my voice be an angel-on-the-spot,
An amen corner?
Can my voice take you there,
Gallant girl with a notebook,
Up, up from the shadows of gallows trees
To the other shore:
A globe bathed in light,
A chalkboard blooming with equations—

I have never seen the likes of you,
Pioneer in dark glasses:
You won't show the mob your eyes,
But I know your gaze,
Steady-on-the-North-Star,
Burning—

With their jerry-rigged faith,
Their spear of the American flag,
How could they dare to believe
You're someone sacred?:
Nigger, burr-headed girl,
Where are you going?

I'm just going to school.

                    Cyrus Cassells

The Battle, Over and Over Again

**(given as testimony in support of the student's case
against racism at columbia university)**

my daughter came home from school one day
when she was four
she ran into the bathroom, crying and
sitting on the floor

i said, —baby, what's the matter, c'mon,
what could be so bad
i bought you a box of cherry fun fruits,
bet that'll make you glad—

she lifted up her little arms, squinted in the light
mommy, she asked, —why didn't god make me white—

she dropped her arms and question hard on her lap
her eyes were closed, my knees were weak, she said,

—they keep saying i'm ugly, and they say
it's because i'm black—
the bathroom had always been our place we ran to
whenever she was hurt

we'd band-aid the cuts, pull out the splinters
and wash away the dirt
but suddenly our refuge had become a place for war

with bombs waiting to explode
the sink's faucet dripped like a timer,
the pipes signaled an enemy code

who said these things, i wanted to ask,
but i didn't let out the words
my child picking away her dark brown skin
had loosened every nerve

and who was not important, more important was the why
that in 1983 america, racism was making my child cry

i sat beside her on the floor, pulled her to my chest
i thought of how often we had sat like this
just to take a rest

—sweetheart—i said, —now you know you're not ugly—
i pasted words in the air,

—you're one of the prettiest girls i've ever seen, anywhere—
her back was warm and sweaty, she held her muscles tight

there was sand on her cheeks,
she was much too young to fight
the air was full of bullet holes, i could smell the dead

—and you have the prettiest smile—
my daughter shook her head
i pushed against that bathroom wall,
trying to gain a balance

trying to find the perfect words
to break this painful silence
i thought of all the great ones
who had died to prevent such a day

the fannie lous, malcolms,
name calling dragons that they slayed
i thought about the marches,
shouts of let freedom ring

busrides, boycotts, sit-ins, speeches, endless praying
the world stood boldly in my bathroom,
between my child and me

and i wondered as i squeezed her hands,
how long will the battle be
her eyes opened and looked in mine,
as if she heard my fear

she hugged my neck and said, —mommy, i don't care,
they're two mean boys and they're always starting fights
they never have anything special for lunch,
they always ask for bites—
she straightened and coughed,
her arms still around my neck

—and i'm going to take my fun fruits to school,
and they won't get a peck—
she said, —and the bigger one is going to ask
until his face gets red—

she wiped her eyes, rubbed sand from her head
pointed to her left arm, swallowed and said,

—one thing i know,—
she placed her hands on her hips,
i saw her strength begin to grow,

—mommy, his face gets like that when he's mad,
i seen it lots of times
mommy, i think his face is more ugly than mine—

i kissed her softly on her mouth, both her sandy cheeks,
washed her face, and studied the draining water
as if it were the last enemy's retreat

Safiya Henderson-Holmes

A Story About Chicken Soup

In my grandmother's house there was always chicken soup
And talk of the old country—mud and boards,
Poverty,
The snow falling down the necks of lovers.

Now and then, out of her savings
She sent them a dowry. Imagine
The rice-powdered faces!
And the smell of the bride, like chicken soup.

But the Germans killed them.
I know it's in bad taste to say it,
But it's true. The Germans killed them all.

■　■　■

In the ruins of Berchtesgaden
A child with yellow hair
Ran out of a doorway.

A German girl-child—
Cuckoo, all skin and bones—
Not even enough to make chicken soup.
She sat by the stream and smiled.

Then as we splashed in the sun
She laughed at us.
We had killed her mechanical brothers,
So we forgave her.

■　■　■

The sun is shining.
The shadows of the lovers have disappeared.
They are all eyes; they have some demand on me—
They want me to be more serious than I want to be.

They want me to stick in their mudhole
Where no one is elegant.
They want me to wear old clothes,
They want me to be poor, to sleep in a room with many others—

Not to walk in the painted sunshine
To a summer house,
But to live in the tragic world forever.

Louis Simpson

Salt

Lisa, Leona, Loretta?
She's sipping a milkshake
In Woolworths, dressed in
Chiffon & fat pearls,
She looks up at me,
Grabs her purse
& pulls at the hem
Of her skirt. I want to say,
"I'm just here to buy
A box of Epsom salt
For my grandmama's feet."
Lena, Lois? I feel her
Strain to not see me.
Lines are now etched
At the corners of her thin,
Pale mouth. Does she know
I know her grandfather
Rode a white horse
Through Poplars Quarters
Searching for black women,
How he killed Indians
& stole land with bribes
& fake deeds? I remember
She was seven & I was five
When she ran up to me like a cat
With a gypsy moth in its mouth

& we played doctor & house
Under the low branches of a raintree
Encircled with red rhododendrons.
We could pull back the leaves
& see Grandmama ironing
At their wide window. Once
Her mother moved so close
To the yardman we thought they'd kiss.
What the children of housekeepers
& handymen knew was enough
To stop biological clocks,
& it's hard now not to walk over
& mention how her grandmother
Killed her idiot son
& salted him down
In a wooden barrel.

Yusef Komunyakaa

Something About Being an Indian

There's something about being an Indian
we say to each other in a Bishop saloon
both of us forty with pony tails
grown down long to our Levi butts.
Yes, brother, it is the heart, and it is
the blood that we share.
The heart alone is not enough.

There's something about being an Indian
we say in soft whiskey voices that remember
many soft, brown women.
We laugh past the window and its vision
of constant traffic, the aimless yuppies
bound for the ski lodges.
Snow must be licentious for such fools:
white sheets to be soiled with temporal chill.
Yes, there's something about being an Indian
we say as we exit into the warmth

of Hell's secondary nature,
a place we call the Fire Water World.

Adrian C. Louis

Poem for the Young White Man Who Asked Me How I, an Intelligent, Well-Read Person, Could Believe in the War Between Races

In my land there are no distinctions.
The barbed wire politics of oppression
have been torn down long ago. The only reminder
of past battles, lost or won, is a slight
rutting in the fertile fields.

In my land
people write poems about love,
full of nothing but contented childlike syllables.
Everyone reads Russian short stories and weeps.
There are no boundaries.
There is no hunger, no
complicated famine or greed.

I am not a revolutionary.
I don't even like political poems.
Do you think I can believe in a war between races?
I can deny it. I can forget about it
when I'm safe,
living on my own continent of harmony
and home, but I am not
there.

I believe in revolution
because everywhere the crosses are burning,
sharp-shooting goose-steppers round every corner,

there are snipers in the schools . . .
(I know you don't believe this.
You think this is nothing
but faddish exaggeration. But they
are not shooting at you.)

I'm marked by the color of my skin.
The bullets are discrete and designed to kill slowly.
They are aiming at my children.
These are facts.
Let me show you my wounds: my stumbling mind, my
"excuse me" tongue, and this
nagging preoccupation
with the feeling of not being good enough.

These bullets bury deeper than logic.
Racism is not intellectual.
I cannot reason these scars away.

Outside my door
there is a real enemy
who hates me.

I am a poet
who yearns to dance on rooftops,
to whisper delicate lines about joy
and the blessings of human understanding.
I try. I go to my land, my tower of words and
bolt the door, but the typewriter doesn't fade out
the sounds of blasting and muffled outrage.
My own days bring me slaps on the face.
Every day I am deluged with reminders
that this is not
my land

and this is my land.

I do not believe in the war between races

but in this country
there is war.

Lorna Dee Cervantes

Election Time

Names will change
faces will change
but not much else
the President will still be white
and male
and wasp
still speak with forked tongue
still wear red, white and blue underwear
still sleep on white sheets
in a white house
still surround himself with white men
still believe that white is the best thing to be
still read all white newspapers
that only talk about Blacks in connection with crime
still fly in white Air Force One
still worship a white Jesus
still pray to a white God
still go on vacation
where white people lie on white sand beaches
still white out his mistakes
still issue white papers
still throw out little white balls
on opening day
still uphold the laws of dead white men
still dream about big white monuments
and big white memorials
ain't nothin' changed
ain't nothin' changed at all

Lamont B. Steptoe

Bicentennial Anti-Poem
for Italian-American Women

On the crowded subway,
riding to the prison to teach
Black and Puerto Rican inmates how to write,
I think of the fable of the shoemaker
who struggles to make shoes for the oppressed
while his own go barefoot over the stones.

I remember Grandma, her olive face
wrinkled with resignation,
content just to survive
after giving birth to twenty children,
without orgasmic pleasures or anesthesia.
Grandpa, immigrant adventurer,
who brought his family
steerage passage to the New World;
his shoemaker shop where he labored
over American factory goods
that made his artisan's craft a useless
anachronism; his Code of Honor
which forced him to starve
accepting not a cent of welfare
from anyone but his sons;
his ironic "Code of Honor"
which condoned jealous rages of wife-beating;
Aunt Elisabetta, Aunt Maria-Domenica,
Aunt Raffaella, Aunt Elena, grown women
huddled like girls in their bedroom in Newark,
talking in whispers, not daring
to smoke their American cigarettes
in front of Pa;
the backyard shrine of the virgin,
somber blue-robed woman,
devoid of sexual passions,
to whom Aunt Elisabetta prayed
daily before dying in childbirth,
trying to have *a son*

against doctor's orders
though she had five healthy daughters;
Dr. Giuseppe Ferrara,
purple-heart veteran of World War II,
told he couldn't have a residency
in a big New York hospital
because of his Italian name;
the mafia jokes, the epithets:
Wop, guinea, dago, grease-ball;
and the stories told by Papa
of Dante, Galileo, Da Vinci,
Marconi, Fermi and Caruso
that stung me with pride
for Italian *men;*
how I was discouraged from school,
told a woman meant for cooking
and bearing doesn't need education.

I remember
Grandma
got out of bed
in the middle of the night
to fetch her *husband* a glass of water
the day she died,
her body wearied
from giving and giving and giving
food and birth.

Daniela Gioseffi

The Yahrtzeit Light

Dusty, with some skeleton of
a flying thing that died
in it, as if the flame
already had been pulling

on things restless and alive.
My mother bought it, an

extra one, the year after
my grandmother died,

when my mother's hair was
still dark and curly. It
haunted 15 years, in the
middle of scales, shoe

polish and liquids to make
what is glow hot, spit
eerie light and the flicker
of death into shadows. I

couldn't throw it out,
more Jewish than anything
I owned and wondered if my
mother would have other

people leaving too fast to
say goodbye to, rub her
hands in front of this
candle, rub what was still

warm numb as any heart rubbed
raw. This morning, my mother,
at 90 lbs, was afraid to
stay alone in the mall,

her face gray as the stone
squares she had trouble,
even holding my arm, getting
across. I take her bag, as

if alone she might collapse
and nobody would know who
she was to claim her. My
uncle's voice on tape

reminds it's the anniversary
of my mother's mother's death
so tonight I give the candle
to her, go down to the room

where no candle could catch.
In the glitz of fire, my
mother's cheeks are caverns
no light fills

                    Lyn Lifshin

After the Anti-Semitic Calls
on a Local Talk Station

I want to check
the mirror, see
if I have a Jewish
nose, always glad
for being supposed

Norwegian or French.
Greek once maybe.
Knowing no Hebrew,
growing up in a
town where kids

supposed if you
didn't go to the
Catholic school you
must be Protestant.
White wasn't even

a point, feeling
strange in a Jewish
sorority later, not
knowing any Yiddish
phrase, the rituals
the past, thinking

I was fat and wore
glasses because I
wasn't Episcopalian

or Methodist or could
confess, thinking my

sister with her Holocaust
books was a little paranoid,
skinny in contact lenses
I'm shaking in front
of all mirrors, glass

as if midnight in
Dresden was now and the
moon caught in a thousand
panes of crystal
was starting
to crack

Lyn Lifshin

An Agony. As Now.

I am inside someone
who hates me. I look
out from his eyes. Smell
what fouled tunes come in
to his breath. Love his
wretched women.

Slits in the metal, for sun. Where
my eyes sit turning, at the cool air
the glance of light, or hard flesh
rubbed against me, a woman, a man,
without shadow, or voice, or meaning.

This is the enclosure (flesh,
where innocence is a weapon). An
abstraction. Touch. Not mine.
Or yours, if you are the soul I had
and abandoned when I was blind and had
my enemies carry me as a dead man
(if he is beautiful, or pitied).

It can be pain. (As now, as all his
flesh hurts me.) It can be that. Or
pain. As when she ran from me into
that forest.
               Or pain, the mind
silver spiraled whirled against the
sun, higher than even old men thought
God would be. Or pain. And the other. The
yes. (Inside his books, his fingers. They
are withered yellow flowers and were never
beautiful.) The yes. You will, lost soul, say
"beauty." Beauty, practiced, as the tree. The
slow river. A white sun in its wet sentences.

Or, the cold men in their gale. Ecstasy. Flesh
or soul. The yes. (Their robes blown. Their bowls
empty. They chant at my heels, not at yours.) Flesh
or soul, as corrupt. Where the answer moves too quickly.
(Where the God is a self, after all.)

Cold air blown through narrow blind eyes. Flesh,
white hot metal. Glows as the day with its sun.
It is a human love, I live inside. A bony skeleton
you recognize as words or simple feeling.

But it has no feeling. As the metal, is hot, it is not,
given to love.

It burns the thing
inside it. And that thing
screams.

Amiri Baraka

Notes for a Poem
on Being Asian American

As a child, I was a fussy eater
and I would separate the yolk from the egg white
as I now try to sort out what is Asian

in me from what is American—
the east from the west, the dreamer from the dream.
But countries are not
like eggs—except in the fragileness
of their shells—and eggs resemble countries
only in that when you crack one open and look inside,
you know even less than when you started.

And so I crack open the egg,
and this is what I see:
two moments from my past that strike me
as being uniquely Asian American.

In the first, I'm walking down Michigan Avenue
one day—a man comes up to me out of the blue and says:
"I just wanted to tell you . . . I was on the plane that
bombed Hiroshima. And I just wanted you to know that
what we did was for the good of everyone." And it
seems as if he's asking for my forgiveness. It's 1983,
there's a sale on Marimekko sheets at the Crate &
Barrel, it's a beautiful summer day and I'm talking to
a man I've never seen before and will probably never
see again. His statement has no connection to me—
and has every connection in the world. But it's not
for me to forgive him. He must forgive himself.
"It must have been a very difficult decision to do what
you did," I say and I mention the sale on Marimekko
sheets across the street, comforters, and how the
pillowcases have the pattern of wheat printed on them,
and how some nights if you hold them before an open
window to the breeze, they might seem like flags—
like someone surrendering after a great while, or
celebrating, or simply cooling themselves in the summer
breeze as best they can.

In the second moment—I'm in a taxi and the Iranian
cabdriver looking into the rearview mirror notices my
Asian eyes, those almond shapes, reflected in the glass
and says, "Can you really tell the difference between
a Chinese and a Japanese?"

Dwight Okita

Portrait of Assimilation

My father sits quietly in his brown Naugahyde chair watching
   TV with the remote control
   held out in his hand
He switches off the sound
at the commercials   while intently gazing at the picture
   His hair is cut short
he wears an electronic watch, white shirt, brown tie, gray sweater
carefully polished black leather shoes
Under his feet a prairie of green gold wall to wall carpet
says nothing
His chair is placed to hide the bad crack in the wall
& to catch the heat from an economy quartz unit
The walls are covered with paintings by his children
   photographs of his grandchildren
A yellow box of Kleenex is on the table near a carved tusk
   made to look like a fish   & a coral rose   he grew
in a turquoise glass vase from Woolworth's
               The way you know
                  it's really him
is the way he's wrapped
                old style
                in a red & blue blanket
He says
               Gets kinda cold nowadays for me

                                    Chrystos

The Jewish Singles Event

Here are those who are challenged by
It's hard to meet someone,
those who have taken to heart,
not only the importance of marriage,
but marriage to the right person.

We surround the dance floor and,
just like in summer camp,
the men are on one side, women on the other.
The band begins with a tune by the Stones.
A bold man, the one with the beard
and the Calvin Klein suit who has no doubt
considered law school, medical school
and is now a photographer,
walks over to the woman in gold lamé shoes.
She seems so uninterested
that an earthquake would not startle her,
that the chandelier, falling from the ceiling,
would seem like an ocean of diamonds.

Moms and dads of the world, look how hard we are trying.
Wasn't it easier forty years ago when marriages
were arranged, and survival was the issue?
You watched lovers holding each other
through barbed wire fences,
and heard about the experiments on the wombs
of Jewish women. You wanted us to have a better life,
so you have given us everything you could not have:
the finest clothing, appliances that can
spin, blend, chop, dice the most wilted produce.
And a world where we can choose what we want to do
and whether or not we want to marry.
We haven't come a long way to want to live alone,
but it is easy. Only the ghosts are there:
their branded arms embrace us.

Stewart Florsheim

Coming of Age

I was sitting on the roof with my grandmother.
I was seven years old. Beyond the roof
It was summer. It was night. It was the Bronx.
She told me about Columbus. A great man,
A very great man. I didn't understand.

Everyone in the world was an Italian,
Everyone was a Catholic. Then I was ten
And the Irish nuns told us all about Columbus.
Nobody ever mentioned that he was Italian,
A guinea. Everyone was very nice.

How Italian was I then? A handful of words—
Counting to ten, hello, goodbye, *fangul*—
What everybody knew. My grandmother
Sent me to buy a jar of parmigian',
I asked the man for a brand called Farmer John.

Inside the house I heard names like Sinatra,
Names like DiMaggio. Everybody knew them.
I was twelve years old. Beyond the wall
It was Westchester. I sounded like a goat.
In right field I missed everything, and the Irish fumed.

The priests had big red faces and big voices,
They poured the Latin out like water faucets.
I was an altar boy. Beyond the Church
It was baseball weather. They told us about Don Bosco
And Dominic Savio. Even then it was funny.

I found out other names, like Pirandello,
Like Leopardi. Everybody laughed.
No one had ever heard of them. Flukey ways,
That was the line on me, and nobody argued.
I was fifteen. I stayed in the house all summer.

Sacco and Vanzetti, these were my people.
Men who sat in bars all day and were whispered about,
These were my people. In nameless Sicilian towns
Made out of solid rock, men spat in the dust
And glared at strangers. I was one of these.

I couldn't understand ten words they said,
Old men after fifty years of construction gangs
And fruitstands and barbershops and railroad gangs
Still sounding like last week's boatload. In the street
They glared at strangers. I was one of them.

Old men in dirty caps and cotton shirts
Were all around me, inside me, when I was twenty.
They dressed up and sang at weddings, they pinched my cheeks.
Alone in the parking lot in a new suit of clothes
I grunted spontaneously in time with the band.

                                                    Michael Palma

At the Nuclear Rally

thinking of my father
who died of cancer of the pancreas
now linked to radiation

thinking of my father
who worked for the Atomic Energy Commission
that ran security checks on him
questioning our neighbors in Woodbridge

thinking of my father
with a pen in his pocket
who could add four columns of figures
in his head but stayed poor
working for the OPA
while colleagues took
expensive presents

thinking of my father
who embarrassed me, singing in the car
with the radio on as I now do
who returned from government trips
with marzipan strawberries, bananas, grapes
who cooked Sunday breakfasts of chocolate
French toast (his special recipe)
and let my mother sleep late

thinking of my father
who was born Jewish

but never went to temple
never was Bar Mitzvahed

thinking of my father
who smelled of Chesterfields
who never hit, never spanked me
told me he was glad I walked home
with the only black woman
in my high school class

thinking of my father
who would have been at this rally
next to me tonight

                                        Laura Boss

The Candy Lady

Aunt Lily stood
behind her candy counter
passing out Mary Janes, Hersheys, and advice.

Everyone listened to Aunt Lily,
Seer of the pinball crowd,
Ann Landers to the neighborhood.

A sapphire ring guarded her finger,
a gift from the man who promised to marry her
but never did.
Six cats slept in her bed
in a room behind the store.
Once she had her advice published.
Publishers put her words to music,
promising her success,
charging her two hundred dollars.

Aunt Lily could never eat candy.
Diabetic, she checked her urine every day.
She used to have me watch

the chemical kaleidoscope: blue, green, yellow, orange.
She was Merlin of the urine test.

After the cat scratched her,
they amputated one leg
and then the other.
It took twelve months for her to die;
she never sold another penny candy.

Aunt Lily left me a song, her advice, and her ring.
The candy was eaten up,
and the cats disappeared.
Last year I took her ring to a jeweler;
the stone was loose.
And he told me her stone was glass.

Laura Boss

My Father and the Figtree

For other fruits my father was indifferent.
He'd point at the cherry trees and say,
"See those? I wish they were figs."
In the evenings he sat by my bed
weaving folktales like vivid little scarves.
They always involved a figtree.
Even when it didn't fit, he'd stick it in.
Once Joha was walking down the road
and he saw a figtree.
Or, he tied his camel to a figtree
and went to sleep.
Or, later when they caught and arrested him,
his pockets were full of figs.

At age six I ate a dried fig and shrugged.
"That's not what I'm talking about!" he said.
"I'm talking about a fig straight from the earth—
gift of Allah!—on a branch so heavy it touches the ground.
I'm talking about picking the largest fattest sweetest fig

in the world and putting it in my mouth."
(Here he'd stop and close his eyes.)

Years passed, we lived in many houses, none had figtrees.
We had lima beans, zucchini, parsley, beets.
"Plant one!" my mother said, but my father never did.
He tended garden half-heartedly, forgot to water,
let the okra get too big.
"What a dreamer he is. Look how many things he starts
and doesn't finish."

The last time he moved, I had a phone call,
my father, in Arabic, chanting a song I'd never heard.
"What's that?"
"Wait till you see!"

He took me out to the new yard.
There, in the middle of Dallas, Texas,
a tree with the largest, fattest, sweetest figs in the world.
"It's a figtree song!" he said,
plucking his fruits like ripe tokens,
emblems, assurance
of a world that was always his own.

                                        Naomi Shihab Nye

Half-Breed

the difference between you and me
is as I bent
over strangers' toilet bowls,
the face that glared back at me
in those sedentary waters
was not my own, but my mother's
brown head floating in a pool
of crystalline whiteness

she taught me how to clean
to get down on my hands and knees
and scrub, not beg

she taught me how to clean,
not live in this body

my reflection has always been
once removed.

Cherríe Moraga

Modern Secrets

Last night I dreamt in Chinese.
Eating Yankee shredded wheat
I said it in English
To a friend who answered
In monosyllables:
All of which I understood.

The dream shrank to its fiction.
I had understood its end
Many years ago. The sallow child
Ate rice from its ricebowl
And hides still in the cupboard
With the china and tea-leaves.

Shirley Geok-lin Lim

Grandfather at the
Indian Health Clinic

It's cold at last and cautious winds creep
softly into coves along the riverbank. At my insistence
he wears his denim cowboy coat high on his neck; averse to
an unceremonious world, he follows me through
hallways pushing down the easy rage he always has
with me, a youngest child, and smiles.
This morning the lodge is closed to the dance

and he reminds me these are not the men who
raise the bag above the painted marks; for the young
intern from New Jersey he bares his chest
but keeps a scarf tied on his steel-gray braids
and thinks of days that have no turning: he wore
yellow chaps and went as far as Canada to ride
Mad Dog and then came home to drive the Greenwood Woman's
cattle to his brother's place,
two hundred miles
along the timber line
the trees were bright
he turned his hat brim down in summer rain.

Now winter's here, he says, in this white lighted place
where lives are sometimes saved by
throwing blankets over spaces where the leaves are brushed away
and giving brilliant gourd-shell rattles
to everyone who comes.

                                            Elizabeth Cook-Lynn

Birdfoot's Grampa

The old man
must have stopped our car
two dozen times to climb out
and gather into his hands
the small toads blinded
by our lights and leaping,
live drops of rain.

The rain was falling,
a mist about his white hair
and I kept saying
you can't save them all,
accept it, get back in
we've got places to go.

But, leathery hands full
of wet brown life,

knee deep in the summer
roadside grass,
he just smiled and said
they have places to go to
too.

Joseph Bruchac

Undressing Aunt Frieda

Undressing Aunt Frieda, I think of how,
undressing me, she would tilt back her head
as if listening for footsteps, the faint marching
of the S.S. men whose one great dream
was her death. They must have feared
how her young Jewish fingers unbuttoned
and buttoned, as if they had continents
to cross, as if here, in East New York,
I was already tiring, and no one at home
to put me to bed.

Undressing Aunt Frieda, I try to imagine her
healthy, undressing herself, slowly at first,
as if for the love of a man, untying
her green checkered apron with the secret pockets,
unwrapping the frail "just shy of five foot" body
whose scarred beauty Rubens would surely have missed,
but Rembrandt, in the loneliness of his dying days,
might have immortalized.

My daughter at my side grows restless.
She unties her shoes, tugs at each sock.
She has learned, recently, to undress herself,
and pausing occasionally for applause,
does so now. Naked, she shimmies up onto the bed,
curls her thin fingers around Frieda who,
as if she wished herself already dead,
doesn't coo or even smile.

"A dream of love," Frieda preached, "is not love,
but a dream." "And bad luck," I'd say, "follows
the bitter heart." But undressing her now,
I remember the lightness of her hands
and their strength which somehow lifted me
above the nightmares she had known.
I'll care for you, she whispered once,
as if you were my own. My daughter yawns.
I lift her gently, hoping she'll sleep
the hour drive home.

Richard Michelson

Rib Sandwich

I wanted a rib sandwich

So I got into my car
and drove as fast as I could
to a little black restaurant-
bar
and walked in
and so doing
walked out
of
America

and didn't even
need a passport

William J. Harris

Going Home

Ngoh m' sick gong tong hwa—
besides the usual menu words,
the only phrase I really know.
I say it loudly,

but he is not listening.
He keeps on talking with his smile,
staring, it would seem, past me
into the night without a moon.

He's lost, presumably.
But I don't know what he's saying.
He is an old man, wearing a hat,
and the kind of overcoat
my father wears:
the super-padded shoulders.
His nostrils trickle with wet drops,
which he does not care to wipe away.

Ngoh m' sick gong tong hwa—
I try again, to no avail.
I try in English: what street?
and think of taking out
some paper and a pen.
                                    Just then,
two young fellows approach us
carrying a chair; one look
and I can tell
that *they* will oblige him.

I sigh, and point them out,
and hastily cross the street,
escaping. Once on the other side,
I glimpse around, and catch
their gestures from afar,
still able to hear those familiar,
yet no less incomprehensible sounds.

I head home, and visualize
this old man with his small beady eyes
and the two glistening lines
below them, vertical,
like makeup for some clown.
Out loud, I wonder:
but Chinamen aren't supposed to cry.

Wing Tek Lum

Upkeep

My father died of a heart attack
during an afternoon nap.
I remember this while salting my salad.
Had he a moment of consciousness before the dark
descended, a moment when he knew the Winner
had collected early? He was overweight,
his veins whitened with the waxy residue of alcohol.
The maiden aunt, who oiled the rosewood table
and clucked if she found a ring of moisture from a highball,
or ashes from his cigarette,
is also dead. Father liked his pleasure,
but did not like her:
her allergies, her apron pockets stuffed with Kleenex,
her thin figure, a reproach.

A libertine and an old maid,
my life is a contest between them.
The rosewood table, moved now
to my living room, is seldom dusted.
Respect for Aunt's work died
with her and the will to keep a house up
dissolved with my divorce.

This year, I hung a 60-watt lamp
over my place at the kitchen table.
Now I read there in the mornings, and at night.
I must be getting old, needing, as father did,
the pool of yellow lamplight to sit under.
When did the active father I remember
give way to the silent, seated man?
He pined for Mother. I sent him
to the sea and it was better.
He sat, a widower in his blue beret,
before the wharf apartments, watching
the gay waiters with tattoos who took him up.

Jews queue for services today, but I'm not
one of them. Why don't I say the Kaddish

for my father? Others rise at the announcement
of the prayer. The aggregate life affirms life
in the prayer that praises its creator.
A woman in a long wool dress hurries her boy
to the service. She has hidden him
in man's clothing: trousers and a starched white shirt.
I see my father in him, the only boy
among four sisters. When he married,
Mother took their place and when she died,
again his sisters fed him.

On Yom Kippur we pray to dwell
in the House of the Lord. Death keeps a house
like that, a place we once were loved and safe.
But who would want to go there?
Father, a creative sleeper,
kicked the sheets and blankets off,
tossing in the bed at night.
And every morning, Mother made them up,
same as the day before.

Miriam Goodman

Armitage Street

Waiting for the elevated train
during a pale, faintly cold afternoon,
I looked down on Armitage Street
full of quaint old buildings,
up-scale stores and fashionably dressed
mothers pushing white-walled baby carriages
on well-heeled sidewalks.
                              And to think.
It seems just like yesterday on Armitage Street
that Alfredo and Cha-Cha played hide and seek
with Quinto the cop while Cosmo and Aidita
made love in the gangway.
            When radios blared out open windows
            dressed in five and dime lace curtains.
            When staccato Spanish bounced between

buildings high above the rolling traffic
because telephones were insultingly impersonal
and it was no secret that the eyes expressed the heart.
        When rice and bean smells
        roamed the hallways covering up
        the tracks of other ethnics who had
        since faded into the American Dream.
When candles danced amber-hued
in roach-sprayed apartments
from all-night vigils for the dead
before being shipped back to their homeland
in self-addressed, stamped coffins.
        And the children kissed their cheeks
        in gratitude for all the nickels and candy
        after payday, for all the stories and
        pony rides on laps and knees they received
        and the dead knew they would be missed.
            When 25-cent haircuts at Don Florencio's
            illegal basement barber shop made you
            smell pretty, doused in brilliantine hair tonic
            ready for Sunday church services.
                And Nereida, the beautiful older cousin
                that you secretly loved, was the official translator
                for school teacher notes pinned to lapels and coats
                because the mothers were all Englishless.
        When the last summer days were spent
        under street rainbow firehydrant showers
        and that night you overheard your parents whisper
        about moving out because the rent was going up.
But you didn't care because last autumn during school
Ms. Greenspan said that someday you would be a great writer,
Rennee finally kissed you during recess
and that was enough for any little boy's lifetime.
                        And to think.
                It seems just like yesterday
                        on Armitage Street.

                                David Hernandez

Laughing Gas

It was near the Coliseum, RKO,
in the Bronx,
on a broad street lined with trees
where the dentist, an old sweetheart
of my mother's, gave me gas
for a six-year-old molar.

I laughed.

      I swam inside
bubbles of laughter
in a leather-smelling office,
while my tooth floated away.

Then out on the street,
on the trolley,
all the way home and through the night,
I vomited.

I vomited my lost babyhood,
separations to come,
the plane over Reno, buses and trains
pulling out, each future diminution:
hair, teeth, breath.

My grandmother said:
laugh before breakfast,
cry before dinner.

                            Ruth Whitman

Elegy

I. WINEMAKING
Eyes shining like wetted sapphires
my sanguine grandfather

pealed out against the night
"let there be light, let there be more light"
quoting poets and madmen he went down
to turn with friends the winding press
expressing grape's blood, carmine,
heady, fragrant juice in great wooden barrels
and touched singing glasses
to toast the first bottle
in their Redman's "freedom, friendship, charity"
Salud!

II. IN THE GARDEN
He journeyed past Liberty and the Island
to a dark wine cellar in this new world
journeyed to light overwhelming hills and fields
a fertile land more bright than haloes
where he moved amid the blaze of noon
through cloisters of vine trellises
rows of tomato plants, viburnum shrubs
gnarled apple trees, smooth silver trees
of figs fleshed purple-scarlet
figs swelling among susurrant leaves
he moved blessing with fruitful gifts
in the garden green I followed.

III. LAMBENT SUNDAYS
Wineglass at hand
ear turned toward radio
listening to his native opera
ruddy face lifted in the hymn of eating
wine-dipped bread
peaches from his trees floating in the ruby glass
face intent in the labor of cutting
gold cane swinging, spats white under striped pants
taking us to the far cemetery to honor our dead
on lambent Sundays
he dealt the cards
so I won.

IV. LAST DAY
Gentle man, groaning, from the dying bed
rose on your last day out of our room

not to disturb my dreams
went gently down to that dark wine cellar—
let the bright sun wake to realms of light—
in this body and blood
dark fire wine still flows,
I followed, seeing face to face
found you fallen on that last day
(not to disturb my dreams you rose!)
and trying to rise again
your shining eyes closed.

                              Arthur L. Clements

Foreign Ways

If I were in China this minute
and running after a friend
spied across from the hotel
I was staying at

waving to him, say
calling his name in Mandarin

Still they'd know me—
the body giving the person away
betrays a mind
of its own—

my voice from Duluth
my lope with its prairie air

                    Diana Chang

Autobiography

in my house we had an elephant named Italy
grazed the parlor for peanuts
stroked the back of your neck with the thumb of her trunk

kept sitting on the chairs and breaking them
when we went out she stayed home and threw straw all over the floor
we didn't know what to do with her
there was no group for people stuck with an elephant
the social worker took one look and left.
we painted her sides with huge pink flowers
marched her in the parade
rented her out for parties
wrote papers about her in school
waiting for her to die, we bought sacks of lead shot
to stuff her with but she refused to go.
we have had to reinforce the floors three times
and are always putting in another sidewalk.

Robert Viscusi

Horse

PARA LA GENTE DE HARGILL, TEXAS

Great horse running in the fields
come thundering toward
the outstretched hands
nostrils flaring at the corn
only it was knives in the hidden hands
can a horse smell tempered steel?

Anoche some kids cut up a horse
it was night and the *pueblo* slept
the Mexicans mutter among themselves:
they hobbled the two front legs
the two hind legs, kids aged sixteen
but they're *gringos*
and the sheriff won't do a thing
he'd just say boys will be boys
just following their instincts.

But it's the mind that kills
the animal the *mexicanos* murmur
killing it would have been a mercy

black horse running in the dark
came thundering toward
the outstretched hands
nostrils flaring at the smell
only it was knives in the hidden hands
did it pray all night for morning?

It was the owner came running
30-30 in his hand
put the *caballo* out of its pain
the Chicanos shake their heads
turn away some rich father
fished out his wallet
held out the folds of green
as if green could staunch red
pools dripping from the ribbons
on the horse's flanks
could cast up testicles
grow back the ears on the horse's head
no ears of corn but sheaths
hiding blades of steel
earth drinking blood sun rusting it
in that small Texas town
the *mexicanos* shuffle their feet
shut their faces stare at the ground.

Dead horse neighing in the night
comes thundering toward the open faces
hooves iron-shod hurling lightning

only it is red red in the moonlight
in their sleep the *gringos* cry out
the *mexicanos* mumble if you're Mexican
you are born old.

Gloria Anzaldúa

Travels in the South

I. EAST TEXAS
When I left the Alabama-Coushatta people,
it was early morning.
They had treated me kindly, given me food,
spoken me words of welcome, and thanked me.
I touched them, their hands, and promised
I would be back.

When I passed by the Huntsville State Pen
I told the Indian prisoners what the people said
and thanked them and felt very humble.
The sun was rising then.

When I got to Dallas I did not want to be there.
I went to see the BIA Relocation man.
He told me, "I don't know how many Indians
there are in Dallas; they come every week."
I talked with Ray, a Navajo; he didn't have a job,
was looking, and he was a welder.
I saw an Apache woman crying for her lost life.

When it was evening of the next day,
I stopped at a lake called Caddo.
I asked a park ranger, "Who was Caddo?"
And he said it used to be some Indian tribe.

I met two Black women fishing at the lake.
I sat by them; they were good to be with.
They were about seventy years old and laughed,
and for the first and only time in my life
I cut a terrapin's head off because,
as the women said, "They won't let go until sundown."

When it was after sundown in East Texas, I prayed
for strength and the Caddo and the Black women
and my young son at home and Dallas and when
it would be the morning, the sun.

II. THE CREEK NATION EAST OF THE MISSISSIPPI
Once, in a story, I wrote that Indians are everywhere.
Goddamn right.

In Pensacola, Florida, some hotdog stand
operator told me about Chief McGee.

"I'm looking for Indians," I said.
"I know Chief Alvin McGee," he said.
I bought a hotdog and a beer.
"He lives near Atmore, Alabama,
cross the tracks, drive by the school,
over the freeway to Atlanta, about a mile.
He lives at the second house on the right."

I called from a payphone in Atmore.
Mr. McGee told me to come on over.
I found his home right away,
and he came out when I stopped in his yard.
He had a big smile on his face.
I'd seen his face before in the history books
when they bothered to put Creeks in them.

He told me about Osceola.
"He was born in this county," Chief McGee said.
He showed me his garden and fields.
"I have seventy acres," he said.
"We used to have our own school,
but they took that away from us.
There ain't much they don't try to take."

We watched the news on TV.
It was election time in Alabama,
George Wallace against something.
People kept coming over to his house,
wanting the Chief's support. "Wallace is the one."
"Brewer is our man." They kept that up all night.
The next morning the election was on,
but I left right after breakfast.

Chief Alvin McGee put his arms around me
and blessed me. I remembered my grandfather,

the mountains, the land from where I came,
and I thanked him for his home, "Keep together,
please don't worry about Wallace, don't worry."

I was on that freeway to Atlanta
when I heard about the killings at Kent State.
I pulled off the road just past a sign which read
NO STOPPING EXCEPT IN CASE OF EMERGENCY
and hugged a tree.

III. CROSSING THE GEORGIA BORDER INTO FLORIDA
I worried about my hair, kept my car locked.
They'd look at me, lean, white, nervous,
their lips moving, making wordless gestures.

My hair is past my ears.
My grandfather wore it like that.
He used to wear a hat, a gray one,
with grease stains on it.
The people called him Tall One
because he was tall for an Acoma.

I had a hard time in Atlanta;
I thought it was because
I did not have a suit and tie.
I had to stay at the Dinkler Plaza,
a classy joint, for an Indian meeting.
The desk clerk didn't believe it
when I walked up, requested a room,
towel rolled up under my arm,
a couple books, and my black bag of poems.
I had to tell him who I really wasn't.
He charged me twenty dollars for a room,
and I figured I'm sure glad
that I'm not a Black man,
and I was sure happy to leave Atlanta.

A few miles from the Florida line,
I picked some flowers beside the highway
and put them with the sage I got in Arizona.
After the Florida line, I went to a State Park,

paid two-fifty, and the park ranger told me,
"This place is noted for the Indians
that don't live here anymore."
He didn't know who they used to be.

When I got to my camping site
and lay on the ground,
a squirrel came by and looked at me.
I moved my eyes. He moved his head.
"Brother," I said.
A red bird came, hopped.
"Brother, how are you?" I asked.
I took some bread, white, and kind of stale,
and scattered some crumbs before them.
They didn't take the crumbs,
and I didn't blame them.

Simon J. Ortiz

Grandmother

FOR GRAZIELLA ZODA

What is the purpose of visits to me twice since you've died?

Downstairs near a woodstove I hear you
in motion, always working,
a long silken dress—
tight sleeves at your wrist, soft above the elbow,
wide top at your shoulder for free movement.

When we were young you didn't visit—
You never baked a cake that I remember
or babysat or held me in your lap,
You were in the men's part of town running a man's business
calling the world to order
six children behind you
raised singlehanded in your large house. You were
moving, always moving.

When I kept losing things like my parents, my children, money,
my time and health,
why did you appear in my room with gifts painted
red, yellow, blue,
brilliant colored toys. What
essential fact did you want me to know,
that the body is the essence of the spirit and so
must be in motion?

Now that I've lost my foothold, my direction, my way,
what is your message, strong spirit,
strong Grandmother,
What is the meaning of your dream-present,
a bright clock shaped like a train—
                                   simply that it moves?

                                              Grace Cavalieri

Living Alone with Jesus—

Can it be
I am the only Jew residing in Danville, Kentucky,
looking for matzoh in the Safeway and the A & P?
The Sears, Roebuck salesman wrapping my potato masher
advises me to accept Christ as my personal savior
or else when I die I'll drop straight down to hell,
but the ladies who come knocking with their pamphlets
say as long as I believe in God that makes us
sisters in Christ. I thank them kindly.

In the county there are thirty-seven churches
and no butcher shop. This could be taken
as a matter of all form and no content.
On the other hand, form can be seen as
an extension of content, I have read that,
up here in the sealed-off wing where my three rooms
are threaded by outdoor steps to the downstairs world.
In the open risers walnut trees are growing.
Sparrows dipped in raspberry juice
come to my one window sill. Cardinals

are blood spots before my eyes.
My bed is a narrow canoe with a fringy throw.
Whenever I type it takes to the open sea
and comes back wrong end to.
Every morning the pillows produce tapioca.
I gather it up for a future banquet.

I am leading a meatless life. I keep
my garbage in the refrigerator. Eggshells
potato peels and the rinds of cheeses nest
in the empty sockets of my daily grapefruit.
Every afternoon at five I am comforted
by the carillons of the Baptist church next door.
I let the rock of ages cleave for me on Monday.
Tuesday I am washed in the blood of the lamb.
Bringing in the sheaves on Wednesday keeps me busy.
Thursday's the day on Christ the solid rock I stand.
The Lord lifts me up to higher ground on Friday so that
Saturday I put my hands in the nail-scarred hands.
Nevertheless, I stay put on the Sabbath. I let
the whiskey bottle say something scurrilous.

Jesus, if you are in all thirty-seven churches,
are you not also here with me
making it alone in my back rooms like a flagpole sitter
slipping my peanut shells and prune pits into the Kelvinator?
Are you not here at nightfall
ticking in the box of the electric blanket?
Lamb, lamb, let me give you honey on your grapefruit
and toast for the birds to eat
out of your damaged hands.

                                        Maxine Kumin

The Sweaters

Used to be, fellows would ask if you were married,
now they just want to know what kind of diseases
you've got. Mother, what did they teach you of the future
in those nun-bred schoolrooms of the sacred heart?

Nobody kept cars in the city. Maybe you'd snuggle
when the subway tunnels ran dark, or take walks
down Castle Hill Avenue, until it ran into the Sound—
the place you called "The End": where, in late summer,

the weeds were rife with burrs, and tomatoes ripened
behind the sheds of the Italians, beside their half-built
skiffs. Out on the water,
bare-legged boys balanced on the gunwales
of those wooden boats, reeling in the silver-bellied fish
that twitched and flickered while the evening dimmed to purple.

What sweater did you wear to keep you from the chill wind
blowing down at the End, that evening you consented
to marry Father? The plain white mohair, or the gray
angora stitched with pearls around the collar?
Or the black cashmere, scoop-necked
and trimmed with gold braid, stored in a box below the bed
to keep it hidden from Grandma? Each one prized,
like a husband, in those lean years during the war.
I see him resting his face against whichever wool it was,
a pearl or a cable of braid imprinting his cheek
while the Sound washed in, crying *again, again.*

Mother, we've abandoned all our treasured things
these days that wear a death-smell in the throat
of each embrace—a death come not by falling to contagion
but by us falling to our knees before those we might have loved
who will kick us and leave us broken. Your sweaters
have long since fallen to the moths of bitter days. And what
will I inherit to soften this hard skin, to make love tender?

Lucia Maria Perillo

Heritage

From my mother, the antique mirror
where I watch my face take on her lines.
She left me the smell of baking bread

to warm fine hairs in my nostrils,
she left the large white breasts that weigh down
my body.

From my father I take his brown eyes,
the plague of locusts that leveled our crops,
they flew in formation like buzzards.

From my uncle the whittled wood
that rattles like bones
and is white
and smells like all our old houses
that are no longer there. He was the man
who sang old chants to me, the words
my father was told not to remember.

From my grandfather who never spoke
I learned to fear silence.
I learned to kill a snake
when you're begging for rain.

And Grandmother, blue-eyed woman
whose skin was brown,
she used snuff.
When her coffee can full of black saliva
spilled on me
it was like the brown cloud of grasshoppers
that leveled her fields.
It was the brown stain
that covered my white shirt,
my whiteness a shame.
That sweet black liquid like the food
she chewed up and spit into my father's mouth
when he was an infant.
It was the brown earth of Oklahoma
stained with oil.
She said tobacco would purge your body of poisons.
It has more medicine than stones and knives
against your enemies.

That tobacco is the dark night that covers me.

She said it is wise to eat the flesh of deer
so you will be swift and travel over many miles.
She told me how our tribe has always followed a stick
that pointed west
that pointed east.
From my family I have learned the secrets
of never having a home.

                                        Linda Hogan

Lakota Sister/Cherokee Mother

we are both from the center of the continent
        i was born there
but my blood is from the east and the south,
my mother said i wandered in, lost
        and came to her one cold and snowy winter night
from a reservation in north dakota

that was one creation story
        for me

but she knew
and she could not pretend
        telling her trickster stories
that i was a stranger
        exchanged in a hospital bed
        lost in a winter storm

the daughter of her people
        i am
the one with the straightest hair
and the warrior spirit
in so many ways like her
i am the daughter of her people
        the people
she learned to deride
        deny

trying to become a modern woman
      not a mountain woman
      an indian woman
that no one could understand.

                    Victoria Lena Manyarrows

Wingfoot Lake

Independence Day, 1964

On her 36th birthday, Thomas had shown her
her first swimming pool. It had been
his favorite color, exactly—just
so much of it, the swimmers' white arms jutting
into the chevrons of high society.
She had rolled up her window
and told him to drive on, fast.

Now this *act of mercy:* four daughters
dragging her to their husbands' company picnic,
white families on one side and them
on the other, unpacking the same
squeeze bottles of Heinz, the same
waxy beef patties and Salem potato chip bags.
So he was dead for the first time
on Fourth of July—ten years ago

had been harder, waiting for something to happen,
and ten years before that, the girls
like young horses eyeing the track.
Last August she stood alone for hours
in front of the T.V. set
as a crow's wing moved slowly through
the white streets of government.
That brave swimming

scared her, like Joanna saying
Mother, we're Afro-Americans now!

What did she know about Africa?
Were there lakes like this one
with a rowboat pushed under the pier?
Or Thomas' Great Mississippi
with its sullen silks? (There was
the Nile but the Nile belonged

to God.) Where she came from
was the past, 12 miles into town
where nobody had locked their back door,
and Goodyear hadn't begun to dream of a park
under the company symbol, a white foot
sprouting two small wings.

                              Rita Dove

After the Funeral
of Assam Hamady

FOR MY MOTHER, DAVID AND LAURA

Cast:
Hajj Abbass Habhab: my grandfather
Sine Hussin: an old friend of my father
Hussein Hamod Subh: my father
me

6 p.m.

middle of South Dakota
after a funeral in Sioux Falls
my father and grandfather
ministered the Muslim burial
of their old friend, Assam Hamady

me—driving the 1950 Lincoln
ninety miles an hour

"STOP! STOP!
stop this car!"

Why?
"STOP THIS CAR RIGHT NOW!"—Hajj Abbass
                    grabbing my arm from back seat
"Hysht Iyat?   (What're you yelling about?)"—my Father
"Shu bikkee? (What's happening?)"—Sine Hussin

I stop

"It's time to pray"—the Hajj
                    yanks his Navajo blanket
                    opening the door

"It's time to pray, sullee
the sun sets
time for sullee"

my Father and Sine Hussin follow
obedient
I'm sitting behind the wheel
watching, my motor still running

car lights scream by
more than I've ever seen in South Dakota

the Hajj spreads the blanket
blessing it as a prayer rug
they discuss which direction is East

after a few minutes it's decided
it must be that way
they face what must surely be South

they face their East, then notice
I'm not with them

"Hamode! get over here, to pray!"

No, I'll watch
and stand guard

"Guard from what—get over here!"

I get out of the car
but don't go to the blanket

My father says to the others:
"He's foolish, he doesn't know how
to pray."

they rub their hands
then their faces
rub their hands then
down their bodies
as if in ablution
their feet bare
together now
they begin singing

Three old men
chanting the Qur'an in the middle
of a South Dakota night

    "Allahu Ahkbar
    Allahu Ahkbar

    Ash haduu n lah illah illilawhh
    Ash haduu n lah illah illilawhh

    Muhammed rasoul illawh"

in high strained voices they chant

    "Bismee lahee
    a rah'manee raheem"

more cars flash by

    "malik a youm a deen
    ehde nuseerota el mustakeem
    seyrota la theena"

I'm embarrassed to be with them

"en umta ailiy him
ghyrug mugthubee aliy him"

people stream by, an old woman strains a gawk at them

"willathouu leen—
Bismee lahee"

I'm standing guard now

"a rah'maneel raheem
khul hu wahu lahu uhud"

They're chanting with more vigor now
against the cars—washing away
in a dry state
Hamady's death
he floats from their mouths
wrapped in white

"Allahu sumud
lum yuulud wa'alum uulud"

striped across his chest, with green

"Walum yakun a kuf one uhud
willa thouu leen"

his head in white, his gray mustache still

"Ameen . . ."

I hear them still singing
as I travel half-way across
America
to another job
burying my dead
I always liked trips, traveling at high speed
but they have surely passed me
as I am standing here now
trying so hard to join them
on that old prayer blanket—

as if the pain behind my eyes
could be absolution

The Muslim prayer in this poem is analogous to The Lord's Prayer.

Hamod (Sam)

Friendly Town #1

it was august, i was inner city
and ten, on a bus with forty
seven inner city tens: small,
pulsing centers of blueblack

of brownbeige faces as public,
as crowded as the schools
we attended. we were leaving
the city quickly, escaping in twos,

going to the country:
—where the grass allowed us
to run, trees allowed us
to sleep and air stretched

across our backs like wings—
at least this is what the counselor said,
as she counted and tapped our seats,
and the bus stood long yellow and green

stripes in front of the gray.
we were going to camp:
—friendly town—the counselor said,
her smile pearly, perfectly even,

her hair: blonde, to her
beaded belt and waist.
she counted us three times
before the bus left the corner.

after each count she smiled.
we were given sandwiches, chips
and red apples in white paper bags.
our names were written in blue

marker on square, white labels,
and stuck, ends curling, to our chests:
we were shirley with the thick black bangs
and blue eyeglasses, maria with thin lips

and long, thin black hair, josé chewing gum
and reading superman, paulette crying,
edward counting trucks, debra eating the apple,
but not swallowing the skin.

i smoothed my name,
wondered about country animals:
cows, goats, pigs, or did friendly
towners have regular cats and dogs

that fight and regular birds
that never fly? edward exploded
his white lunch bag. the counselor
jumped, her smile popped into a scream,

—my god—she said—i thought
it was a gun.—edward laughed.
i closed my eyes, listened to paulette's
crying, imagined dogs barking

their teeth chasing our bus.

Safiya Henderson-Holmes

My First Riot: Bronx, NYC

we are ten, two
boys and a girl,
walking home from
dracula's matinee.

in a vacant lot
we see smoke and
flame, run into
the heat with our mouths

and eyes locked open.
find jarcaps and
cardboard to scoop
dirt and cover fire.

smokey the bear
taught us dousing
and smothering.
good citizens, we work

to save free space. somewhere
in the smoke we see
and hear a man
shouting,—hey you bastards.—

his pale face growing
larger in the smoke.
—you black bastards,
with your gadamn fires,

i'm calling the cops.—
i watch him run,
think of dracula
entering a grave, taste

ashes on my teeth.
—fuck him—gerald

says, finds a small
flame, carries it to

a pile of sticks and
paper. it stretches and
cracks the summer
we stare until our eyes

burn and the dirt is
hot and mean again.
sirens screech and howl
up our backs, we run

from the charred emptiness,
blood racing, vampires
not far enough away.

Safiya Henderson-Holmes

The Truth Is

In my left pocket a Chickasaw hand
rests on the bone of the pelvis.
In my right pocket
a white hand. Don't worry. It's mine
and not some thief's.
It belongs to a woman who sleeps in a twin bed
even though she falls in love too easily,
and walks along with hands
in her own empty pockets
even though she has put them in others
for love not money.

About the hands, I'd like to say
I am a tree, grafted branches
bearing two kinds of fruit,
apricots maybe and pit cherries.
It's not that way. The truth is
we are crowded together

and knock against each other at night.
We want amnesty.

Linda, girl, I keep telling you
this is nonsense
about who loved who
and who killed who.

Here I am, taped together
like some old civilian conservation corps
passed by from the great depression
and my pockets are empty.
It's just as well since they are masks
for the soul, and since coins and keys
both have the sharp teeth of property.

Girl, I say,
it is dangerous to be a woman of two countries.
You've got your hands in the dark
of two empty pockets. Even though
you walk and whistle like you aren't afraid
you know which pocket the enemy lives in
and you remember how to fight
so you better keep right on walking.
And you remember who killed who.
For this you want amnesty
and there's that knocking on the door
in the middle of the night.

Relax, there are other things to think about.
Shoes for instance.
Now those are the true masks of the soul.
The left shoe
and the right one with its white foot.

Linda Hogan

Hanging Fire

I am fourteen
and my skin has betrayed me
the boy I cannot live without
still sucks his thumb
in secret
how come my knees are
always so ashy
what if I die
before morning
and momma's in the bedroom
with the door closed.

I have to learn how to dance
in time for the next party
my room is too small for me
suppose I die before graduation
they will sing sad melodies
but finally
tell the truth about me
There is nothing I want to do
and too much
that has to be done
and momma's in the bedroom
with the door closed.

Nobody even stops to think
about my side of it
I should have been on Math Team
my marks were better than his
why do I have to be
the one
wearing braces
I have nothing to wear tomorrow
will I live long enough
to grow up
and momma's in the bedroom
with the door closed.

Audre Lorde

In the Way Back

FOR MY FATHER

One must go around for news of home.
                    —Japanese proverb

The Friday before Labor Day
after a day's hard work
my father'd come home, read the paper
then tell my mother:
"Mo' bettah take da kids around da island."

Next morning, up early, mother'd be
telling us to turn off the TV
and packing a picnic lunch:
musubi, scrambled eggs, Spam,
a thermos of watered-down Exchange.

Stuck in the way back of the Valiant
I faced the closed rear window
already hot, thinking how much
I hated this.
At my back my grandma sat,
next to her my brother and sisters dozed.
In front of them my parents sat,
in front of them the long way back.
My mother drove.
Beside her on the seat,
the lunch she'd packed.
My father hung an elbow out the window.

Out of the city and into "scenery"
that blurred ocean, sand and trees,
I pulled out my pack of cards
and played solitaire. My shuffling woke
my sister. She reached past
the back of the front seat
to turn on the radio.
Back in her seat she reached behind
and tapped me on the shoulder.
She leaned and whispered,

"Having one good time already?"
She laughed and climbed
into the way back.

And then
we were four kids laughing
and singing in the way back
with the Rascals, "How Can I Be Sure?"
and Bill Withers, "Lean on Me"
while in between
my grandma sang the chorus:
"*Matte, matte* you, damn kids,
Look the view!"
which sounded to us kids like
"Rook the few."

And in between the singing and the laughing
one of us kept asking,
"We stay dere or what?"
all the way to Hauula Beach
where Grandma smoked a cigarette
and gathered stones along the shore.

The rest of us ate silently.
And silently when we were done
we piled into the car. My father drove,
slowing or stopping now and again to show us
the Crouching Lion,
Chinaman's Hat,
the Blow Hole,
Koko Head, Diamond Head
then Honolulu after dark.
As if he meant to tell us:
When you let the island in you
the road both does and doesn't lead you back.

Four kids in the way back of the Valiant
leaning one upon the other,
we didn't have to watch the road.
Our parents left us free to look in both directions,
behind us and ahead.

Debi Kang Dean

Cultures

vete
go out take the pick axe
take the shovel
my mother would tell me

hard brown earth with the axe
I'd pick at its dark veins
disinter a rotting tin can
unmold a shell from a lost ocean
bones of an unknown animal

with my eyes I'd measure out a rectangle
I'd swing and shove and lift
my sweat dripping on the swelling mounds

into the hole I'd rake up and pitch
rubber-nippled baby bottles
cans of Spam with twisted umbilicals
I'd overturn the cultures
spawning in Coke bottles
murky and motleyed

my brothers never helped
woman's work and beneath them
under the clothesline
three times a year, two feet apart

I'd dig and sweat and grunt
above me clothes flapping like banners
wire taut between the crossed posts
crucifixes over earlier graves

when it rots
trash replenishes the soil
my mother would say
but nothing would grow in
my small plots except
thistle sage and nettle.

Gloria Anzaldúa

Re-Envisioning

■   ■   ■

By reclaiming their ethnic backgrounds and their names, many poets redefine what it means to be American and begin to embrace much of what they previously had denied—immigrant parents, a dark skin, a mixed tongue, working-class roots. While many of these poems wonder at the survival of people who, in Joy Harjo's words, "were never meant to survive," they are not simply positive affirmations of ethnicity. Rather, as Al Young demonstrates in "A Dance for Ma Rainey," *re-envisioning* is also a painful confrontation of personal and national history:

> Ma,
> the beautiful people
> our beautiful brave black people
> who no longer need to jazz
> or sing to themselves in murderous vibrations
> or play the veins of their strong tender arms
> with needles
> to prove we're still here

I Ask My Mother to Sing

She begins, and my grandmother joins her.
Mother and daughter sing like young girls.
If my father were alive, he would play
his accordion and sway like a boat.

I've never been in Peking, or the Summer Palace,
nor stood on the great Stone Boat to watch
the rain begin on Kuen Ming Lake, the picnickers
running away in the grass.

But I love to hear it sung;
how the waterlilies fill with rain until
they overturn, spilling water into water,
then rock back, and fill with more.

Both women have begun to cry.
But neither stops her song.

Li-Young Lee

I Walk in the History of My People

There are women locked in my joints
    for refusing to speak to the police
My red blood full of those
    arrested   in flight   shot
My tendons stretched brittle with anger
    do not look like white roots of peace
In my marrow are hungry faces
    who live on land the whites don't want
In my marrow women who walk 5 miles every day for water
In my marrow the swollen hands of my people who are not allowed
    to hunt

```
            to move
            to be
In the scars of my knees you can see
            children torn from their families
            bludgeoned into government schools
You can see through the pins in my bones
            that we are prisoners of a long war
My knee is so badly wounded no one will look at it
The pus of the past oozes from every pore
This infection has gone on for at least 300 years
            Our sacred beliefs have been made into pencils
            names of cities   gas stations
My knee is wounded so badly that I limp constantly
            Anger is my crutch   I hold myself upright with it
                        My knee is wounded
                    see
                        How I Am Still Walking
```

                                        Chrystos

I Have Not Signed a Treaty
with the United States Government

ESPECIALLY FOR CELESTE GEORGE

nor has my father nor his father
nor any grandmothers
We don't recognize these names on old sorry paper
Therefore we declare the United States a crazy person
    nightmare   lousy food   ugly clothes   bad meat
    nobody we know
No one wants to go there   This US is theory   illusion
terrible ceremony   The United States can't dance   can't cook
    has no children   no elders   no relatives
They build funny houses no one lives in but papers
    Everything the United States does to everybody is bad
No this US is not a good idea   We declare you terminated
    You've had your fun now go home we're tired   We signed
no treaty   WHAT are you still doing here   Go somewhere else and

build a McDonald's   We're going to tear all this ugly mess
down now   We revoke your immigration papers
   your assimilation soap suds   your stories are no good
your colors hurt our feet   our eyes are sore
   our bellies are tied in sour knots   Go Away Now
   We don't know you from anybody
You must be some ghost in the wrong place   wrong time
   Pack up your toys   garbage   lies
We   who are alive now
   have signed no treaties
Burn down your stuck houses   you're sitting
   in a nowhere gray glow   Your spell is dead
Go so far away we won't remember you ever came here
   Take these words back with you

                                                      Chrystos

The Real Indian Leans Against

FOR NANCY EMERY

the pink neon lit window full of plaster of paris & resin
Indians in beadwork for days with fur trim
turkey feathers dyed to look like eagles
abalone & bones
The fake Indians if mechanically activated
would look better at the Pow Wow than the real one in plain jeans
For Sale For Sale with no price tag
One holds a bunch of Cuban rolled cigars
One has a solid red bonnet & bulging eyes ready for war
Another has a headdress from hell
with painted feathers no bird on earth
would be caught dead in
All around are plastic inflatable hot pink palm trees
grinning skulls   shepherd beer steins   chuckling check books
black rhinestone cats & a blowup blonde fuck me doll for horny men
who want a hole that will never talk back
There are certainly more fake Indians
than real ones but this is the usa
What else can you expect from the land of sell

your grandma   sell our land   sell your ass
You too could have a fake Indian in your parlor
who'll never talk back
Fly in the face of it I want a plastic white man
I can blow up again & again
I want turkeys to keep their feathers
& the non-feathered variety to shut up
I want to bury these Indians dressed like cartoons of our long dead
I want
to live
somewhere
where nobody is sold

Chrystos

Night Vision

the girl fits her body in
to the space between the bed
and the wall. she is a stalk,
exhausted. she will do some
thing with this. she will
surround these bones with flesh.
she will cultivate night vision.
she will train her tongue
to lie still in her mouth and listen.
the girl slips into sleep.
her dream is red and raging.
she will remember
to build something human with it.

Lucille Clifton

In the Inner City

in the inner city
or
like we call it
home
we think a lot about uptown
and the silent nights
and the houses straight as
dead men
and the pastel lights
and we hang on to our no place
happy to be alive
and in the inner city
or
like we call it
home

Lucille Clifton

The House on Moscow Street

It's the ragged source of memory,
a tarpaper-shingled bungalow
whose floors tilt toward the porch,
whose back yard ends abruptly
in a weedy ravine. Nothing special:
a chain of three bedrooms
and a long side porch turned parlor
where my great-grandfather, Pomp, smoked
every evening over the news,
a long sunny kitchen
where Annie, his wife,
measured cornmeal
dreaming through the window
across the ravine and up to Shelby Hill
where she had borne their spirited,
high-yellow brood.

In the middle bedroom's hard,
high antique double bed
the ghost of Aunt Jane,
the laundress
who bought the house in 1872,
though I call with all my voices,
does not appear.
Nor does Pomp's ghost,
with whom one of my cousins believes
she once had a long and intimate
unspoken midnight talk.
He told her, though they'd never met,
that he loved her; promised
her raw widowhood would heal
without leaving a scar.

The conveniences in an enclosed corner
of the slant-floored back side porch
were the first indoor plumbing in town.
Aunt Jane put them in,
incurring the wrath of the woman
who lived in the big house next door.
Aunt Jane left the house
to Annie, whose mother she had known
as a slave on the plantation,
so Annie and Pomp could move their children
into town, down off Shelby Hill.
My grandmother, her brother, and five sisters
watched their faces change slowly
in the oval mirror on the wall outside the door
into teachers' faces, golden with respect.
Here Geneva, the randy sister,
damned their colleges,
daubing her quicksilver breasts
with gifts of perfume.

As much as love,
as much as a visit
to the grave of a known ancestor,
the homeplace moves me not to silence
but to righteous, praise Jesus song:

Oh, catfish and turnip greens,
hot-water cornbread and grits.
Oh, musty, much-underlined Bibles;
generations lost to be found,
to be found.

                              Marilyn Nelson Waniek

To Jesus Villanueva,
with Love

my first vivid memory of you
mamacita,
we made tortillas together
yours, perfect and round
mine, irregular and fat
we laughed
and named them: *ose, pajarito, gatito.*
my last vivid memory of you
     (except for the very last
     sacred memory
     i won't share)
mamacita,
beautiful, thick, long, gray hair
the eyes gone sad
with flashes of fury
when they wouldn't let you
have your chilis, your onions, your peppers
     —what do these damned gringos know of *my* stomach?—*
so when I came to comb
your beautiful, thick, long, gray hair
as we sat for hours
(it soothed you
my hand
on your hair)
I brought you your chilis, your onions, your peppers.
and they'd always catch you

because you'd forget
and leave it lying open.
they'd scold you like a child
and you'd be embarrassed like a child
silent, repentant, angry
and secretly waiting for my visit, the new supplies
we laughed at our secret
we always laughed
            you and I

you never could understand
the rules
at clinics, welfare offices, schools
any of it.
I did.
you lie. you push. you get.
I learned to do all this by
the third clinic day of being persistently
sent to the back of the line by 5 in the afternoon
and being so close to done by 8 in the morning.
so my lungs grew larger
and my voice got louder
and a doctor consented
to see an old lady,
and the welfare would give you the money
and the landlady would remember to spray for cockroaches
and the store would charge the food till the check came
and the bank might cash the check if I got the nice man this time
and I'd order hot dogs and Cokes for us
at the old "Crystal Palace" on Market Street
and we'd sit on the steps
by the rear exit, laughing
            you and I

mamacita,
I remember you proudly at Christmas
time, church at midnight services:
you wear a plain black dress
your hair down, straight and silver
(you always wore it up
tied in a kerchief,

knotted to the side)
your face shining, your eyes clear,
your vision intact.
you play Death.
you are Death.
you quote long stanzas from a poem I've long
forgotten;
even fitful babies hush
such is the power of your voice,
your presence
fills us all.
the special, pregnant
silence.
eyes and hands lifted up
imploringly and passionately
the vision and power
offered to us,
eyes and hands cast down
it flows through you
to us,
a gift.

your daughter, my mother
told me a story I'd never
heard before:
    you were leaving Mexico
    with your husband and two
    older children, pregnant
    with my mother.
    the U.S. customs officer
    undid everything you so
    preciously packed, you
    took a sack, blew it up
    and when he asked about
    the contents of the sack,
    well, you popped it with
    your hand and shouted
    MEXICAN AIR!*

aiiiiiiiiii mamacita, Jesus,
I won't forget my visions and reality.

to lie, to push, to get
just isn't
enough.

*Translated from Spanish; she refused (and pretended not to be able) to speak
English.

Alma Luz Villanueva

They Didn't Get Me

TO SAN FRANCISCO'S MISSION DISTRICT,
MY CHILDHOOD GROUND

They didn't get me.
I feel like the hunted prey that
escaped

　　schools
　　churches
　　office jobs
　　city streets
　　morals
　　anglo culture / western civilization / the democratic process
　　dutiful sex free sex no sex
　　9–5
　　the perfect mother
　　&　　"　　wife
IQs / MDs / PHDs / USA
delivery rooms with drs. in a hurry
project walls a ½ inch thick
white kids who hate black kids
black kids who hate white kids
mexican kids who hate light kids
people who hate themselves & hate everyone
The city was the hunter
and the streets of my childhood were
peopled with many like me—
　　the streets soaked up
oil & blood & rain & tears & dog shit & footsteps &

love &
children's games & lives & piss & stunted trees & the
      blossoming
trees on Guerrero St. & the hardy weeds that burst
      through
the cracks in spring, especially spring,
and the people, the people, the people.

They told us in school one
time that a beautiful creek
ran down Dolores St. and that on
Noe St. Indians fished for their supper, we were told—
      Can't you just see cornfields
spreading all over the Mission?
And all that time,
the earth wasn't confined
to backyards and fences and the "country"—
      the weeds kept telling
me something I couldn't hear—
the earth was laughing and listening and singing
all that time. All our destruction
can't touch it. It lies in wait.

They can't touch us.
They didn't get us.

Under my flesh/this skin
my heart keeps pumping
      my blood
            laughing and listening and singing inside me
            all on its own
and I'm amazed.

                                        Alma Luz Villanueva

My People Are
the Color of the Earth

you cannot leave
my aunt's house
without a
full stomach
   she would be
   offended;
she's small
and earth color,   her
face records
her mother's people
    the hills and desert of Sonora.
her eyes hold
an eclipse
   of clarity/pain:
      once,
        when I was small
     I remember
      her and me eating
        a cluster of grapes
          in a matter of minutes
        each one so delicious
        we couldn't wait
          for the next, and
            when the last
              grape was gone
                we laughed because
                  the grape's skeleton
                    looked so funny—
before she was born
her father recognized
her mother and converted (he was a minister)
and married her; his indian
blood mixed with that
of the spanish
conqueror. I saw a
picture of his congregation

in Mexico, his wife's brother
holding their first born
who died before five,
and the majority of his
followers indian/eyes stared
out at me and I
recognized them,
    my aunt, not yet born
among them.

I grew up hearing
my aunt's visions and dreams,
she had no one but
a child to tell them to—
she saw the bombing
of Japan and the
back of God
   and a neighbor's son opened
the front door and called her
the day he was reported missing
in action, and she
dreamt my house and knew
where the trees stood before
she ever came—and she's
always apologetic for staying
"too long" and she's always
sorry you're leaving "too soon"—
    talking and telling in spanish
to english
in english for the skeleton
in spanish for the flesh,
we sit for hours
   she being older for a while
   I being oldest in my turn
taking turns as we've
always done—
and she tells me
she tried going to
an anglo church, but their
faces were blank
and their
eyes

mute; they did not
recognize her—
and with the spontaneity of
a laugh held long
within her
        she smiles
as she tells me:
        —Mi gente son el color de la
                tierra.—
and the clarity overshadows
the pain.

    and she lapses and offers
me a cup of coffee and I
drink it or she
will be offended.

                Alma Luz Villanueva

From a Heart of Rice Straw

Ma, my heart must be made of rice straw,
the kind you fed a fire in Papa's home village
so Grandma could have hot tea upon waking,
so Grandma could wash her sleepy eyes. My heart
knocks as silently as that LeCoultre clock
that Papa bought with his birthday money.
It swells like a baby in your stomach.

Your tears have flooded the house, this life.
For Canton? No, you left home forty years ago
for the fortune Papa sought in Gum San.
In Gold Mountain you worked side by side
in the lottery with regular pay offs
to the Oakland cops. To feed your six daughters
until one day Papa's cousin shot him.

I expected you to fly into the clouds, wail
at Papa's side, but you chased Cousin instead.
Like the cops and robbers on the afternoon radio.

It didn't matter that Papa lay bleeding.
It didn't matter that Cousin accused Papa
of cheating him. You ran, kicking
your silk slippers on the street, chasing
Cousin until you caught him, gun still in hand.
My sister and I followed you, crying.

If Cousin had shot you, you would have died.
The cops showed up and you told them how Cousin
gunned Papa down, trusted kin who smoked
Havana cigars after filling his belly with rice
and chicken in our big yellow house.

Papa lay in his hospital bed, his kidney removed.
Three bullets out. They couldn't find the last
bullet. A search was made, hands dove into Papa's
shirt pocket. A gold watch saved Papa's life.

Ma, you've told this story one hundred times.
The cops said you were brave. The neighbors said
you were brave. The relatives shook their heads,
the bravery of a Gold Mountain woman unknown
in the old home village.

The papers spread the shooting all over town.
One said Papa dueled with his brother like
a bar room brawl. One said it was the beginning
of a tong war, but that Occidental law
would prevail. To them, to the outside,
what was another tong war, another dead Chinaman?

But Papa fooled them. He did not die
by his cousin's hand. The lottery closed down.
We got food on credit. You wept.
I was five years old.

My heart, once bent and cracked, once
ashamed of your China ways.
Ma, hear me now, tell me your story
again and again.

Nellie Wong

April Fool Birthday Poem
for Grandpa

Today is your
birthday and I have tried
writing these things before,
but now
in the gathering madness, I want to
thank you
for telling me what to expect
for pulling
no punches, back there in that scrubbed Bronx parlor
thank you
for honestly weeping in time to
innumerable heartbreaking
italian operas for
pulling my hair when I
pulled the leaves off the trees so I'd
know how it feels, we are
involved in it now, revolution, up to our
knees and the tide is rising, I embrace
strangers on the street, filled with their love and
mine, the love you told us had to come or we
die, told them all in that Bronx park, me listening in
spring Bronx dusk, breathing stars, so glorious
to me your white hair, your height your fierce
blue eyes, rare among italians, I stood
a ways off, looking up at you, my grandpa
people listened to, I stand
a ways off listening as I pour out soup
young men with light in their faces
at my table, talking love, talking revolution
which is love, spelled backwards, how
you would love us all, would thunder your anarchist wisdom
at us, would thunder Dante, and Giordano Bruno, orderly men
bent to your ends, well I want you to know
we do it for you, and your ilk, for Carlo Tresca,
for Sacco and Vanzetti, without knowing
it, or thinking about it, as we do it for Aubrey Beardsley

Oscar Wilde (all street lights
shall be purple), do it
for Trotsky and Shelley and big/dumb
Kropotkin
Eisenstein's Strike people, Jean Cocteau's ennui, we do it for
the stars over the Bronx
that they may look on earth
and not be ashamed.

Diane di Prima

Bully

Boston, Massachusetts, 1987

In the school auditorium,
the Theodore Roosevelt statue
is nostalgic
for the Spanish-American war,
each fist lonely for a saber
or the reins of anguish-eyed horses,
or a podium to clatter with speeches
glorying in the malaria of conquest.

But now the Roosevelt school
is pronounced Hernández.
Puerto Rico has invaded Roosevelt
with its army of Spanish-singing children
in the hallways,
brown children devouring
the stockpiles of the cafeteria,
children painting Taíno ancestors
that leap naked across murals.

Roosevelt is surrounded
by all the faces
he ever shoved in eugenic spite
and cursed as mongrels, skin of one race,
hair and cheekbones of another.

Once Marines tramped
from the newsreel of his imagination
now children plot to spray graffiti
in parrot-brilliant colors
across the Victorian mustache
and monocle.

Martín Espada

Anchorage

FOR AUDRE LORDE

This city is made of stone, of blood, and fish.
There are Chugach Mountains to the east
and whale and seal to the west.
It hasn't always been this way, because glaciers
who are ice ghosts create oceans, carve earth
and shape this city here, by the sound.
They swim backwards in time.

Once a storm of boiling earth cracked open
the streets, threw open the town.
It's quiet now, but underneath the concrete
is the cooking earth,
                      and above that, air
which is another ocean, where spirits we can't see
are dancing   joking   getting full
on roasted caribou, and the praying
goes on, extends out.

Nora and I go walking down 4th Avenue
and know it is all happening.
On a park bench we see someone's Athabascan
grandmother, folded up, smelling like 200 years
of blood and piss, her eyes closed against some
unimagined darkness, where she is buried in an ache
in which nothing makes
                      sense.

We keep on breathing, walking, but softer now,
the clouds whirling in the air above us.
What can we say that would make us understand
better than we do already?
Except to speak of her home and claim her
as our own history, and know that our dreams
don't end here, two blocks away from the ocean
where our hearts still batter away at the muddy shore.

And I think of the 6th Avenue jail, of mostly Native
and Black men, where Henry told about being shot at
eight times outside a liquor store in L.A., but when
the car sped away he was surprised he was alive,
no bullet holes, man, and eight cartridges strewn
on the sidewalk
                    all around him.

Everyone laughed at the impossibility of it,
but also the truth. Because who would believe
the fantastic and terrible story of all of our survival
those who were never meant
                              to survive?

                                                        Joy Harjo

For Alva Benson, and for Those Who Have Learned to Speak

And the ground spoke when she was born.
Her mother heard it. In Navajo she answered
as she squatted down against the earth
to give birth. It was now when it happened,
now giving birth to itself again and again
between the legs of women.

Or maybe it was the Indian Hospital
in Gallup. The ground still spoke beneath
mortar and concrete. She strained against the

metal stirrups, and they tied her hands down
because she still spoke with them when they
muffled her screams. But her body went on
talking and the child was born into their
hands, and the child learned to speak
both voices.

She grew up talking in Navajo, in English
and watched the earth around her shift and change
with the people in the towns and in the cities
learning not to hear the ground as it spun around
beneath them. She learned to speak for the ground,
the voice coming through her like roots that
have long hungered for water. Her own daughter
was born, like she had been, in either place
or all places, so she could leave, leap
into the sound she had always heard,
a voice like water, like the gods weaving
against sundown in a scarlet light.

The child now hears names in her sleep.
They change into other names, and into others.
It is the ground murmuring, and Mt. St. Helens
erupts as the harmonic motion of a child turning
inside her mother's belly waiting to be born
to begin another time.

As we go on, keep giving birth and watch
ourselves die, over and over.
And the ground spinning beneath us
goes on talking.

Joy Harjo

Chinese Hot Pot

My dream of America
is like *dá bìn lòuh*
with people of all persuasions and tastes
sitting down around a common pot

chopsticks and basket scoops here and there
some cooking squid and others beef
some tofu or watercress
all in one broth
like a stew that really isn't
as each one chooses what he wishes to eat
only that the pot and fire are shared
along with the good company
and the sweet soup
spooned out at the end of the meal.

Wing Tek Lum

The Seder

This is a strange seder.
Some of us are Irish,
Italian, French-Canadian.
One is Chinese, from the mainland.
Most of us are Jews.

There are at least 3 types
of socialists here.
We have to keep the Bundists
separate from the Communists
who still maintain that Uncle Joe
had a bad press.
The anarchist glowers.   He won't
drink to the health of Israel
or any other state.

We sing Dayanu,
Go Down Moses,
and Solidarity Forever.

The host-person has designed
a non-sexist Haggadah
stressing the universals.
She's forgotten the hard-boiled eggs,
but it doesn't matter.

We've got horse radish
apples and honey
warm sticky wine.

We fill up the glasses   drain them
four times   set aside
a cup for Elijah.
The ritual flows around us
we start to connect.

But I think of
my secular relatives.
They'd shake their heads   call us nostalgic
warming our hands above
an unnecessary fire.

My orthodox relatives
would be disgusted
at our heresies   our bad
pronunciations.
They'd get up and leave.

It's time for Elijah.
Apprehensive,
I open the door.
He's come so far, been to so many
holy official places.
What will he think
of our oddly assorted communion?

He wanders in smiling
empties his wine cup
calls me aside:

"Don't worry   my daughter   don't worry
you see
we keep on   we keep going on."

Enid Dame

The Bucket

Why is it I can't sleep tonight?
My teeth are brushed,
my alarm is set, yet
something is rising in me.
I'm thinking of the way
her eyebrows rose,
small, black eyebrows
over wide, brown eyes,
and the way she said—
But how would they know?

So simple, an obvious solution—
no one need ever know
I'm Italian. My grandmother
said so. She told me
to shut up, in her Neapolitan.
Her phrases sing through my life
and no one need ever know. This
is Italian wisdom—shut up.
If no one knows
they won't be able to
find us; therefore
they won't rape us anymore
they won't lynch us anymore
they won't shoot us anymore
they won't deny us jobs anymore
they won't deny us apartments anymore
they won't deny us education anymore
and it seems to be working very well.

It's almost my fault
I didn't get those jobs
or those apartments. I could
have changed my name, kept
my mouth shut. I'm light enough.

My father thinks it's wise
to laugh at ethnic jokes.

This is the old Italian strategy
of rising above your problems.
We don't ignore our problems—
we become people for whom these problems
are not problems. Americans
don't understand—they believe
this means we have no problems.
But Americans don't recognize Italian
wisdom—they wouldn't find it
if it smelled like provolone.
I know, because
wisdom smells like provolone.
But I heard
a good one the other day—
what's the difference between an Italian
and a bucket of shit?

It's almost my fault
I didn't get those jobs
or those apartments or
those friends. I could
have changed my name, kept
my mouth shut. I'm light enough.
Not all Italians can say that.
With her rising eyebrows,
she tossed aside my heritage
not because
she thinks it's worthless,
but because
she doesn't know it's there.
But how would she know? It seems
to be working very well. Our enemies
cannot find us; therefore
our friends cannot find us.
Why is it I can't sleep tonight?
Something is rising in me.

Rose Romano

Speaking with Hands

There were no markets in Watts.
There were these small corner stores
we called *marketas*
who charged more money
for cheaper goods than what existed
in other parts of town.
The owners were often thieves in white coats
who talked to you like animals,
who knew you had no options;
who knew Watts was the preferred landfill
of the city.

One time, Mama started an argument
at the cash register.
In her broken English,
speaking with her hands,
she had us children stand around her
as she fought with the grocer
on prices & quality & dignity.

Mama became a woman swept
by a sobering madness;
she must have been what Moses saw
in the burning bush,
a pillar of fire,
consuming the still air
that reeked of overripe fruit
and bad meat from the frozen food
section.

She refused to leave
until the owner called the police.
The police came and argued too,
but Mama wouldn't stop.

They pulled her into the parking lot,
called her crazy . . .
and then Mama showed them crazy!

They didn't know what to do
but let her go, and Mama took us children
back toward home, tired of being tired.

Luis J. Rodriguez

Song: I Want a Witness

Blacks in frame houses
call to the helicopters,
their antlered arms
spinning; jeeps pad
these glass-studded streets;
on this hill are tanks painted gold.

Our children sing
spirituals of *Motown*,
idioms these streets suckled
on a southern road.
This scene is about power,
terror, producing
love and pain and pathology;
in an army of white dust,
blacks here to *testify*
and *testify*, and *testify*,
and *redeem*, and *redeem*,
in black smoke coming,
as they wave their arms,
as they wave their tongues.

Michael S. Harper

In the Good Old U.S.A.

Here in the good old U.S.A.
where being Puerto Rican is taboo.

Where the language passed on by generations
is a curse.

Where our culture is a prison term given
for life.
Where I am a prisoner with no rights to my own identity.
I wonder how America welcomes us all?

In 1974 I was seventeen,
living in Paterson. I met my first
white girlfriend. Her father
cursed me for being Puerto Rican.

He said, "He is a nigger
and I will lock him up
if you continue to see him!"
She was not as brave
as the love we thought we had.

This was my first lesson in racism 101.

During my first two years of college
one of my teachers said,
"You won't make it here,
you're just another spic
who will amount to nothing."
Other teachers did not say it,
but I could hear the words anyway;
"You cannot be educated, why stay in school?"
"Niggers like you will never learn their place!"
So I tried to change my accent,
to hide my Puerto Rican culture
and changed my name from José to Joseph;
I even straightened my hair with Classic Curls
So that I could be accepted
by White America.

It did not matter
I was still a young Brown boy with nappy hair.
I could not hide my Puerto Rican heritage
passed on to me by generations.

This was my second lesson in being educated in White America.

Today, I am no longer ashamed.
I am proud of being Afro-Puerto Rican.
I am proud of my heritage.
my language,
my brillo hair,
and my name.

José Angel Villalongo, Sr.

Today We Will Not Be Invisible Nor Silent

today
we will not be invisible nor silent
as the pilgrims of yesterday continue their war of attrition
forever trying, but never succeeding
        in their battle to rid the americas of us
convincing others and ourselves
        that we have been assimilated & eliminated,

but we remember who we are

we are the spirit of endurance that lives
in the cities and reservations of north america
and in the barrios and countryside of Nicaragua, Chile
Guatemala, El Salvador

and in all the earth and rivers of the americas

Victoria Lena Manyarrows

The View from
Skates in Berkeley

FOR OLIVER JACKSON, HOMEBOY & PAINTER

the clouds were mountains, that day, behind the real mountains
sideways, from san francisco, across the tossed bay, the beauty
    we saw
from skates, in berkeley, was real, there, stretched out behind
    sailboats
the wind driven waves bucking, like rodeo horses carrying
    cowboys
breaking across the frothing, gray water, like sand dunes

rippling across an empty expanse of desert, mirrored & beautiful
here, near sunset, we looked out through the wide, open
    windows & took in
the view, unbroken under sinking sunlight, the hills, breasts,
    the gulls
resembling small planes, banked over the waves, searching
    for fish
they snapped up in their beaks under fleecing clouds

streaming high up, across, in the jetstream, the pricking mist
    hung low
over angel island, like the day after too many drinks fogged up
    your head
in an afternoon sunlight, on a day further back in cobwebs than
    you care
to remember, but there, anyway, as a still life you clung to once
as in a long gone memory, the skyline changing, now

behind the tumbling clouds, the architecture trembling through
    the mist
of the "shining pearl by the bay," grown up from split open
    gums of the land
like chipped shark teeth, or tombstones leaning white & bright
into the light, shimmering, like the friendship of this meeting is
    luminous

here, because we knew we were what we always thought
　　we were

finally, homeboys, at last, laughing like joyous paint in sprayed
　　mist
the fog overhead hung low, over oakland, thick as a mattress
where you laid down your head full of dreams & painted images
　　in full view
of the bay bridge, stretching, like one of your elegant lines
　　stretches through
our view, here, outside skates window, the sun plunging like one
　　of your colors

bright into the rabid wash of gray waves, the wind slapping salt
　　tears across
our faces, creased, as the american flag is streaked with a rain-
　　bow of colors
here, where we were what we always thought we were, on this
　　day
here, when the moment kicked up, the water surging, like our
　　dreams
homeboy, & we were riding these bucking horse waves breaking
　　across

the bobbing, duned, foaming waters, mirrored & beautiful, we
　　were strong
as we always knew we would be, our view unbroken from here,
　　on skates
under the dazzling sunlight of our dreams, streaming across the
　　jetstream
high up in the turbulent afternoon of our heads, light &
　　luminous
you & me, homeboys, Oliver, on this shimmering, rare day filled
　　with flight

Quincy Troupe

I Defy You

I defy you Wallace Stevens
to prove "the exquisite truth."
Your thirteen blackbirds rolled in one
continuous seamless world
bob in and out of my world
as do the black men and women
in Durban who skitter
on my tv screen. There is something else
than mere vision, mere imagination,
fat man of language. Something other
than words and quiet time and cold mind,
although you have emptied your pockets
and peeked over the horizon of our desires
and turned back preferring your onanistic treasures.
The young Cambodian whose father drowned
in monsoon ocean knows
his sister's raped eyes are truth;
the hungry and dead are his "exquisite truth,"
and you an American fiction.

                              Shirley Geok-lin Lim

Prayer

Let my words
be bright with animals,
images the flash of a gull's wing.
If we pretend
that we are at the center,
that moles and kingfishers,
eels and coyotes
are at the edge of grace,
then we circle, dead moons
about a cold sun.
This morning I ask only
the blessing of the crayfish,
the beatitude of the birds;

to wear the skin of the bear
in my songs;
to work like a man with my hands.

Joseph Bruchac

Lamenting the Inevitable

The world dances with hate
Like heat waves
Coming up off blacktop.

In Jerusalem, city of zeal,
Tante Zillah, intelligent
And compassionate, pours black

Coffee in the checkered shade
Of the oleanders,
Laments that your Arab

Friends finally always
Betray you, they cheat on you,
They presume on your friendship

To put you
In the way
Of danger,

Inviting you where the bombs
Will detonate, the crowd
Will riot. This is of course just

As the Nicaraguan revolutionaries
Invite their American
Sympathizers

To the Honduran
Border where
They are shot at

And barely escape,
And just as the nine year old
Black girl in the Project

Whose haughtiness I admired
When I bravely asked her to play
Looked me up and down

And spit on my shoes. To prove
Something, to share
Something, to throw us safe ones also

Like sticks
Into the fire
Of the burning world.

Alicia Ostriker

Speaking Through White:
For My Mother

I
Twenty years ago today, your death changed
our house into a white world of mourning:
the undertaker's drapes billowed over your

yellow couch and in the doorway where you'd
stood listening to my piano; incense smoke
wrote endless columns of mantra, and

your red-covered diary was taken away—
everything locked in white, I cannot now
remember what dress or kimono they'd put

on you, what color I saw as I bent down to
commit every detail of you to memory. Today
in Wisconsin, hail like paper bullets

dissolves into rain and then turns to snow.
I drive with my friends Wendy and Andrea
to give a seminar on women's literature,

mothers and daughters in poetry. I
read my poems about you. Everyone
loves you through me. We drive back

on the highway, our tire tracks blackening
the white scroll of snow. In Madison, we
order ginger tea and curried yellow

squash, sit in our pink nightgowns around
Wendy's fireplace. Laughing with two friends
in this after-the-storm world turned gold, I

regret all the hours you spent alone in
that north-facing house on a hill,
the world outside your window tilted.

II
After the morning of honeybell oranges,
omelettes, toasted nuts and more talk, I

drive back north. Twenty miles away from home,
the sun sets in my rearview mirror, paving

the road behind me into a ribbon of
light. I understand your life

as a series of significant refusals—
to marry or live except as you chose, to leave

me a legacy of helplessness. *You will
overcome my death and become a strong*

woman, you wrote in your last hour while
I was writing circles of hard ice with

the blades of my skates. Though I will never
overcome your death, I am a woman

driving into and out of sunsets to
speak about you. The world balances, again,

mid-March, daffodils breaking through
snow like our words through silence.

Kyoko Mori

Certificate of Live Birth

I
Shuffling papers
      rushing to find some critical
      form or letter or journal
      mired amid the stacks that have collected
      that I've hidden in every corner of the room

Tiny newborn footprints step out of flatland
      a xerox copy of my birth certificate
Nostalgia
      no time—
Yet as I hold the single sheet
      it shapes itself and curves out of my hand

Chubby ankle circled firmly
      protesting kicking held still
      foot inked
      the page indelibly marked
      with my unwilling signature
Perhaps some memory of that first helplessness
      makes me struggle still against capture
      against hint of bonds—
You won't imprint me again

II
Or perhaps it was your capture
      that so enraged my yet unconscious mind
      that brought me kicking into the world
For yours was the more torturous:
      Father, caucasian.

Mother, caucasian.
What pain what shame what fear
          must have forced that check in that flatland box?

Mother, should I correct it?

But no it is more accurate
          just as it stands
In that mark I read your life
I read the history of Indian people in this country
It is my heritage more truly than any account of bloodlines
It tells the story of a people's capture
It tells the story of a people's struggle to survive

And, Mother, this poem is the certificate of our live birth
For together we have escaped their capture
Our time together outdistances their prison

It stands in ruins within the circle of our lives:
          Father, caucasian.
          Mother, American Indian.
          Daughter, mixedblood.

                                        Kimberly M. Blaeser

Cortez's Horse

Return, Sweet Horse, rise
from this warm lake and carry me
high above treetops, two of us
again pressing forward into the wind.

Rise, Sweet Horse, gather your bones
and let me hold your breath hot in my hands.
I will feed you the freshest grasses and tart
purple petals. I promise no beans, no corn.

We didn't know. You were the first horse.
When Cortez left you, we feared your teeth

and hooves. We hid each time you stamped
and snorted or raised your head, tossed your mane.

But didn't I come to you? Didn't I stroke
your face and flank even though I knew
your yellow teeth could chew my flesh?
I put out my hand and offered you my newest seeds.

Why did you die, Sweet Horse?
Why did you let our food rot in your mouth?
Why did you lie down, your skin loose on your bones
and never rise again, your eyes brimming with flies?

I sang to you when we were alone. I covered you
with leaves, boiled herbs, poured the brew
into your slack mouth. I danced around you, rattled
rattles to frighten spirits feasting on your heart.

I did what a girl could, Sweet Horse.
Others turned their eyes in shame, wished
some lightning bolt would strike you into dust.
Elders muttered far from your smell.

Remember the honey, Sweet Horse?
I closed my eyes as I walked to that loud tree
then climbed into that swirling buzz, the smell
thick as the liquid amber I found for you.

I hoped the golden drops would slide down
your throat and remind you of wildflowers,
of the taste of cold dew, of our rides
under sun and stars into the wind.

When you died, men left to find an enormous rock,
to carve another horse. Far away they shaped one,
and then magicians breathed into its mouth
until the stone stirred, and its eyes opened.

A stone horse. Imagine the thunder when it thudded
to the lake. They made a raft to sail it back,
but a storm rose, waves taller than trees pounded
until the horse sank into welcoming water.

My people's shame shows, and they dread Cortez.
But it's you I miss. I swim here to be near you.
Together we could fly, Sweet Horse. Rise.
Carry me into the stars.

                                              Pat Mora

OYE MUNDO/ Sometimes

sometimes (
            when the night air feels *chevere*
) when i can hear the real sound
of *el barrio*
on *la conga   y timbales*
coke bottles
& garbage can tops

            when i can feel
            & reallyreally touch
            la música latina/   africana

& the fingerpoppin soul
emergin from tears/   sweet tears of laughter

            & i can feel
            a conglomeration of vibrations/
            heat waves
            body waves
            people waves
            of real *gente*
            /& i feel gooooooood

when i can taste the rare culture
of *cuchifritos   y lechón*
chitterlins   & black-eyed peas
& corn bread

            & *la pompa* is open
            & cooooooools the hot tar
            of summer heated streets

where children play
kick-the-can (
& sirens
cannot be heard)

/sometimes

sometimes
when the last of the ghetto poets
writes of flowers
growin in gutters   /& i know it's real

/sometimes

sometimes/   sometimes
when i can almost hear   /being echoed back
an answer
to my ghetto cry

sometimes/   sometimes
i run up the fire escape/   not to escape
& climb on the roof
& stand on the ledge
& look down
& yell out
to the midnight world
below
above
around
within:

OYE MUNDO TÚ ERES BONITO!!!

& i forget about the junkies
on the stoop.

Jesús Papaleto Meléndez

The Men

What then shall we say to this?
If God is for us, who is against us?
                    —Romans 8:31

I
Today I saw black men
carrying babies,
pushing carriages,
holding their own.

II
Our streets filled
with good news,
we must write the
headlines ourselves.

III
When the world
makes a fist
we duck and counterpunch,
we jab and swing.

IV
Black men
at construction sites
lifting black earth,
black hearts, black
hands.

V
The young men
dress in black,
their clothes
just big enough
for love.

E. Ethelbert Miller

The New Apartment:
Minneapolis

The floorboards creak.
The moon is on the wrong side of the building,

and burns remain
on the floor.

The house wants to fall down
the universe when earth turns.

It still holds the coughs of old men
and their canes tapping on the floor.

I think of Indian people here before me
and how last spring white merchants hung an elder

on a meathook and beat him
and he was one of The People.

I remember this war
and all the wars

and relocation like putting the moon in prison
with no food and that moon already a crescent,

but be warned, the moon grows full again
and the roofs of this town are all red

and we are looking through the walls of houses
at people suspended in air.

Some are baking, with flour on their hands,
or sleeping on floor three, or getting drunk.

I see the businessmen who hit their wives
and the men who are tender fathers.

There are women crying or making jokes.
Children are laughing under beds.

Girls in navy blue robes talk on the phone all night
and some Pawnee is singing 49s, drumming the table.

Inside the walls
world changes are planned, bosses overthrown.

If we had no coffee,
cigarettes, or liquor,

says the woman in room twelve,
they'd have a revolution on their hands.

Beyond walls are lakes and plains,
canyons and the universe;

the stars are the key
turning in the lock of night.

Turn the deadbolt and I am home.
I have walked dark earth,

opened a door to nights where there are no apartments,
just drumming and singing;

The Duck Song, The Snake Song,
The Drunk Song.

No one here remembers the city
or has ever lost the will to go on.

Hello aunt, hello brothers, hello trees
and deer walking quietly on the soft red earth.

Linda Hogan

A Dance for Ma Rainey

I'm going to be just like you, Ma
Rainey this monday morning
clouds puffing up out of my head
like those balloons
that float above the faces of white people
in the funnypapers

I'm going to hover in the corners
of the world, Ma
& sing from the bottom of hell
up to the tops of high heaven
& send out scratchless waves of yellow
& brown & that basic black honey
misery

I'm going to cry so sweet
& so low
& so dangerous,
Ma,
that the message is going to reach you
back in 1922
where you shimmer
snaggle-toothed
perfumed &
powdered
in your bauble beads

hair pressed & tied back
throbbing with that sick pain
I know
& hide so well
that pain that blues
jives the world with
aching to be heard
that downness
that bottomlessness
first felt by some stolen delta nigger
swamped under with redblooded american agony;

reduced to the sheer shit
of existence
that bred
& battered us all,
Ma,
the beautiful people
our beautiful brave black people
who no longer need to jazz
or sing to themselves in murderous vibrations
or play the veins of their strong tender arms
with needles
to prove that we're still here

                              Al Young

I Ain't Going
to Hurry No More

I ain't going to hurry up for the white man no more
I don't care if he calls me Mexikan Joe
I am going to take my time plowing his fields
He don't care how I feel
He can't teach me something I already don't know
Sooner or later the white man
Going to send my son to war
I'll be working the fields
He'll be sent out to kill
For the white man
Protecting his fears

I ain't going to hurry up for the white man no more
I'll be out in the hot sun
Picking the white man's cotton
He'll be in Disneyland
Eating cotton candy having fun
Living in the land of freedom
But only he can be governor
I ain't got no money
I haven't even a car to go to the store

My house is a shack
I can't even afford a rat
No indoor plumbing only a gas stove
Catalogs and corn cobs in the out-house in the back
The day I die the rest will be my reward
The white man sure won't cry

If you can't be white
There's no future to life
I ain't going to hurry up for the white man no more.

Jesse F. García

Praise the Tortilla,
Praise the Menudo,
Praise the Chorizo

I praise the tortilla in honor of El Panzón,
who hit me in school every day and made me see
how the bruises on my arms looked like
the brown clouds on my mother's tortillas.
I praise the tortilla because I know
they can fly into our hands like
eager flesh of the one we love,
those soft yearnings we delight in biting
as we tear the tortilla and wipe the plate clean.

I praise the menudo as visionary food that it is,
the tripas y posole tight flashes of color
we see as the red caldo smears across our notebooks
like a vision we have not had in years,
our lives going down like the empty bowl
of menudo exploding in our stomachs
with the chili piquin of our poetic dreams.

I praise the chorizo and smear it
across my face and hands,

the dayglow brown of it painting me
with the desire to find out
what happened to la familia,
why the chorizo sizzled in the pan
and covered the house with a smell
of childhood we will never have again,
the chorizo burrito hot in our hands,
as we ran out to play and show the vatos
it's time to cut the chorizo,
tell it like it is before la manteca runs down
our chins and drips away.

                                        Ray González

The Last Word

i'd rather my fist be made of steel
than my heel made of iron
i'd rather water the earth with my tears
than lose feeling
i'd rather walk
than ride the backs of workers
i'd rather die fighting
than live slaving
i'd rather be criticized for protest poetry
than write lines indifferent to my people's lives
leave me to my "propaganda"
let my songs call for Freedom
turn down my manuscripts
poem after poem
tell me i'm repetitious
the word oppression is used too much
i'd rather complain
than say nothing at all
i hope my last words
call for revolution
i'd rather my pen
be at least as mighty as the sword

                                        Amina Baraka

Martin and My Father

Martin was too peaceful for me.
He let those Deep-South dogs bite him
Police club his head
Suburbanites stone him
Cowards bomb his house
Firemen hose him down
and judges throw him in jail.

I used to pack a .357 Magnum
and if anybody messed with me,
I would aim, pull the trigger
and feel the kick of the gun
saturated in spic anger.
I wanted to kill all the
racist pigs in the world
and marching peacefully
like Martin did, wasn't
about to do it.

One time while arguing with my father
I pulled a knife on him.
That night he cried himself to sleep
and I felt like an assassin.
The next day I heard that Martin
was shot dead and my heart crumbled
for him and my father.

My anger turned ice-blue hot,
well-kept, on target,
proportionately forever and
it was on this anvil that
my pen was forged.

So I took my gun and knife,
threw them in the lake
and watched them drown.
Then I went home and while
my father took a nap on the couch

with the t.v. blaring about
Martin's death,
I kissed him with a poem.

And I'll tell you,
          That Martin,
                    He was something else.

David Hernandez

My Ringless Fingers on the Steering Wheel Tell the Story

Never before without a ring,
The first, gold, with a heart etched in the center.
I still have it.
Still have the memory of its being pressed into my
four-year-old finger by Aunt Lily who worried I'd get
lost as we stood on a crowded bus filled with Christmas
shoppers going down Smith Street in Perth Amboy—
and I, thrilled to be out in the dark among the crowd,
resenting, accepting the protective pressure on my ring finger.

And the amethyst birthday ring from my parents
(though amethyst is not my birthstone)
rewarding me for being their good girl,
reminding me to be their good girl.

All the instant identity rings
the eighth grade going steady rings to show which boy I
belonged to that month; the Girl Scout ring; an Iota Phi
high school ring that proclaimed I was Jewish, pseudo snob,
and couldn't get into Rainbow Girls; and my Woodbridge High
School ring that like my high school never felt comfortable,
though I almost made cheerleader but left finals to make a train
to Lawrenceville and keep my date with a preppie whose
roommate discussed Schopenhauer (whom I'd never heard of),
his apartment on Sutton Place South, his dates with Susan

Strasberg, his producer father, and with whom I fell madly
in love though he didn't know and came to my Sweet Sixteen
and later, instead of going to Harvard where my date went,
joined the Marines, disappeared—
that afternoon was worth giving up two years of cheerleading for
although none of my friends agreed.

Finally, his succession of rings—
the NYU one that kept falling off my finger even when
I bandaged up the back, replaced by a huge diamond marquis,
supposedly flawless, chosen by his mother,
a ring that the other Douglass freshmen recognized as a
definite world with a definite picture
of the wife and mother this ring shaped me into.
A year later, a platinum band—
getting tighter and tighter,
my fingers heavier and heavier.

Last month, my fingers once again slim,
the band of twenty years
slid off almost by itself.
My fingers never looked so free.

Laura Boss

The Women

My cotton shirts float on the line,
this one from India, those, from Africa, Guatemala—
And suddenly my grandmother appears,
in the South, in a straw hat, gathering
clothes before the rain,
while the clouds stall, the sun sinks
below a selvage of pine, and the dog days
unleash their soporific heat—
In the desert afternoon my mother stands, taking
the cottons from the line,
so I imagine them together, light-skinned, lyrical women,
each one describing
the same indelible motions—till I feel myself

through my mothers, my women selves
pausing among the sudden colors . . . a fluttering of
        sheets, shirts,
a childhood of breezes by the yard.

                                    Cyrus Cassells

I Am Singing Now

                        the moon is a white sliver
                        balancing the last of its contents
                        in the final curve of the month
my daughters sleep
in the back of the pickup
breathing small clouds of white in the dark
they lie warm and soft
under layers of clothes and blankets
how they dream, precious ones, of grandma
                and the scent of fire
                the smell of mutton
                they are already home.

i watch the miles dissolve behind us
in the hazy glow of taillights and
the distinct shape of hills and mesas loom above
                then recede slowly in the clear winter night.

i sing to myself and
think of my father
                teaching me, leaning towards me
                listening as i learned.
                "just like this," he would say
                and he would sing those old songs

                        into the fiber of my hair,
                        into the pores of my skin,
                        into the dreams of my children

and i am singing now
for the night

the almost empty moon
and the land swimming beneath cold bright stars.

Luci Tapahonso

To Hell and Back, with Cake

it was spring, saturday.
the small, soundview
bakery was stuffed

but i was the only kid.
the only black. i stood firmly
in front of the cupcakes:

polite desserts in pleated paper
skirts and thick icing hats;
chocolate, vanilla, pistachio,

pure glaze. my allowance melted
in my pocket. i wanted two
vanilla and two chocolate.

i wanted the four in a bakery box,
separated by bakery tissue,
tied in red bakery string.

i wanted to walk home
with this special box
softly swaying in my hand,

a clue of something good occurring.
after seven pies, two ice cream cakes
a dozen blueberry muffins,

and three pounds of mixed cookies,
i was next. i laid a steamy finger
on the bakery glass and said,

—two chocolate and two vanilla
please—the woman behind the counter
was new to neighborhood and bakery.

her apron loosely tied
and still unfolding, fresh razor
creases deflecting flour and syrup spills.

she didn't know my name,
or notice how each week
i grew an inch higher than

the counter, no inquiry into
my parents' health or pastry
needs. she held her arms across

her chest as shield, patrolled
the rows of cupcakes, her blue eyes:
fierce as bullets looked at the cupcakes

and killed them. said,—we don't have
what you want. we have white
cupcakes or black cupcakes.

what you want is someplace else.—
my finger, as if plugging a hole
in a dam, to keep the bakery

from flooding, drowning all
the sweet and good, stayed on
the glass. the blood leaving the tip.

my coins almost stones.—i want two
chocolates and two vanilla.—i said
—cupcakes.—i said—please.—

she cocked and aimed again.
direct.—we got white, we got black.
that's it, you take that or you go

on.—i removed my finger.
the dead sweetness, bloated
belly-up, in waves, carried me

out the bakery door, alive,
but holding my breath.

                    Safiya Henderson-Holmes

Friendly Town #3

(One Day When I Was Strong)

for thirteen days
she had threatened
and forced me dark:

made my baby doll
black and navyblue clothes
when i cried for a dress

as pink as her daughter's
with red lace trim. she said
never comb my hair

with anything but the big
black comb she had bought
for me in woolworths,

along with a black handle
brush with bristles from the
ass of a black boar.

these were her gifts
to me, pledges of an allegiance
she dared me to know.

and for thank yous
she wanted all my white teeth
whenever i smiled,

and then she'd kiss me,
hold me between her large
baby powdered breast, rock me.

after dinner, there was
always ice cream for dessert.
she'd give me fist scoops

of chocolate when i wanted
vanilla, melted, dropping with
butterscotch syrup from the spoon,

like the rest of the family,
like the others.
chocolate or none at all,

she'd say, placing the lone
chocolate in the center
of the table. without

looking or feeling, i'd bring
it to me, dig holes in the mountain
and stare through.

at the bottom of the bowl
i'd see my face burying
my tongue with heaps

from a spoon. one night
a white tooth loosened.
i tasted salt all the next day,

held my face and refused dinner.
of course she asked what was wrong.
it was her job, part of camp,

part of forty five dollars a week.
she offered immediate cure by biting on
a frozen chocolate kiss. i said no.

she said she could tie a black
thread around the tooth, tie
the thread to a doorknob

and slam the door. i said no.
she said if you don't get it out
it'll grow into a huge mouth,

and eat you alive. i left her
advice, went to the bathroom.
in the mirror i opened

my mouth. spit as thin
as tears over my tongue.
i grabbed the tooth,

and pulled. wiped my
bloody fingers on the mirror.
that night i watched the others

eat their cold desserts,
smiled, sucked her into my
new, dark, empty space

slowly.

Safiya Henderson-Holmes

Out of Our Hands

FOR WING TEK LUM

Out of a hat
on a piece of paper
someone once gave me your name.

Your name flew
out of my hand,
the black letters

dismantling the air
above the school.
I watched the letters

form the bird
seeds of a language
I needed to know,

a language borrowed
from the children I taught
who shivered in borrowed coats.

Toward evening they scattered
outside the school,
red-bricked and torn

on the edge of Chinatown.
I watched them disappear
into their lives,

undisciplined like starlings,
they disappeared
in the broken shoes of the wind.

One day your name
came back
in a poem you were   •

writing in another city,
a poem you were determined
to write for the rest of your life.

The poem a subversive act.
The poem about being Chinese,
skin the glorious color of chicken fat.

Cathy Song

The Old Man's Lazy,

I heard the Indian Agent say,
has no pride, no get up
and go. Well, he came out
here and walked around my
place, that agent. Steps
all thru the milkweed and
curing wormwood; tells me
my place is overgrown
and should be made use
of.

The old split cedar
fence stands at many
angles, and much of it
lies on the ground like
a curving sentence of
stick writing. An old
language, too, black with
age, with different
shades of green of moss
and lichen.
      He always
says he understands us
Indians,
      and why don't
I fix the fence at least;
so I took some fine
hawk feathers fixed
to a miniature woven
shield
      and hung this
from an upright post
near the house.
      He
came by last week
and looked all around
again, eyed the feathers

for a long time.
          He didn't
say anything, and he didn't
smile even, or look within
himself for the hawk.

Maybe sometime I'll
tell him that the fence
isn't mine to begin with,
but was put up by
the white guy who used
to live next door.
          It was
years ago. He built a cabin,
then put up the fence. He
only looked at me once,
after his fence was up,
he nodded at me as if
to show that he knew I
was here, I guess.
          It was
a pretty fence, enclosing
that guy, and I felt lucky
to be on the outside
of it.
          Well, that guy
dug holes all over his
place, looking for gold,
and I guess
          he never
found any. I watched
him grow old for over
twenty years, and bitter,
I could feel his anger
all over the place.
          And
that's when I took to
leaving my place to do
a lot of visiting.
          Then
one time I came home
and knew he was gone
for good.

My children would
always ask me why I
didn't move to town
and be closer to them.

Now, they
tell me I'm lucky to be
living way out here.
                              And
they bring their children
and come out and visit me,
and I can feel that they
want to live out here
too, but can't
for some reason, do it.

Each day
a different story is
told me by the fence,
the rain and wind and snow,
the sun and moon shadows,
this wonderful earth,
            this Creation.
I tell my grandchildren
many of these stories,
            perhaps
this too is one of them.

Peter Blue Cloud

America

America, you ode for reality!
Give back the people you took.

Let the sun shine again
on the four corners of the world

you thought of first but do not
own, or keep like a convenience.

People are your own word, you
invented that locus and term.

Here, you said and say, is
where we are. Give back

what we are, these people you made,
us, and nowhere but you to be.

Robert Creeley

Naayawva Taawi

Left in the field
among big-bellied ewes
tightly rusted stuff of borders,
bales of fence wire
sit in the wind
solid
as if on full bellies

and it was not
the garbage you thought
nor discarded nor useless
but look   the small birds
with speckled wings and black heads
have made their nests there
with barley chaff and string,
bits of alfalfa,
singing as sweetly in the wire
as in the willow.

        In the wind
        of sage, sweetgrass,
        you called us
                guteater and squaw
                savage and drunk
        we who finished in the field
        the job you began,
        we who honored your fine foreign steers

as you did not
leaving them where they fell
dead for nothing, to rot

as you laughed in your sherry
from porches and doors
washed white with your joke
that we seemed so satisfied
with what you left

and nothing you can do
will stop us
as we re-make
your weapons into charms,
send flying back to you the bullets.

See
we are strong,
we who are so small
we survive unseen;
hear
our beautiful songs
building from the hills
like thunderheads;
watch
the children we weave
from wire bales and string,
from bottles and bullets,
from steer guts and borders—
See, Pahana,
how we nest
in your ruins.

Naayawva Taawi: Fight Song (Hopi)
Pahana: Whiteman (Hopi)

Wendy Rose

Story Keeper

The stories
would be braided in my hair
between the plastic comb
and blue wing tips
but as the rattles would spit,
the drums begin,
along would come someone
to stifle and stop
the sound
and the story keeper
I would have been
must melt
into the cave
of things discarded

and this is a wound
to be healed
in the spin of winter
or the spiral
of beginning.
This is the task—
to find the stories now
and to heave at the rocks,
dig at the moss
with my fingernails,
let moisture seep
along my skin
and fall within
soft and dark
to the blood

and I promise
to find them
even after so long
that underground
they have turned albino
to listen, to shine,
to wait with tongues shriveled

into blackberries;
and fearful of their names
they will crystallize,
burrow, become fossils
with the feathers on their backs
frozen hard like beetle shells.

But spring is floating
to the canyon,
needles burst yellow
from the sugar pine;
the stories
have built
a new house.
Oh they make us dance
the old animal dances
that go a winding way
back and back
to the red clouds
of our first
Hopi morning.

∎ ∎ ∎

Where I saw them last
they are still—
antelope and bear
dancing in the dust,
prairie dog and lizard
whirling just whirling,
pinyon and willow
bending, twisting,
we women
rooting into earth,
our feet becoming water
and our hair pushing up
like tumbleweeds
and the spirits
should have noticed
how our thoughts wandered
those first days,
how we closed our eyes against them

and forgot all the signs;
the spirits were never
smart about this
but trusted us
to remember it right
and we were distracted,
we were
so new.

I feel the stories
rattle under my hand
like sun-dried greasy
gambling bones.

Wendy Rose

The Upside Down Basket

FOR CONNIE YOUNG YU,
CHINESE AMERICAN SCHOLAR

*"the chinese came to california for gold, they worked on the railroad and wore funny
hats that looked like upside down baskets."*
                    —from a california state history textbook now in use

my grandmother
rakes up chicken shit
mixed with mud
to feed her roses

head protected
by an upside down basket
dares the sun to get closer

her shirt ablaze
with hawaiian pineapples
she imitates the cackle of hens
as they run merry off nests
wings flapping dust

an egg
still warm
cuddles the round
of my chin

a tickle unbearable
so i laugh
and she does too
so hard

the upside down
basket trembles
as though shaking
a fist
at the heat

we walk home
the musk of rotten apples everywhere
incense curling into skin

on the porch the upside down basket
sits rightside up

we drink gallons
of lemonade

Alan Chong Lau

La Migra

I
Let's play *La Migra*
I'll be the Border Patrol.
You be the Mexican maid.
I get the badge and sunglasses.
You can hide and run,
but you can't get away
because I have a jeep.
I can take you wherever
I want, but don't ask

questions because
I don't speak Spanish.
I can touch you wherever
I want but don't complain
too much because I've got
boots and kick—if I have to,
and I have handcuffs.
Oh, and a gun.
Get ready, get set, run.

II
Let's play *La Migra*
You be the Border Patrol.
I'll be the Mexican woman.
Your jeep has a flat,
and you have been spotted
by the sun.
All you have is heavy: hat,
glasses, badge, shoes, gun.
I know this desert,
where to rest,
where to drink.
Oh, I am not alone.
You hear us singing
and laughing with the wind,
Agua dulce brota aquí,
aquí, aquí, but since you
can't speak Spanish,
you do not understand.
Get ready.

La migra: term along the border for Border Patrol agents
Agua dulce brota aquí, aquí, aquí: sweet water gushes here, here, here

Pat Mora

What the Gypsy Said
to Her Children

We are like the dead
invisible to those who do not
want to see,
and color is our only protection against
the killing silence of their eyes,
the crimson of our tents pitched
like a scream
in the fields of our foes,
the amber warmth of our fires
where we gather to lift our voices
in the purple lament of our songs.
And beyond the scope of their senses
where all colors blend into one
we will build our cities of light,
we will carve them
out of the granite of their hatred,
with our own brown hands.

Judith Ortiz Cofer

The Floral Apron

The woman wore a floral apron around her neck,
that woman from my mother's village
with a sharp cleaver in her hand.
She said, "What shall we cook tonight?
Perhaps these six tiny squid
lined up so perfectly on the block?"

She wiped her hand on the apron,
pierced the blade into the first.
There was no resistance,
no blood, only cartilage

soft as a child's nose. A last
iota of ink made us wince.

Suddenly, the aroma of ginger and scallion fogged our senses,
and we absolved her for that moment's barbarism.
Then, she, an elder of the tribe,
without formal head-dress, without elegance,
deigned to teach the younger
about the Asian plight.

And although we have traveled far
we would never forget that primal lesson—
on patience, courage, forbearance,
on how to love squid despite squid,
how to honor the village, the tribe,
that floral apron.

Marilyn Chin

I Give You Back

I release you, my beautiful and terrible
fear. I release you. You were my beloved
and hated twin, but now, I don't know you
as myself. I release you with all the
pain I would know at the death of
my daughters.

You are not my blood anymore.

I give you back to the white soldiers
who burned down my home, beheaded my children,
raped and sodomized my brothers and sisters.
I give you back to those who stole the
food from our plates when we were starving.

I release you, fear, because you hold
these scenes in front of me and I was born
with eyes that can never close.

I release you, fear, so you can no longer
keep me naked and frozen in the winter,
or smothered under blankets in the summer.

I release you
I release you
I release you
I release you

I am not afraid to be angry.
I am not afraid to rejoice.
I am not afraid to be black.
I am not afraid to be white.
I am not afraid to be hungry.
I am not afraid to be full.
I am not afraid to be hated.
I am not afraid to be loved,

to be loved, to be loved, fear.

Oh, you have choked me, but I gave you the leash.
You have gutted me, but I gave you the knife.
You have devoured me, but I lay myself across the fire.
You held my mother down and raped her,
                    but I gave you the heated thing.

I take myself back, fear.
You are not my shadow any longer.
I won't hold you in my hands.
You can't live in my eyes, my ears, my voice
my belly, or in my heart my heart
my heart   my heart

But come here, fear
I am alive and you are so afraid
                    of dying.

Joy Harjo

For the Color of My Mother

I am a white girl gone brown to the blood color of my mother
speaking for her through the unnamed part of the mouth
the wide-arched muzzle of brown women

at two
my upper lip split open
clear to the tip of my nose
it spilled forth a cry that would not yield
that traveled down six floors of hospital
where doctors wound me into white bandages
only the screaming mouth exposed

the gash sewn back into a snarl
would last for years

I am a white girl gone brown to the blood color of my mother
speaking for her

at five, her mouth
pressed into a seam
a fine blue child's line drawn across her face
her mouth, pressed into mouthing english
mouthing yes yes yes
mouthing stoop lift carry
(sweating wet sighs into the field
her red bandana comes loose from under the huge brimmed hat
moving across her upper lip)

at fourteen, her mouth
painted, the ends drawn up
the mole in the corner colored in darker larger mouthing yes
she praying no no no
lips pursed and moving

at forty-five, her mouth
bleeding into her stomach
the hole gaping growing redder
deepening with my father's pallor

finally stitched shut from hip to breastbone
   an inverted V
   Vera
   Elvira

I am a white girl gone brown to the blood color of my mother
speaking for her

as it should be
dark women come to me
                       sitting in circles
I pass through their hands
the head of my mother
painted in clay colors

touching each carved feature
                    swollen eyes and mouth
they understand the explosion the splitting
open   contained within the fixed expression

they cradle her silence
            nodding to me

Cherríe Moraga

Present

This woman vomiting her
hunger over the world
this melancholy woman forgotten
before memory came
this yellow movement bursting forth like
coltrane's melodies all mouth
buttocks moving like palm trees,
this honeycoatedalabamianwoman
raining rhythm of blue/black/smiles
this yellow woman carrying beneath her breasts
pleasures without tongues
this woman whose body weaves
desert patterns,

this woman, wet with wandering,
reviving the beauty of forests and winds
is telling you secrets
gather up your odors and listen
as she sings the mold from memory.

        there is no place
for a soft / black / woman.
there is no smile green enough or
summertime words warm enough to allow my growth.
and in my head
i see my history
standing like a shy child
and i chant lullabies
as i ride my past on horseback
tasting the thirst of yesterday tribes
hearing the ancient/black/woman
me, singing   hay-hay-hay-hay-ya-ya-ya.
                  hay-hay-hay-hay-ya-ya-ya.
like a slow scent
beneath the sun
      and i dance my
creation and my grandmothers gathering
from my bones like great wooden birds
spread their wings
while their long/legged/laughter
stretched the night.
      and i taste the
seasons of my birth. mangoes. papayas.
drink my woman/coconut/milks
stalk the ancient grandfathers
sipping on proud afternoons
walk like a song round my waist
tremble like a new/born/child troubled
with new breaths
      and my singing
becomes the only sound of a
blue/black/magical/woman. walking.
womb ripe. walking. loud with mornings. walking.
making pilgrimage to herself. walking.

Sonia Sanchez

Norma

As a teen-ager I was very shy. I always felt so conspicuous that I talked with my head down, walked with my head down and would have slept with my head down if sleeping had demanded a standing position. It was with difficulty that I mustered up courage to ask Mr. Castor again and again, "But how do you factor that equation? I don't understand how it's done."

And he kept pointing to the book and looking upward, as if the combination of those actions would give me the immediate joy of an answer.

A sound from the back of the class made me turn around. It was the "people"—the "people" who sat in the back and talked when they wanted to, ate their lunches when they wanted to, and paid attention when they wanted to. They were paying attention to Mr. Castor and me. And I shook. I always wanted to be inconspicuous around the "people."

Odessa screamed, "Sit down, Mr. Castor. You don't know crap. Norma, go up front and teach that little 'pip-squeak' how to do this Algebra."

As Mr. Castor moved to the sidelines, like some dejected player, Norma got up and began her slow walk up to the blackboard.

Have you ever seen a river curve back on itself? That was Norma as she walked on the edge of the classroom. She was heavy with white petticoats as she questioned, "Whatcha wanna know, Sonia?"

Indeed. What did I want to know? It was all so very simple. I just wanted to know how to factor the problems so I could do my homework. Nothing else. I had a father waiting for me at home who would take no excuses concerning homework. He said, "The teachers are there. If you don't know, ask them. They know the answers." He didn't know Mr. Castor though.

As I asked the question, she sighed, and explained the factoring process in such an easy manner. I wrote it all down and closed my math notebook. I could do my homework now. There would be no problem with the family.

Norma was still at the blackboard. She hadn't moved and I knew that she was waiting for Lewis to say something. Lewis was the other brain in the class. They were always discussing some complex math problem. As if on cue, Lewis called out a more difficult question. She smiled. The smile ripened on her mouth like pomegranates.

Her fingers danced across the board. I watched her face. I was transfixed by her face that torpedoed the room with brilliance. She pirouetted problem after problem on the blackboard. We all thought genius. Norma is a mathematical genius.

I used to smile at Norma and sometimes she smiled back. She was the only one in the group who spoke to the "pip-squeaks" sitting up front. The others spoke, but it was usually a command of sorts. Norma would sometimes shake off her friends and sit down with the "pip-squeaks" and talk about the South. She was from Mississippi. She ordained us all with her red clay Mississippi talk. Her voice thawed us out from the merciless cold studding the hallways. Most of the time though, she laughed only with her teeth.

One day Norma called out a question in our French class. I understood part of the question. French was my favorite class. Mrs. LeFevebre was startled. She was a hunchback who swallowed her words so it was always difficult to understand her. But Norma's words were clear.

Mrs. LeFevebre spoke her well-digested English, "No rudeness, please, Norma. You are being disrespectful. I shall not tolerate this."

Norma continued the conversation in French. Her accent was beautiful. I listened while her words fell like mangoes from her lips. The "people" laughed, "Talk that talk, Norma. Go on, girl. Keep on doin' it; whatever you're saying."

Mayhem. The smell of mayhem stalked the room. I wondered if the "people" would lock us all in the closet again.

Mrs. LeFevebre screamed, "Silence. Silence. Savages. How dare you ask me about my affliction. It is none of your business." As she talked, her large owl-head bobbed up and down on her waist. I wondered if she had trouble each night taking off her black dress. Her head was so large.

Norma stood up and started to pack her books. The noise subsided. She walked to the door, turned and said, "I just wanted to talk to you in your own language so you wouldn't be so lonely. You always look so lonely up there behind your desk. But screw you, you old bitch. You can go straight to hell for all I care. Hunchback and all."

She exited; the others followed, dragging their feet and mumbling black mourning words.

Mrs. LeFevebre stood still like a lizard gathering the sun.

I never liked that class after that. I still got good grades, but Norma, when she came to the French class, just sat and watched us struggle with our accents in amusement. I wondered what she did after school. I wondered if she ever studied.

George Washington High School was difficult. Our teachers had not prepared us for high school. The first year was catch-up time. My sister and I spent long nights in our small room, reading and studying our material.

I don't remember who it was. It was announced one day at lunchtime that Norma was pregnant. She had been dismissed from school. I had almost forgotten Norma. The mathematical genius. Norma. The linguist. The year had demanded so much work and old memories and faces had faded into the background.

I was rushing to the library. The library had become my refuge during the Summer of '55. As I turned the corner of 145th Street, I heard her hello. Her voice was like stale music in barrooms. There she stood. Norma. Eyelids heavy. Woman of four children, with tracks running on her legs and arms.

"How you be doing, Norma? You're looking good, girl."

"I'm making it, Sonia. You really do look good, girl. Heard you went to Hunter College. Glad you made it."

"You should have gone too, Norma. You were the genius. The linguist. You were the brain. We just studied and got good grades. You were the one who understood it all."

And I started to cry. On that summer afternoon, I heard a voice from very far away paddling me home to a country of incense. To a country of red clay. I heard her laughter dancing with fireflies.

Tongue-tied by time and drugs, she smiled a funny smile and introduced me to her girls. Four beautiful girls. Norma predicted that they would make it. They wouldn't be like their mother. They would begin with a single step, then they would jump mountains.

I agreed.

She agreed.

We agreed to meet again.

Then I pulled myself up and turned away; never to agree again.

Sonia Sanchez

An Anthem

FOR THE ANC AND BRANDYWINE PEACE COMMUNITY

Our vision is our voice
we cut through the country
where madmen goosestep in tune to Guernica.

we are people made of fire
we walk with ceremonial breaths
we have condemned talking mouths.

we run without legs
we see without eyes
loud laughter breaks over our heads.

give me courage so I can spread
it over my face and mouth.

we are secret rivers
with shaking hips and crests
come awake in our thunder
so that our eyes can see behind trees.

for the world is split wide open
and you hide your hands behind your backs
for the world is broken into little pieces
and you beg with tin cups for life.

are we not more than hunger and music?
are we not more than harlequins and horns?
are we not more than color and drums?
are we not more than anger and dance?

give me courage so I can spread it
over my face and mouth.

we are the shakers
walking from top to bottom in a day
we are like Shango
involving ourselves in acts

that bring life to the middle
of our stomachs

we are coming towards you madmen
shredding your death talk
standing in front with mornings around our waist
we have inherited our prayers from
the rain
our eyes from the children of Soweto.

red rain pours over the land
and our fire mixes with the water.

give me courage so I can spread
it over my face and mouth.

                                        Sonia Sanchez

Arturo

I told everyone
your name was Arthur,
tried to turn you
into the imaginary father
in the three-piece suit
that I wanted instead of my own.
I changed my name to Marie,
hoping no one would notice
my face with its dark Italian eyes.

Arturo, I send you this message
from my younger self, that fool
who needed to deny the words
—Wop! Guinea! Greaseball!—
slung like curved spears,
the anguish of sandwiches
made from spinach and oil,
the roasted peppers on homemade bread,
the rice pies of Easter.

Today, I watch you,
clean as a cherub,
your ruddy face shining,
closed by your growing deafness
in a world where my words
cannot touch you.

At 80, you still worship
Roosevelt and J.F.K.,
read the newspaper carefully,
know with a quick shrewdness
the details of revolutions and dictators,
the cause and effect of all wars,
no matter how small.
Only your legs betray you
as you limp from pillar to pillar;
yet your convictions remain
as strong now as they were at 20.

For the children, you carry chocolates
wrapped in gold foil
and always find for them
your crooked grin and a $5 bill.

I smile when I think of you.
Listen, America,
this is my father, Arturo;
I am his daughter, Maria.
Do not call me Marie.

                    Maria Mazziotti Gillan

Public School No. 18: Paterson, New Jersey

Miss Wilson's eyes, opaque
as blue glass, fix on me:
"We must speak English.

We're in America now."
I want to say, "I am American,"
but the evidence is stacked against me.

My mother scrubs my scalp raw, wraps
my shining hair in white rags
to make it curl. Miss Wilson
drags me to the window, checks my hair
for lice. My face wants to hide.

At home, my words smooth in my mouth,
I chatter and am proud. In school,
I am silent, grope for the right English
words, fear the Italian word
will sprout from my mouth like a rose,

fear the progression of teachers
in their sprigged dresses,
their Anglo-Saxon faces.

Without words, they tell me
to be ashamed.
I am.
I deny that booted country
even from myself,

want to be still
and untouchable
as these women
who teach me to hate myself.

Years later, in a white
Kansas City house,
the Psychology professor tells me
I remind him of the Mafia leader
on the cover of *Time* magazine.

My anger spits
venomous from my mouth:

I am proud of my mother,
dressed all in black,

proud of my father
with his broken tongue,
proud of the laughter
and noise of our house.

Remember me, ladies,
the silent one?
I have found my voice
and my rage will blow
your house down.

Maria Mazziotti Gillan

Growing Up Italian

When I was a little girl,
I thought everyone was Italian,
and that was good. We visited
our aunts and uncles,
and they visited us.
The Italian language smooth
and sweet in my mouth.

In kindergarten, English words fell on me,
thick and sharp as hail. I grew silent,
the Italian word balanced on the edge
of my tongue and the English word, lost
during the first moment
of every question.

It did not take me long to learn
that dark-skinned people were greasy
and dirty. Poor children were even dirtier.
To be dark-skinned and poor was to be dirtiest of all.

Almost every day
Mr. Landraf called Joey
a "spaghetti bender."
I knew that was bad.
I tried to hide

by folding my hands neatly
on my desk and
being a good girl.

Judy, one of the girls in my class,
had honey-blonde hair and blue eyes.
All the boys liked her. Her parents and
grandparents were born in America.
They owned a local tavern.
When Judy's mother went downtown
she brought back coloring books and candy.
When my mother went downtown, she brought back
one small brown bag with a towel or a sheet in it.

The first day I wore my sister's hand-me-down coat,
Isabelle said, "That coat looks familiar. Don't
I recognize that coat?" I looked at the ground.

When the other children brought presents
for the teacher at Christmas, embroidered silk
handkerchiefs and "Evening in Paris" perfume,
I brought dish cloths made into a doll.

I read all the magazines that told me
why blondes have more fun,
described girls whose favorite color was blue.
I hoped for a miracle that would turn my dark skin light,
that would make me pale and blonde and beautiful.

So I looked for a man
with blond hair and blue eyes
who would blend right in,
and who'd give me blond, blue-eyed children
who would blend right in
and a name that could blend right in
and I would be melted down
to a shape and a color
that would blend right in,
till one day, I guess I was 40 by then,
I woke up cursing
all those who taught me
to hate my dark, foreign self,

and I said, "Here I am—
with my olive-toned skin
and my Italian parents,
and my old poverty,
real as a scar on my forehead,"
and all the toys we couldn't buy
and all the words I didn't say,
all the downcast eyes
and folded hands
and remarks I didn't make
rise up in me and explode

onto paper like firecrackers
                    like meteors

and I celebrate
          my Italian American self,
rooted in this, my country, where
all those black/brown/red/yellow
olive-skinned people
soon will raise their voices
and sing this new anthem:

Here I am
          and I'm strong
          and my skin is warm in the sun
          and my dark hair shines,

and today, I take back my name
and wave it in their faces
like a bright, red flag.

                              Maria Mazziotti Gillan

Contributors

Sherman Alexie is an enrolled Spokane and Coeur d'Alene Indian from Wellpinit, Washington, on the Spokane Indian Reservation. His books include *The Business of Fancydancing, Old Shirts & New Skins, First Indian on the Moon, The Lone Ranger and Tonto Fistfight in Heaven*, and *Coyote Springs*.

Born in Puerto Rico, **Miguel Algarín** grew up in Spanish Harlem and Queens. He founded the Nuyorican Poets Café in New York City. He has published four books of poetry including *The Time Is Now/Ya es tiempo*. With Miguel Piñero, he edited *Nuyorican Poetry: An Anthology of Puerto Rican Words and Feelings*.

Gloria Anzaldúa, born in the Río Grande Valley of South Texas, explores her Chicana tejana background in her book *Borderlands/La frontera: The New Mestiza*. She is also co-editor of the award-winning *This Bridge Called My Back: Writings by Radical Women of Color* and *Making Face, Making Soul/Haciendo caras*.

Jimmy Santiago Baca, born in Santa Fe, New Mexico, is the author of three books of poetry including *Immigrants in Our Own Land* and *Martín & Meditations on the South Valley*, for which he won the 1988 American Book Award. His most recent book is *Working in the Dark: Reflections of a Poet of the Barrio*.

Amina Baraka is a poet and singer and former dancer. Her first book of poetry was *Songs For The Masses*. She has co-produced two books with Amiri Baraka: *Confirmation: An Anthology of Afro American Women*, which she co-edited and *The Music: Reflections On Blues & Jazz*, which she co-authored.

Amiri Baraka is a poet, political activist and teacher. He has three books coming out in the next year: *Eulogies*, a book of eulogies given over the last twenty years; *Why's/Wise*, a book of poetry; and *Jesse Jackson and Black People*, essays collected since 1972 about Jackson and his politics, both from Third World Press.

Stanley H. Barkan is the editor/publisher of Cross-Cultural Communications. For the past twenty years, he has directed the International Festival of Poetry, Writing, and Translation, which includes the reading series at the United Nations in New York City. His collection, *Bubbes & Bubbemeises*, is forthcoming.

Helen Barolini, of Italian ancestry, was married to the late Italian poet and author Antonio Barolini and divided her time between the U.S. and Italy. She is the author of several books, including *Umbertina*, and is the editor of *The Dream Book: An Anthology of Writings by Italian American Women*.

Carole Bernstein is descended from Polish-Russian Jews and lives in Brooklyn, where she was born in 1960. Her poems have appeared in *Poetry, Yale Review, Antioch Review, Shenandoah, Chelsea, Bridges, Confrontation*, and other magazines.

Kimberly M. Blaeser, of Ojibway and German ancestry, is an enrolled member of the Minnesota Chippewa Tribe and grew up on White Earth Reservation. She is currently an assistant professor in the English and Comparative Literature department at the University of Wisconsin–Milwaukee. She is also the author of a critical study, *Gerald Vizenor: Writing—in the Oral Tradition*.

Peter Blue Cloud (Aroniawenrate) is a member of the Mohawk Nation at Kahnawake, Quebec. His seven published books include *Sketches in Winter, With Crows* and *The Other Side of Nowhere*. His forthcoming collection of poems is entitled *Clans of Many Nations*.

Mary Jo Bona is an assistant professor of American literature in the English department at Gonzaga University. She is the editor of *The Voices We Carry*, an anthology of Italian American women writers.

Laura Boss is the founder and editor of *LIPS*. Her books of poetry include *Stripping* and the Alta Award–winning *On the Edge of the Hudson*, which recently went into its second printing and bilingual editions.

Joseph Bruchac is a storyteller and writer of Abenaki, English, and Slovak ancestry. As a storyteller, he is the author of six retellings of traditional tales from the Abenaki and the Iroquois. He has also edited several anthologies including *Songs from This Earth on Turtle's Back* and *New Voices from the Longhouse*.

Giovanna (Janet) Capone, a working-class lesbian writer of Neapolitan descent, co-edited with Denise Nico Leto the *Sinister Wisdom* issue on Italian American women: *Il Viaggio delle Donne*. A chapter of her first novel, *Olive and Lavender*, appears in *The Voices We Carry: Recent Italian/American Women's Fiction*, edited by Mary Jo Bona.

Robert Carnevale, born in Benevento, Italy, was raised in New Jersey. His poems have appeared in *The Paris Review* and *The New Yorker*. He was principal literary researcher for the *Voices & Visions* film series on American poets and is assistant poetry coordinator for the Geraldine R. Dodge Foundation.

Cyrus Cassells is the author of *The Mud Actor*, one of the winners of the 1982 National Poetry Series, and the forthcoming *Soul Make a Path through Shouting*, a 1992 AWP Poetry Award finalist. He is a recipient of a 1992 Peter I. B. Lavan Younger Poet Award from the Academy of American Poets.

Grace Cavalieri, a "second-generation Italian," is the author of six books of poetry; the most recent is *Trenton*. She is the producer/host of the radio program "The Poet and the Poem," which she has broadcast weekly from WPFW-FM in Washington, D.C., for sixteen years. In 1993, she edited *The WPFW Poetry Anthology*.

Lorna Dee Cervantes is the author of *Emplumada*, a collection of poems rooted in her Chicana heritage. She is the recipient of the 1982 American Book Award. Her second book is entitled *From the Cables of Genocide*. Currently, she resides in Boulder, Colorado, where she co-edits *Red Dirt*, a crosscultural poetry journal.

Diana Chang is the author of five novels including *The Frontiers of Love* and three poetry chapbooks. She has taught creative writing at Barnard College and edited *The American Pen*, a quarterly once published by American Center of PEN.

Marilyn Chin, born in Hong Kong and raised in Portland, Oregon, is the author of *Dwarf Bamboo*. Recently, her poetry has appeared in *The Kenyon Review* and *The Iowa Review*, as well as *The Norton Introduction to Poetry*. She has just completed her second manuscript of poems, entitled *The Phoenix Gone, The Terrace Empty*.

Chrystos is a political activist and speaker as well as an artist and writer. Her tireless momentum is directed at better understanding how issues of colonialism, genocide, class, and gender affect the lives of women and Native people.

Cheryl Clarke is an African American lesbian poet, college administrator, and AIDS activist with four books in print: *Narratives, Living as a Lesbian, Humid Pitch*, and, most recently, *Experimental Love*.

Arthur L. Clements (Americanized from Clemente by his grandfather) teaches modern and Renaissance literature and creative writing at SUNY, Binghamton. His book of poems, *Common Blessings*, received the American Literary Translators Association Award for translation into Italian and publication in a bilingual edition, *Benedizioni Comuni*.

Susan Clements is of Blackfeet, Mohawk, Seneca, and European heritage. Her chapbook, *The Broken Hoop*, was published in 1988. Her most recent book, *In the Moon When the Deer Lose Their Horns*, was published in 1993.

Lucille Clifton was born in Depew, New York. Her awards include the Juniper Prize for Poetry, two nominations for the Pulitzer Prize, and an Emmy Award. Presently she is Distinguished Professor of Humanities at St. Mary's College of Maryland. She is the author of eight books of poetry, fifteen books for children, and a memoir, *Generations*.

Judith Ortiz Cofer, a native of Hormigueros, Puerto Rico, is the author of a novel, *The Line of the Sun*, of *Silent Dancing*, a collection of essays and poetry, and of two books of poetry, *Terms of Survival* and *Reaching for the Mainland*. *The Latin Deli* is her most recent collection of prose and poetry.

Elizabeth Cook-Lynn, a member of the Crow Creek Sioux Tribe, is a founding editor of *The Wicazo Sa Review* (*The Red Pencil Review*). Her poetry collections include *The Badger Said This* and *Seek the House of Relatives*.

Robert Creeley is the director of the Poetics Program at the University of Buffalo–SUNY. State poet of New York from 1989 to 1991, Robert Creeley has published many collections of prose and poetry over the years, among them *For Love, Pieces, The Island*, and the recent collections *Windows* and *Selected Poems*.

Enid Dame is a poet, writer, and teacher. Her most recent book of poems is *Anything You Don't See*. Her poems have appeared in a number of publications, including *New York Quarterly* and *Negative Capability*. She is currently working on a novel about two generations in a radical Jewish family.

Debi Kang Dean, is a third-generation American of Korean and Okinawan ancestry. Her poems, first published in *The Greenfield Review* and *Tar River Poetry*, have since appeared in *Ploughshares, CutBank*, and other magazines. Her essay, "Telling Differences," is also forthcoming in *New England Review*.

Toi Derricotte, an African American woman, has published three collections of poetry: *Natural Birth, The Empress of the Death House*, and, most recently, *Captivity*. Her poems have appeared in *American Poetry Review* and *The Iowa Review*.

Rachel Guido deVries is an Italian American poet and novelist. Her novel, *Tender Warriors*, was published in 1986, and she has recently completed a manuscript of poems, *How to Sing to a Dago*.

Diane di Prima, born in Brooklyn, New York, is a second-generation American of Italian descent. She is the author of thirty-two books of poetry and prose, including *Pieces of a Song* and *Seminary Poems*. Her autobiographical memoir is *Recollections of My Life as a Woman*.

Originally from India, **Chitra Banerjee Divakaruni** lives in the San Francisco Bay Area. She teaches creative writing at Foothill College, where she is a director for the annual multicultural Writing Conference. Her most recent poetry collection is *Black Candle*.

Gregory Djanikian was born of Armenian parentage in Alexandria, Egypt, in 1949, and emigrated to the United States with his family in 1957. His poems have appeared in *The Nation, The American Scholar, Poetry*, and other journals. He is the author of *The Man in the Middle* and *Falling Deeply into America*.

Rita Dove won the 1987 Pulitzer Prize in poetry for *Thomas and Beulah*, becoming the second African American to do so. In addition, she was named the 1993 Poet Laureate at the Library of Congress. Her other poetry books are *The Yellow House on the Corner, Museum*, and *Grace Notes*. Her first novel is *Through the Ivory Gate*.

Alfred Encarnacion is a mestizo of Filipino, German, and English descent. His chapbook is entitled *At Winter's End*. His poems have appeared in *The Open Boat: Poems from Asian America, Indiana Review*, and *Oklawaha Review*.

Louise Erdrich is of mixed German, Chippewa, and French ancestry. Her books include *The Bingo Palace, Tracks, The Beet Queen*, and *Love Medicine* (novels), and two collections of poetry, *Jacklight* and *Baptism of Desire*. She is the co-author of *The Crown of Columbus* written with her husband, Michael Dorris.

Martín Espada was born in Brooklyn, New York, of Puerto Rican and Jewish parentage. He is the author of four books: *The Immigrant Iceboy's Bolero* (1982), *Trumpets from the Islands of Their Eviction* (1987), *Rebellion Is the Circle of a Lover's Hands* (1990), and most recently *City of Coughing and Dead Radiators* (1993).

Sandra María Esteves is a Nuyorican poet. Her poems have been collected in *Yerba Buena* and *Tropical Rains: A Bilingual Downpour*. Her most recent book of poetry is entitled *Bluestown Mockingbird Mambo*.

Lawrence Ferlinghetti, born in New York of Italian ancestry, is the author of more than sixteen books. *When I Look at Pictures* and *Love in the Days of Rage* are two of his most recent publications. He is the founder of City Lights Booksellers and Publishers in San Francisco.

Stewart Florsheim's poetry has appeared in various small press publications throughout the world. He is the editor of *Ghosts of the Holocaust*, an anthology of poetry by children of Holocaust survivors.

Jesse F. García, born of migrant working parents in the early 1950s in Devine, Texas, traveled the state and beyond throughout his childhood in search of cottonfields to be picked. His work has been published in *Red Dirt* and *Top Heavy.*

Sandra Mortola Gilbert is a feminist critic and poet of Italian descent. She has published four collections of poetry, including *Blood Pressure.* She is the co-editor with Susan Gubar of several anthologies and critical studies, including *The Norton Anthology of Literature by Women* (1985).

Maria Mazziotti Gillan, born of southern Italian immigrant parents, is director of the Poetry Center at Passaic County Community College in Paterson, New Jersey, and editor of *Footwork: The Paterson Literary Review*, as well as the author of *Winter Light, The Weather of Old Seasons, Taking Back My Name*, and *Where I Come From: New and Selected Poems.*

Daniela Gioseffi is the editor of *Women on War: Essential Voices for the Nuclear Age*, a National Book Award winner. Her first novel, *The Great American Belly . . .* , was optioned by Michael Christopher for a screenplay by Warner Brothers. Most recently, she edited *On Prejudice: A Global Perspective.*

Nikki Giovanni, born in Knoxville, Tennessee, and raised in Cincinnati, is the author of seventeen poetry collections, including *Black Feeling Black Talk/ Black Judgement* and *My House.* Her most recent work is *Sacred Cows . . . And Other Edibles*, a collection of essays. Her work has been widely anthologized and recorded.

Michael S. Glaser is a professor of literature and creative writing at St. Mary's College of Maryland and serves as a poet-in-the-schools through the Maryland State Arts Council. He was editor of *The Cooke Book: A Seasoning of Poets.* His latest collection of poems is *A Lover's Eye.*

Ray González is literature director of The Guadalupe Cultural Arts Center in San Antonio, Texas. He is the author of a book of essays, *Memory Fever: A Journey Beyond El Paso del Norte*, and two books of poetry. He is the editor of ten anthologies, including *Without Discovery: A Native Response to Columbus.*

Miriam Goodman is a Jewish American writer whose poems have appeared most recently in *The Prose Poem—An International Journal.* She is the author of *Permanent Wave* and *Signal: Noise.*

Janice Gould is a mixed-blood of American Indian, English, French, and Irish ancestry, and is a member of the Maidu tribe of Northern California. She is the author of *Beneath My Heart.*

Born and raised in the Philippines, **Jessica Hagedorn** is well known as a performance artist, poet, and playwright. Her first novel, *Dogeaters*, was nominated for the National Book Award. Her most recent works are *Danger and Beauty*, a collection of new and selected writings, and

Charlie Chan Is Dead: An Anthology of Contemporary Asian American Fiction.

Kimiko Hahn was born just outside New York City to a Japanese American mother and German American father. Her influences primarily come from her Asian background. Her poetry collections include *Air Pocket* and *Earshot.*

Shalin Hai-Jew is a Chinese American born to immigrant parents in Huntsville, Alabama. She has worked for newspapers in the Northwest as a reporter, interviewer, and columnist. Her poetry has appeared in over a hundred publications and she has a chapbook forthcoming.

Hamod (Sam) is a professor of English at Howard University and the author of seven books, most recently *Dying with the Wrong Name: New and Selected Poems.* Hamod's work has appeared in numerous anthologies and magazines, including *Grape Leaves: A Century of Arab American Poetry.*

Joy Harjo is an enrolled member of the Creek Tribe. She has published four books of poetry, including *She Had Some Horses* and *In Mad Love and War.* She is also the editor of an anthology of Native American women's writing, *Reinventing the Enemy's Language.*

Michael S. Harper has published nine books of poetry and is co-editor of *Chant of Saints,* an anthology of African American writing, art, and scholarship. He is also co-editor of an anthology of Black American poetry from 1945 to the present. He is the first Poet Laureate of Rhode Island.

William J. Harris, a professor at Pennsylvania State University, is the author of two books of poetry, *Hey Fella Would You Mind Holding This Piano a Moment* and *In My Own Dark Way,* and of a critical study, *The Poetry and Poetics of Amiri Baraka.* He is the editor of *Leroi Jones/Amiri Baraka Reader.*

Safiya Henderson-Holmes's first book of poems, *Madness and a Bit of Hope,* won the Poetry Society of America's William Carlos Williams Award in 1990. Her story "Snapshots of Grace" appeared in Terry McMillan's *Breaking Ice,* and her play "Testimony" premiered at the Henry Street Theater of New York City.

David Hernandez has published several books of poems, including *Despertando/Waking Up* and *Satin City Lullaby.* He also wrote the introduction to Walter Lowenfels's anthology *From the Belly of the Shark* and poet Ken Serrito's book *Saturn Calling.* In addition, he has edited and published three poetry anthologies.

Linda Hogan is a Chickasaw poet, novelist, and essayist. She is the author of a novel, *Mean Spirit,* and of several poetry books, including

Savings and *Seeing Through the Sun*, which received the American Book Award.

Garrett Hongo was born in Volcano, Hawaii, and grew up on the North Shore of Oahu and, later, Los Angeles. He is the author of *Yellow Light* and *The River of Heaven*, which was the Lamont Poetry Selection for 1987 and a finalist for the Pulitzer Prize. Most recently, Hongo edited *The Open Boat: Poems from Asian America*.

Lawson Fusao Inada is the author of *Before the War*, the first volume of poetry by an Asian American to be published by a major firm. He also is an editor of two Asian American anthologies: *Aiiieeeee!* and *The Big AIIIEEEEE!*

Reuben Jackson, an archivist with the Smithsonian Institution's Duke Ellington Collection, has been published in the *Indiana Review, Black American Literature Forum*, and elsewhere. His first book of poems, *fingering the keys*, won the 1992 Columbia Book Award.

June Jordan is the author of twenty books. Her most recent titles are *Technical Difficulties*, a book of political essays, and *Haruko/Love Poetry of June Jordan*. She is professor of African American and Women's Studies at U.C. Berkeley.

Allison Joseph was born in London to parents of Caribbean heritage— her mother was from Jamaica, her father from Grenada. She grew up in Toronto, Canada, and the Bronx, New York. Her first book, *What Keeps Us Here*, was the first winner of the Ampersand Press Women Poets Series.

Claire Kageyama is a third-generation Japanese American from Los Angeles, California. For the past two years, she has been a Hoyns Fellow and undergraduate writing instructor in the MFA program at the University of Virginia. Her poem "Dying" appeared in the Spring 1993 issue of *The Antioch Review*.

Shirley Kaufman has published six collections of poetry and several volumes of translations of contemporary Israeli poetry. Her most recent book is *Rivers of Salt*. Among her many honors are a National Endowment Fellowship and the 1991 Shelley Memorial Award of the Poetry Society of America.

Milton Kessler, born in Brooklyn, worked in the garment industry and as an optician before becoming a university teacher. His five poetry collections include *The Grand Concourse*. His book *Riding First Car* is forthcoming.

Yusef Komunyakaa is co-editor (with Sascha Feinstein) of *The Jazz Poetry Anthology*. His latest collections of poems are *Magic City* and *Neon*

Vernacular: New and Selected. He is professor of English and African-American Studies at Indiana University.

Maxine Kumin has published ten books of poetry, most recently *Looking for Luck.* She won the Pulitzer Prize in poetry in 1973 for *Up Country: Poems of New England* and has served as the Poet Laureate at the Library of Congress. Kumin has also published four novels, two essay collections, and a collection of short stories.

Dale M. Kushner is founder/director emerita of The Writers' Place, a literary center located in Madison, Wisconsin. Her father was born in Lithuania, and her Russian grandmother lived with the family most of her life. Her poetry collection, *Another Kingdom*, was translated into Serbo-Croatian.

Jennifer Lagier is affiliated with the Regional Alliance for Progressive Policy, a Salinas-based organization working for social justice and progressive change. She is the author of *Coyote Dream Cantos.* She owes her Italian ancestry to her grandmother, Clementina Canclini Peini.

Alan Chong Lau's books include a collection of poetry entitled *Songs from Jadina.* His poetry has appeared in several publications, including *The Open Boat: Poems from Asian America.*

Li-Young Lee is of Chinese descent, born in Indonesia. His two published books are *Rose* and *The City in Which I Love You.* His work has also been published in *The American Poetry Review* and *Grand Street*, as well as in numerous anthologies including five volumes of *The Pushcart Prize.*

Denise Nico Leto, of Sicilian and Southern Italian decent, co-edited a special issue of *Sinister Wisdom* on Italian American women, titled "Il Viaggio delle Donne." Her work has appeared in publications including *Voices in Italian Americana* and the anthology *We Speak for Peace.*

Philip Levine, the son of Russian and Jewish immigrants, has published fifteen books of poetry, most recently *What Work Is* and *New Selected Poems.* He won the National Book Award twice, most recently in 1991 for *What Work Is.* His forthcoming books of poetry are *Another America* and *The Simple Truth.*

Lyn Lifshin is the author of over ninety chapbooks, books, and collections, including *Not Made of Glass, Upstate Madonna, Black Apples*, and *Raw Opals.* She has edited four anthologies, including two versions of *Tangled Vines.*

Shirley Geok-lin Lim grew up in the often-colonized Malacca, Malaysia. She received the 1980 Commonwealth Poetry Prize for *Crossing the Peninsula.* She is the author of *No Man's Grove, Modern Secrets, Another*

Country (stories), and the editor of *The Forbidden Stitch: An Asian American Women's Anthology*, an American Book Award winner.

Born and raised in Queens, New York, **Julia Lisella** is a third-generation Italian American. She has been a resident at the MacDowell and Millay art colonies and her poems have appeared in *West Branch, Embers, Sojourner*, and other publications.

Audre Lorde was born in New York of West Indian parents. She cofounded, with Barbara Smith, Kitchen Table: Women of Color Press. She published nine volumes of poetry, including *Our Dead Behind Us*, before dying in 1992.

Adrian C. Louis, an enrolled member of the Lovelock Paiute Indian Tribe, resides on the Pine Ridge Reservation. He is the author of *Among the Dog Eaters* and *Fire Water World*, which won the book award from the Poetry Center at San Francisco State University. His forthcoming collection is *Blood Thirsty Savage*.

Wing Tek Lum is a Honolulu businessman and poet. His first collection of poetry, *Expounding the Doubtful Points*, was published in 1987.

Haki R. Madhubuti has published eighteen books of poetry, literary criticism, and essays. He is the founder of the Third World Press and the Institute of Positive Education in Chicago, Illinois. In 1991, he received the American Book Award.

Lisa Suhair Majaj is a Palestinian American born in Iowa, raised in Jordan, and educated in Beirut. She is currently writing a dissertation on Arab American literature for the University of Michigan. Her work has appeared in the *Worcester Review, Woman of Power, Red Dirt, Mr. Cogito*, and is forthcoming in an anthology of Arab American women's writing.

Victoria Lena Manyarrows is of Native/mestiza (Eastern Cherokee/Italian) heritage. Her work has been published in various publications, including *Without Discovery: A Native Response to Columbus; Piece of My Heart*; and *Voices of Identity, Rage and Deliverance*.

A Puerto Rican originally from New York City, **Jesús Papoleto Meléndez** is the author of several volumes of poetry: *Street Poetry & Other Poems, Have You Seen Liberation*, and *Casting Long Shadows*. His work has appeared in numerous anthologies, including *La Línea Quebrada/The Broken Line*.

David Meltzer was born of commingled Polish, Lithuanian, Anglo-Saxon genes, and raised as a Jew in Brooklyn in a neighborhood of first- and second-generation European Jews and Italians. His recent books are *Arrows: Selected Poetry 1982–1992* and the anthology *Reading Jazz: The White Invention of Jazz*.

Richard Michelson, a Jewish American poet who was born in Brooklyn, is the recipient of the 1990 Felix Pollak Prize for Poetry. He is the author of *Tap Dancing for the Relatives* and *Did You Say Ghosts?*

E. Ethelbert Miller is the director of the African American Resource Center at Howard University, as well as the founder and director of the Ascension Poetry Reading Series. He is the host of a weekly radio program on WDCU-FM and a commentator for National Public Radio. His forthcoming book is entitled *First Light: Selected and New Poems.*

Janice Mirikitani, a Sansei (third-generation Japanese American), authored two books of poetry and prose: *Awake in the River* and *Shedding Silence.* Mirikitani has also edited numerous anthologies, including *Making Waves, An Asian Women's Anthology.*

James Masao Mitsui is a Nisei (second-generation Japanese American) born in Skykomish, Washington. His parents immigrated from Nagano-Ken, Japan. He is the author of three books: *Journal of the Sun, Crossing the Phantom River*, and *After the Long Train.*

Pat Mora, a latina native of El Paso, Texas, is the author of a nonfiction collection, *Nepantla: Essays from the Land in the Middle*, and three poetry collections, *Chants, Borders*, and *Communion.* She has also written several children's books and received a Kellogg National Fellowship in 1986.

Cherríe Moraga is a contributor and editor of *Cuentos: Stories by Latinas* and *This Bridge Called My Back.* Her plays, *Heroes & Saints, Shadow of a Man*, and *Giving Up the Ghost*, were published in a 3-volume series in 1993. Her most recent collection of poetry and essays is entitled *The Last Generation.*

Kyoko Mori, born in Kobe, Japan, has lived in the American Midwest since 1977. Her poems have appeared in *The American Scholar* and *The Beloit Poetry Journal.* Her novel, *Shizuko's Daughter*, was published in 1993.

David Mura, a Sansei (third-generation Japanese American), is the author of *Turning Japanese: Memoirs of a Sansei* and *A Male Grief: Notes on Pornography & Addiction.* His book of poetry, *After We Lost Our Way*, won the 1989 National Poetry Series Award.

Naomi Shihab Nye was born in St. Louis of a Palestinian father and an American mother, lived in Jerusalem in 1966–1967, and currently resides in San Antonio, Texas. Her books of poems include *Different Ways to Pray, Hugging the Jukebox*, and *Yellow Glove.* She edited *This Same Sky*, a collection of international poems.

Dwight Okita, a third-generation Japanese American poet and playwright, won an Illinois Arts Council fellowship for poetry in 1988.

Crossing with the Light is his first book of poems. He recently premiered two stage plays: *The Salad Bowl Dance* and *The Rainy Season*.

Simon J. Ortiz, poet, short fiction writer, essayist, and lately a documentary and feature filmwriter, is a native of Acoma Pueblo. His most recent collection, *Woven Stone*, is an omnibus of three previous works—*Going for the Rain, A Good Journey*, and *Fight Back: For the Sake of the People, for the Sake of the Land*.

Alicia Ostriker is a poet-critic, born in Brooklyn, third-generation Jewish; her grandparents were Russian and Lithuanian Jews. She is the author of seven volumes of poetry, most recently *Green Age*. As a critic she writes on women's poetry and, in recent years, on the Bible. Her latest book is *Feminist Revision and the Bible*.

Michael Palma, a professor at Iona College, has published *The Egg Shape* (poems) and translations of Guido Gozzano's and Diego Valeri's work. He collaborated with Dana Gioia on *New Italian Poets* and with Ernest Menze on *Selected Early Works of Johann Gottfried Herder*.

Joseph Papaleo has published two novels, one novella, and thirty-six or so stories in magazines, from small literary journals to *Harper's* and *The New Yorker*. He has also published a book of poems, *Picasso at Ninety-One*, and has recently helped produce a second production of his translations of Dario Fo plays.

Lucia Maria Perillo is of Italian and Yugoslavian ancestry. Her book *Dangerous Life* received the Poetry Society of America's Farber Award in 1989, and she has since published poems in *The Atlantic, The Kenyon Review*, and elsewhere.

Marge Piercy is the author of twelve books of poetry and eleven novels, including *Mars and Her Children*, and *He, She and It*, a novel. The anthology she edited, *Early Ripening*, is available again in the United States.

Pedro Pietri is a poet and playwright of Puerto Rican heritage living in New York City. He has authored several books of poetry, including *Puerto Rican Obituary, Uptown Train, Traffic Violations*, and *Masses Are Asses*.

Ishmael Reed is the author of seven novels, five books of poetry, and several essay collections. His collected poems was published in 1988. He is the co-founder of the Before Columbus Foundation, the sponsor of the American Book Awards.

Vittoria repetto is an Italian American lesbian poet who lives, works, and plays in downtown Manhattan where she was born in 1951. She has organized readings at the W.O.W. Café and mosaicBooks. Her work has appeared in *Earth's Daughters, Amethyst*, and *Mudfish*; she has forthcoming work in *Footwork: The Paterson Literary Review*.

The most recent book by Chicano/Hispanic/Latino writer **Alberto Alvaro Ríos** is *Teodoro Luna's Two Kisses*; other books include *The Lime Orchard Woman, The Warrington Poems, Five Indiscretions, The Iguana Killer*, and *Whispering to Fool the Wind*.

Luis J. Rodriguez is publisher of Tía Chucha Press, Chicago. His first book, *Poems across the Pavement*, won a 1989 Book Award from the Poetry Center, San Francisco State University. His second, *Concrete River*, won a 1991 PEN-Oakland/Josephine Miles Literary Award. His most recent book is *Always Running: A Memoir of La Vida Loca, Gang Days in L.A.*

Rose Romano, born and raised in Brooklyn, is the granddaughter of Neapolitan and Sicilian immigrants. Her first book, *Vendetta*, has been used in multicultural and women's literature courses at colleges and universities across the country and is included in several Italian American and women's archives. Her publications include *Differentia, Italian Americana*, and many others.

Wendy Rose, of Hopi-Miwok ancestry, currently lives near her mother's ancestral land in the Sierra foothills at the southern end of the Mother Lode country. She is an instructor in American Indian Studies at Fresno City College. *Bone Dance: New & Selected Poems, 1967–1993* is her most recent collection.

Liz Rosenberg has published two books of poems, *The Fire Music* (1986) and *Children of Paradise* (1993), as well as books for children, including her latest, *Monster Mama*. She teaches creative writing and English at Binghamton University.

Carol Lee Saffioti is of Italian, Scots, and German descent. Her poetry has appeared in publications including *The Malahat Review* and *Poetry Studies*. Her first collection of poetry is forthcoming.

Dixie Salazar, a visual artist and poet, is half Spanish on her father's side and French and English on her mother's. She is the author of a chapbook, *Hotel Fresno*. Her poems and stories and have appeared in numerous small press magazines.

Sonia Sanchez is the author of thirteen books, including *Homecoming, Homegirls and Handgrenades*, and, most recently, *Under a Soprano Sky*. In addition to being a contributing editor to *Black Scholar* and *Journal of African Studies*, she has edited *We Be Word Sorcerers: 25 Stories by Black Americans* and *360° of Blackness Coming at You*.

Yvonne V. Sapia, born in New York City, traces her heritage to Puerto Rico. One of her collections of poetry, *Valentino's Hair*, was awarded the Samuel French Morse Poetry Prize. In 1991, she received the Nilon

Award for Excellence in minority fiction and her first novel, *Valentino's Hair*, was published.

Ruth Lisa Schechter, of Russian and Polish descent, was the executive editor of the *Croton Review*, a prize-winning literary magazine. The author of nine poetry books, she died in 1989.

Barry Seiler, the son of Jewish parents who were born in what is now a part of Ukraine, is the author of several volumes of poetry. Currently, he is an editor of the *American Book Review*.

Ntozake Shange is probably best known for her choreoplay, *For Colored Girls Who Have Considered Suicide, When the Rainbow Is Enuf*. She has subsequently had a number of plays produced and is the author of several novels, poetry, and prose collections including the novel *Betsey Brown* and *From Okra to Greens: Poems*.

Gregg Shapiro was born in Chicago and raised in Skokie, Illinois. He is of Russian, Hungarian, Polish descent. "Tattoo" is the title section of his work in *Troika II*.

Louis Simpson has published twelve books of verse; five books of literary criticism; a novel, *Riverside Drive*; an autobiography, *North of Jamaica*; and *An Introduction to Poetry*. He was awarded the Pulitzer Prize for a book of poems, *At the End of the Open Road*, and has received many other honors and awards.

Patricia Smith is the author of *Close to Death, Big Towns, Big Talk*, and *Life According to Motown*. *Life According to Motown* and *Close to Death* have been adapted for theatrical presentation, the latter for Boston University Playwright's Theater under the direction of Nobel Prize winner Derek Walcott.

Cathy Song, the daughter of a Chinese American mother and a Korean American father, was born in Honolulu, Hawaii. *Picture Bride*, her first book, won the Yale Series of Younger Poets Award in 1982. Her second book is *Frameless Windows, Squares of Light*.

Gary Soto, born, raised, and educated in Fresno, California, is author of more than eighteen books, including *Living Up the Street, A Summer Life, Baseball in April*, and *Home Course in Religion*. He has produced two films for Spanish-speaking children. He teaches occasionally at the University of California-Berkeley.

Felix Stefanile, born in Long Island City, New York, of Southern Italian immigrant parents, authored five poetry collections, including *A Fig Tree in America*. With Selma Stefanile, he publishes *Sparrow*, one of the oldest poetry journals in the country.

Lamont B. Steptoe is an African American with Cherokee blood. He has published four books of poetry, *Crimson River, American Morning/ Mourning, Mad Minute*, and *Small Steps and Toes* with Bob Small. He served in the Republic of South Vietnam from July 1969 to December 1970; *Mad Minute* focuses on that experience.

Gerald Stern was born in Pittsburgh, Pennsylvania, of immigrant Ukrainian and Polish Jews. One grandfather owned a small stogie factory and the other was a shechet (ritual butcher) and Yiddish scholar. He has published eight volumes of poetry, including *Lucky Life*, winner of the Lamont Prize, *Leaving Another Kingdom, Selected Poems*, and *Bread Without Sugar*.

Mary TallMountain was born in 1918 in Nulato, Alaska. She left her village when she was six with her adopted parents and did not return for fifty years. She published seven collections of poetry, including *There Is No Word for Goodbye*, before she died.

Luci Tapahonso is a Navajo Indian born in Shiprock, New Mexico. She is the author of *A Breeze Swept Through, One More Shiprock Night*, and *Seasonal Woman*. She is an assistant professor at the University of New Mexico, Albuquerque.

Quincy Troupe, author of nine books, including four volumes of poetry, the latest of which is *Weather Reports*, edited *James Baldwin: The Legacy* and co-authored *Miles: The Autobiography*. He is the recipient of two American Book Awards and a Peabody Award for the Miles Davis Radio project, which he wrote and co-produced.

José Angel Villalongo, Sr. (Justo Machíche) was born in New York and is of Puerto Rican descent. He is a photographer and poet. His poetry has appeared in *Temas, Footwork, The Mill Street Forward*.

Alma Luz Villanueva is the author of four poetry books—*Bloodroot, Mother, May I?, Life Span*, and *Planet*—as well as two novels, *The Ultraviolet Sky*, recipient of an American Book Award, and *Naked Ladies*.

Tino Villanueva, a Chicano originally from Texas, is the author of three books of poetry. His poems recently have appeared in the anthologies *An Ear to the Ground* and *After Aztlan*. His most recent book is entitled *Scenes from the Movie "Giant."*

Robert Viscusi is the author of the novel-memoir *Astoria* and the long poem *An Oration upon the Most Recent Death of Christopher Columbus*. Executive officer of the Wolfe Institute for the Humanities at Brooklyn College, Viscusi is also president of the Italian American Writers Association.

Justin Vitiello, of Neapolitan origin, has published numerous literary and scholarly essays and translations. His books include *Vanzetti's Fish*

Cart, poetry, and *Confessions of a Joe Rock*, an experimental novel. He is a professor at Temple University in Philadelphia and Rome, Italy.

Maryfrances Cusumano Wagner is the granddaughter of four Italian immigrants. She has two books of poetry: *Bandaged Watermelons and Other Rusty Ducks* and *Tonight Cicadas Sing*; a third book, *Salvatore's Daughter*, is forthcoming. She also co-edited *Missouri Poets: An Anthology*.

Marilyn Nelson Waniek is the author of *For the Body, Mama's Promises, Partial Truth*, and *The Homeplace*, which won the Annisfield-Wolf Award and was a finalist for the 1991 National Book Award.

Winner of the Gwendolyn Brooks Significant Illinois Poets Award, **Michael Warr** is executive director of the Guild Complex—an award-winning multicultural literary arts center. His first book of poetry is *We Are All the Black Boy*.

Michael S. Weaver is an African American poet and playwright. A graduate of Brown University, he is a former NEA Fellow. His second full-length book of poems is *My Father's Geography*. His play, *Rosa*, was produced in Philadelphia by Venture Theatre.

Ruth Whitman is author of eight books of poetry, the most recent of which is *Hatshepsut, Speak to Me*. Her awards and honors include a Senior Fulbright Writer-in-Residence to Hebrew University, Jerusalem, the Alice Fay di Castagnola Award from the Poetry Society of America, and the Guinness International Poetry Award.

Nellie Wong is the author of two collections of poetry: *Dreams in Harrison Railroad Park* and *The Death of Long Steam Lady*. She is co-featured in the documentary film "Mitsuye and Nellie, Asian American Poets," produced by Allie Light and Irving Saraff (1981).

Mitsuye Yamada's writings are heavily focused on her bicultural heritage. She is the author of *Camp Notes and Other Poems* and *Desert Run: Poems and Stories*. She is co-editor of *The Webs We Weave: Orange County Poetry Anthology* and *Sowing Ti Leaves: Writings by MultiCultural Women*.

Al Young is the author of more than a dozen books. These include the novels *Sitting Pretty* and *Seduction by Light; Mingus Mingus: Two Memoirs* (with Janet Coleman); and *Heaven: Collected Poems, 1956–1990*. A screenwriter who has written scripts for Sidney Poitier, Bill Cosby, and Richard Pryor, Young lives near San Francisco.